WATERMARKING – VOLUME 1

Edited by **Mithun Das Gupta**

Watermarking – Volume 1
Edited by Mithun Das Gupta

Published by InTech
Janeza Trdine 9, 51000 Rijeka, Croatia

Publishing Process Manager Sasa Leporic

Technical Editor Teodora Smiljanic

Cover Designer InTech Design Team

Additional hard copies can be obtained from orders@intechopen.com

Watermarking – Volume 1, Edited by Mithun Das Gupta
p. cm.
ISBN 978-953-51-0618-0

For EU product safety concerns:
IN TECH d.o.o., Prolaz Marije Krucifikse Kozulić 3, 51000 Rijeka, Croatia,
info@intechopen.com or visit our website at intechopen.com.

Meet the editor

Dr Mithun Das Gupta received his bachelors from the prestigious Indian Institute of Technology, Kharagpur in 2001. He got his masters and PhD from the ECE Department at the University of Illinois Urbana Champaign in 2008. He was a member of the Image Formation and Processing Lab at the Beckman Institute of Advanced Science and Technology. His areas of interest include computer vision and image processing, graphical models for image classification, machine learning, approximate inference, convex optimization techniques and dimensionality reduction. He has published in a wide variety of prestigious conferences and journals. He is currently a Lead Scientist at GE Global Research Bangalore India.

Contents

Preface

This collection of books brings some of the latest developments in the field of watermarking. Researchers from varied background and expertise propose a remarkable collection of chapters to render this work an important piece of scientific research. The chapters deal with a gamut of fields where watermarking can be used to encode copyright information. The work also presents a wide array of algorithms ranging from intelligent bit replacement to more traditional methods like ICA. The current work is split into two books. Book one is more traditional in its approach dealing mostly with image watermarking applications. Book two deals with audio watermarking and describes an array of chapters on performance analysis of algorithms.

Mithun Das Gupta
Bio Signals and Analysis lab at GE Global Research Bangalore
India

1

Quantization Watermarking for Joint Compression and Data Hiding Schemes

D. Goudia[1], M. Chaumont[2], W. Puech[2] and N. Hadj Said[3]
[1]*University of Montpellier II, University of Science and Technologies of Oran (USTO)*
[2]*University of Nîmes, University of Montpellier II,Laboratory LIRMM, UMR CNRS 5506, 161, rue Ada, 34095 Montpellier cedex*
[3]*University of Science and Technologies of Oran (USTO), BP 1505 El Mnaouer, Oran*
[1,2]*France*
[1,3]*Algeria*

1. Introduction

Enrichment and protection of JPEG2000 images is an important issue. Data hiding techniques are a good solution to solve these problems. In this context, we can consider the joint approach to introduce data hiding technique into JPEG2000 coding pipeline. Data hiding consists of imperceptibly altering multimedia content, to convey some information. This process is done in such a way that the hidden data is not perceptible to an observer. Digital watermarking is one type of data hiding. In addition to the imperceptibility and payload constraints, the watermark should be robust against a variety of manipulations or attacks.

We focus on trellis coded quantization (TCQ) data hiding techniques and propose two JPEG2000 compression and data hiding schemes. The properties of TCQ quantization, defined in JPEG2000 part 2, are used to perform quantization and information embedding during the same time. The first scheme is designed for content description and management applications with the objective of achieving high payloads. The compression rate/imperceptibility/payload trade off is our main concern. The second joint scheme has been developed for robust watermarking and can have consequently many applications. We achieve the better imperceptibility/robustness trade off in the context of JPEG2000 compression. We provide some experimental results on the implementation of these two schemes.

This chapter will begins with a short review on the quantization based watermarking methods in Section 2. Then, the TCQ quantization is introduced along with its application in data hiding and watermarking in Section 3. Next, we present the joint compression and data hiding approach in Section 4. Afterward, we introduce the JPEG2000 standard and the state of the art of joint JPEG2000 coding and data hiding solutions in Section 5.1. We present the proposed joint JPEG2000 and data hiding schemes in Section 6. Finally, Section 7 concludes this chapter.

2. Quantization watermarking

Quantization watermarking techniques are widely used in data hiding applications because they provide both robustness to the AWGN [1] channel and high capacity capabilities while preserving the fidelity of the host document. Quantization watermarking is a part of watermarking with side information techniques . The watermarking problem is considered as a communication problem and can be modeled as a communications system with side information. In this kind of communication system, the transmitter has additional knowledge (or side information) about the channel. Quantization techniques are based on informed coding inspired from the work of Costa (1983) in information theory. Costa's result suggests that the channel capacity of a watermarking system should be independent of the cover Work. In informed coding, there is a one-to-many mapping between a message and its associated codewords. The code or pattern that is used to represent the message is dependent on the cover Work. The reader is directed to Cox et al. (2008) for a detailed discussion of these concepts.

Chen & Wornell (2001) are the first to introduce a practical implementation of Costa's scheme, called Quantization Index Modulation (QIM). The QIM schemes, also referred as lattices codes, have received most attention due to their ease of implementation and their low computational cost. Watermark embedding is obtained by quantizing the host feature sequence with a quantizer chosen among a set of quantizers each associated to a different message. In the most popular implementation of QIM, known as dither modulation or DM-QIM (Chen & Wornell (2001)), as well as in its distortion-compensated version (DC-DM), the quantization codebook consists of a certain lattice which is randomized by means of a dither signal. This signal introduces a secret shift in the embedding lattice. Although the QIM schemes are optimal from an information theoretic capacity-maximization point of view, their robustness may be too restricted for widespread practical usage. They are usually criticized for being highly sensitive to valumetric scaling. Significant progress has been made these last past years toward resolving this issue, leading to the design of improved QIM schemes, such as RDM (Pérez-Gonzàlez et al. (2005)) and P-QIM (Li & Cox (2007)). Scalar Costa scheme (SCS), proposed by Eggers et al. (2003), is also a suboptimal implementation of the Costa's scheme using scalar embedding and reception functions.

Another important watermarking with side information class of methods are dirty paper trellis codes (DPTC), proposed by Miller et al. (2004). These codes have the advantage of being invariant to valumetric scaling of the cover Work. However, the original DPTC scheme requires a computational expensive iterative procedure during the informed embedding stage. Some works have been proposed to reduce the computational complexity of this scheme (Chaumont (2010); Lin et al. (2005)).

3. TCQ and its use for data hiding

3.1 Generalities on TCQ

Trellis coded quantization (TCQ) is one of the quantization options provided within the JPEG2000 standard. It is a low complexity method for achieving rate-distortion performance greater to that of scalar quantization. TCQ was developped by Marcellin & Fischer (1990) and borrowed ideas from trellis coded modulation (TCM) which have been proposed by Ungerboeck (1982). It is based on the idea of an expanded signal set and it uses coded

[1] Additive White Gaussian Noise.

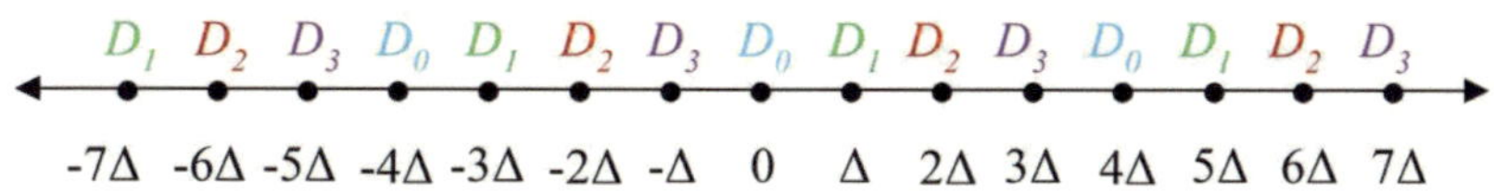

Fig. 1. Scalar codebook with subset partitionning. D_0, D_1, D_2 and D_3 are the subsets, Δ is the step size and ..., -2Δ, -Δ, 0, Δ, 2Δ,..., are the TCQ indices.

modulation for set partitioning. For an encoding rate of R bits/sample, TCQ takes an output alphabet A (scalar codebook) of size 2^{R+1} and partitions it into 4 subsets called D_0, D_1, D_2 and D_3, each of size 2^{R-1}. The partitioning is done starting with the left-most codeword and proceeding to the right, labeling consecutive codewords D_0, D_1, D_2, D_3, D_0, D_1, D_2, D_3,..., until the right-most codeword is reached, as illustrated in Fig. 1. Subsets obtained in this fashion are then associated with branches of a trellis having only two branches leaving each state. Given an initial state, the path can be specified by a binary sequence, since there are only two possible transitions from one state to another. Fig. 2 shows a single stage of a typical 8-state trellis with branch labeling.

In order to quantize an input sequence with TCQ, the Viterbi algorithm (Forney Jr (1973)) is used to choose the trellis path that minimizes the mean-squared error (MSE) between the input sequence and output codewords. The sequence of codewords can be specified by a sequence of R bit indices. Each R bit index consists of a single bit specifying the chosen subset (trellis path) and R-1 bits specifying an index to a codeword within this subset (index value). The dequantization of TCQ indices at the decoder is performed as follows. Given the initial state, the decoder is able to reproduce the reconstructed values by using the sequence of indices specifying which codeword was chosen from the appropriate subset D_0, D_1, D_2 or D_3 at each transition or stage.

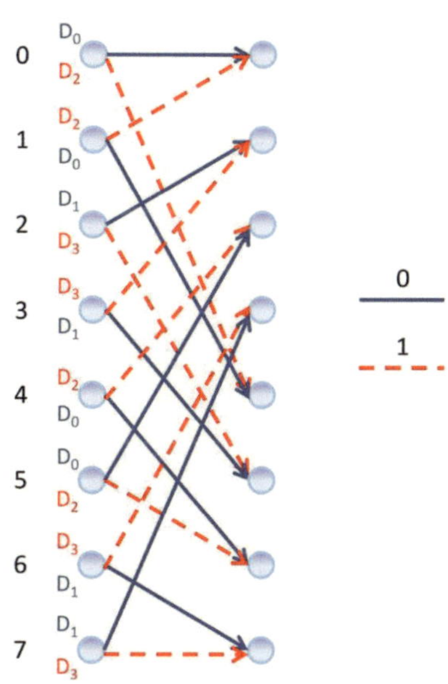

Fig. 2. A single stage of an 8-state trellis with branch labeling.

3.2 TCQ in data hiding and watermarking

TCQ was first used in data hiding to build practical codes based on quantization methods. Exploiting the duality between information embedding and channel coding with side information, Chou et al. (1999) proposed a combination of trellis coded modulation (TCM) and TCQ. This method is referred as TCM-TCQ and consists of partitionning a TCM codebook into TCQ subsets to approach the theory bound. Another data hiding technique based on the TCM-TCQ scheme has been proposed by Esen & Alatan (2004) and Wang & Zhang (2007). This method is called the TCQ path selection (TCQ-PS). In this algorithm, similarly to Miller et al. (2004), the paths in the trellis are forced by the values of the message and the samples of the host signal are quantized with the subset corresponding to the trellis path. Esen & Alatan (2004) also explore the redundancy in initial state selection during TCQ to hide information and compare the results with QIM (Chen & Wornell (2001)) and TCQ-PS. Wang & Zhang (2007) show that the trellis used in TCQ can be designed to achieve more robustness by changing the state transition rule and quantizer selection rule. Le-Guelvouit (2005) explores the use of TCQ techniques based on turbo codes to design a more efficient public-key steganographic scheme in the presence of a passive warden.

Watermarking techniques based on the TCQ-PS method appeared recently in the literature. Braci et al. (2009) focused on the security aspects of informed watermarking schemes based on QIM and proposed a secure version of the TCQ-PS adapted to the watermarking scenario. The main idea is to cipher the path at the encoder side by shifting randomly each obtained codeword to a new one taking from another subset. Then, according to the secret key, a codebook different from the one used for the transmitted message is chosen. Le-Guelvouit (2009) has developed a TCQ-based watermarking algorithm, called TTCQ, which relies on the use of turbo codes in the JPEG domain. Ouled-Zaid et al. (2007) have adapted the TTCQ algorithm to the wavelet domain and have studied its robustness to lossy compression attacks.

4. Joint compression and data hiding approach

Data hidden images are usually compressed in a specific image format before transmission or storage. However, the compression operation could remove some embedded data, and thus prevent the perfect recovery of the hidden message. In the watermarking context, the compression process also degrades the robustness of the watermark. To avoid this, it is better to combine image compression and information hiding to design joint solutions. The main advantage to consider jointly compression and data hiding is that the embedded message is robust to compression. The compression is no longer considered as an attack. Another important advantage is that it allows the design of low complex systems compared to the separate approach.

The joint approach consists of directly embedding the binary message during the compression process. The main constraints that must be considered are trade offs between data payload, compression bitrate, computational complexity and distortion induced by the insertion of the message. In other words, the embedding of the message must not lead to significant deterioration of the compressor's performances (compression rate, complexity and image quality). On the other hand, the data hiding process must take into account the compression impact on the embedded message. The latter should resist to quantization and entropy coding steps of a lossy compression scheme. In the watermarking scenario, we must also consider the watermark robustness against common image attacks after compression. The watermark needs to be robust enough to allow a correct message extraction after some acceptable manipulations of the decompressed/watermarked image.

The data hiding technique must be adapted and integrated into the compressor's coding framework. One or several modules can be used to compress and hide data. Three strategies are commonly used as shown in fig. 3 for a lossy wavelet-based coder :

- data is hidden just after the wavelet transform step: embedding is performed on the wavelet coefficients,
- data is hidden just after the quantization stage: embedding is performed on the quantized wavelet coefficients (quantization indices),
- data is hidden during the entropy coding stage: embedding is performed directly on the compressed bitstream.

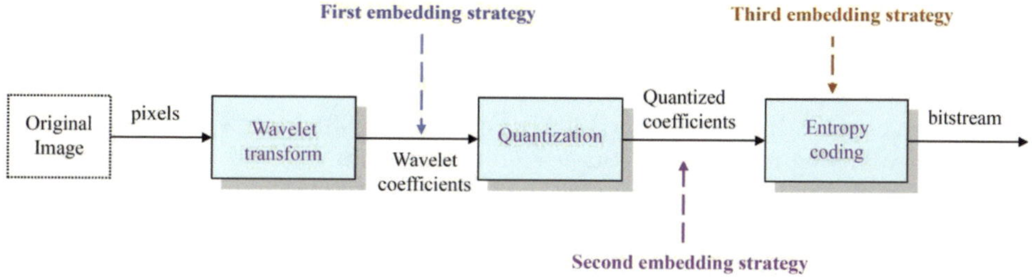

Fig. 3. Data hiding embedding strategies into a lossy wavelet-based coder.

The extraction of the hidden message can be done in two different ways. The first one consists to extract the message from the coded bitstream during the decompression stage. The second one consists to retrieve the hidden message from the data hidden or watermarked image. In this case, the extraction stage is performed after decompression and the knowledge of the compression parameters used during joint compression and data hiding is necessary. For example, if the coder used is a wavelet-based coding system, we need to know the type of wavelet transform used, the number of resolution levels and selected sub-bands.

5. JPEG2000 standard and data hiding in the JPEG2000 domain

5.1 JPEG2000 standard

The international standard JPEG2000 (Taubman & Marcellin (2001)) has been developed by the Joint Photographic Experts Group (JPEG) to address different aspects related with image compression, transmission and manipulation. JPEG2000 is a wavelet-based codec, which supports different types of still images and provides tools for a wide variety of applications, such as Internet, digital cinema and real-time transmission through wireless channels. JPEG2000 provides many features. Some of them are: progressive transmission by quality or resolution, lossy and lossless compression, region of interest (ROI) and random access to bitstream.

The main encoding procedures of JPEG2000 Part 1 are the following: first, the original image undergoes some pre-processing operations (level shifting and color transformation). The image is partitioned into rectangular non-overlapping segments called tiles. Then, each tile is transformed by the discrete wavelet transform (DWT) into a collection of sub-bands:

LL (horizontal and vertical low frequency), HL (horizontal high frequency and vertical low frequency), LH (horizontal low frequency and vertical high frequency) and HH (horizontal high frequency and vertical high frequency) sub-bands which may be organized into increasing resolution levels. The wavelet coefficients are afterwards quantized by a dead-zone uniform scalar quantizer. The quantized coefficients in each sub-band are partitioned into small rectangular blocks which are called *code-blocks*. Next, the EBCOT [2] algorithm encodes each *code-block* independently during the Tier 1 encoding stage and generates the embedded bitstreams. An efficient rate-distortion algorithm called Post Compression Rate-Distortion Optimization (PCRD) provides effective truncation points of the bitstreams in an optimal way to minimize distortion according to any given target bitrate. The bitstreams of each *code-block* are truncated according to the chosen truncation points. Finally, the Tier 2 encoder output the coded data in packets and defines a flexible codestream organization supporting quality layers.

5.2 Data hiding in the JPEG2000 domain

Several data hiding techniques integrated into the JPEG2000 coding scheme have been proposed Chen et al. (2010); Fan & Tsao (2007); Fan et al. (2008); Meerwald (2001); Ouled-Zaid et al. (2009); Schlauweg et al. (2006); Su & Kuo (2003); Thomos et al. (2002). Some of these schemes Chen et al. (2010); Fan & Tsao (2007); Fan et al. (2008) take into account the bitstream truncation of the JPEG2000 bitstream during the rate control stage.

Chen et al. (2010) proposed to perform hiding in the compressed bitstream from rate allocation by simulating a new rate-distortion optimization stage. The new bitrate must be smaller than the original one. A simulated layer optimization induces readjustments of bits in the output layers of the compressed bitstream. These readjustments cleared space in the last output layer for hiding data. Ouled-Zaid et al. (2009) proposed to integrate a QIM-based watermarking method in JPEG2000 part 2. This variant of QIM consists of reducing the distortion caused during quantization-based watermarking by using a non-linear scaling. The watermark is embedded in the LL sub-band of the wavelet decomposition before the JPEG2000 quantization stage. Fan et al. (2008) proposed region of interest (ROI)-based watermarking scheme. The embedded watermark can survive ROI processing, progressive transmission and rate-distortion optimization. The only drawback of this method is that it works only when the ROI coding functionality of JPEG2000 is activated. Fan & Tsao (2007) proposed hiding two kinds of watermarks, a fragile one and a robust one by using a dual pyramid watermarking scheme. The robust pyramid watermark is designed to conceal secret information inside the image so as to attest to the origin of the host image. The fragile pyramid watermark is designed to detect any modification of the host image. Schlauweg et al. (2006) have developed a semi-fragile authentication watermarking scheme by using an extended scalar quantization and hashing scheme in the JPEG2000 coding pipeline. This authentication scheme is secure but the embedding of the watermark induces poor quality performances. Su & Kuo (2003) proposed to hide data in the JPEG2000 compressed bitstream by exploiting the *lazy mode* coding option. Information hiding is achieved after the rate-distortion optimization stage (Tier2 coding) by modifying the data in the magnitude refinement passes. The main drawback of this scheme is that the data hiding procedure is operated in the special JPEG2000 lazy mode which requires a target bitrate higher than 2 bpp. Thomos et al. (2002) presented a sequential decoding of convolutional codes for data hiding in JPEG2000 images. Meerwald (2001) developed a watermarking process based on QIM integrated to JPEG2000 coding chain.

[2] Embedded Block Coding with Optimized Truncation.

Despite its robustness, this method does not fulfill the visual quality requirement. It should be noted that all these schemes integrate an additional embedding/extraction stage in the JPEG2000 compression/decompression process.

6. TCQ based data hiding and JPEG2000 coding schemes

We investigate the design of compression and data hiding schemes in the JPEG2000 domain. The main objective is to develop quantization-based data hiding methods to simultaneously quantize and hide data during JPEG2000 compression. Several quantization options are provided within JPEG2000 Part 2 (ISO/IEC JTCI/SC29 WG1 (2000)) such as TCQ. We propose quantization data hiding strategies based on TCQ to quantize and hide data at the same time by using a single component. This TCQ-based quantization module replaces the TCQ component used in JPEG2000 part 2. Hiding information during the quantization stage ensures that the distortion induced by the information embedding will be minimized and thus obtaining a good image quality. It represents a real joint solution because the quantization and the data hiding aspects are considered together. The proposed schemes can be viewed as "data hiding or watermarking within JPEG2000 Coding".

6.1 TCQ data hiding scheme in the JPEG2000 part 2 coding framework

The first joint scheme investigates the use of TCQ quantization to embed the maximum amount of data in the host image during JPEG2000 compression while minimizing perceptual degradations of the reconstructed image (Goudia et al. (2011b)). The hidden data is extracted during JPEG2000 decompression.

6.1.1 The TCQ-based data hiding strategy

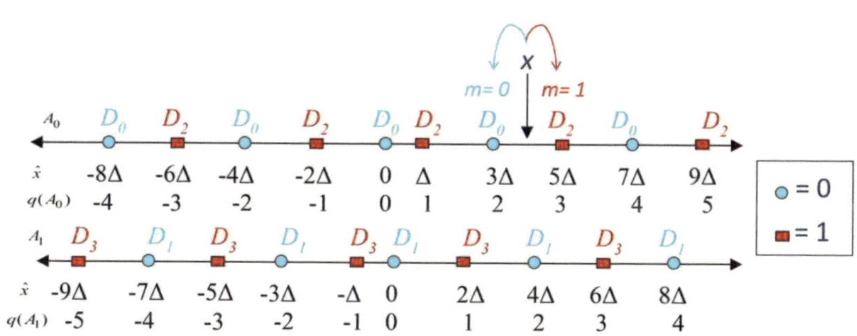

Fig. 4. The QIM principles applied to JPEG2000 part 2 union quantizers.

Our data hiding strategy is derived from the QIM (Chen et al. (2010)) principles and is integrated into a TCQ approach. It is a variant of the TCQ-PS method (Section 3.2). In the TCQ quantization specified in JPEG2000 part 2 recommendations, the two scalar quantizers associated with each state in the trellis are combined into *union quantizers* $A_0 = D_0 \cup D_2$ and $A_1 = D_1 \cup D_3$. The trellis is traversed by following one of the two branches that emanate from each state. The straight branch is labeled by D_0 or D_1 and the dotted branch with D_2 or D_3 as shown in Fig. 2. We propose the following principle as illustrated fig. 4:

- For union quantizer A_0: if the bit to embed is the bit 0, then the quantizer D_0 is used to quantize the wavelet coefficient. Otherwise the quantizer D_2 is used.

- For union quantizer A_1: if the bit to embed is the bit 0, then the quantizer D_1 is used to quantize the wavelet coefficient. Otherwise the quantizer D_3 is used.

The choice of the branch to traverse is determined by the value of the bit to be embedded. This is achieved by removing dotted branches when we embed a 0-bit, and supressing straight branches when we embed a 1-bit. In other words, the path corresponds to the hidden data. However, there is a problem when we integrate this method in the JPEG2000 coding pipeline. EBCOT and the rate-distortion optimization stage must be taken into account in the design of a joint data hiding and JPEG2000 scheme. In JPEG2000, the bitstream truncation produces some bit discards after rate allocation, as described in Section 5.1. Significant coefficients with higher bit-planes have a greater chance of having their TCQ indices being kept complete after JPEG2000 compression. We propose to embed data only in the significant coefficients which have a better chance of survival. These coefficients are called *selected coefficients*. Therefore, the trellis is pruned only at the transitions which correspond to the *selected coefficients*. Moreover, in order to be sure that the LSB value (the path information) will be unchanged after rate allocation, we move the LSB bit-plane of the TCQ indices of the *selected coefficients* to a higher bit-plane.

The message to hide is noted $\mathbf{m} \in \{0,1\}^N$. In order to secure the data to hide, we shuffle (scatter) pseudo randomly the bits of the message $\mathbf{m}$ with a secret key. We obtain another message noted $\mathbf{b} \in \{0,1\}^N$. It prevents all unauthorized users to retrieve the proper values of the hidden data during JPEG2000 decompression. For each *code-block*, the trellis is pruned at the transitions associated to the *selected wavelet coefficients*. The pruning consists of selecting the right branch depending on the value of the bit to embed $\mathbf{b}_k, k \in [0, N]$ at the considered transition step. The process of quantization produces the sequence of TCQ quantization indices $\mathbf{q}$ given by:

$$\mathbf{q}[i] = Q_{D_j}(\mathbf{x}[i]), \tag{1}$$

where Q is the quantization function and D_j is the quantizer used to quantize $\mathbf{x}$[i]. D_j is selected according to the bit to hide $\mathbf{b}_k$. For a given step size Δ, $\mathbf{q}$[i] can be computed as: $\mathbf{q}[i] = sign(\mathbf{x}[i]) \left\lfloor \frac{|\mathbf{x}[i]|}{\Delta} \right\rfloor$. We are able to extract the embedded message during the inverse TCQ quantization stage of JPEG2000 decompression by retrieving the path bits at the transitions which correspond to the *selected coefficients*. For each *code-block*, the decoder produces an estimate of $\mathbf{x}$ as follows:

$$\hat{\mathbf{x}}[i] = \bar{Q}_{D_j}^{-1}(\mathbf{q}[i]), \tag{2}$$

where $\bar{Q}^{-1}$ is the dequantization function. For a given step size Δ, the reconstructed value $\hat{\mathbf{x}}$ can be computed as: $\hat{\mathbf{x}}[i] = sign(\mathbf{q}[i])(|\mathbf{q}[i]| + \delta)\Delta$, where δ is a user selectable parameter within the range $0 < \delta < 1$ (typically $\delta = 0.5$).

6.1.2 The proposed joint JPEG2000 and data hiding scheme

The block diagram of the joint JPEG2000 encoder and data hiding scheme is shown in Fig. 5. First, the original image is processed by some pre-processing operations. Then, it is decomposed by the DWT into a collection of sub-bands. Afterwards, we select the coefficients included in the data hiding process within the wavelet coefficients of the HL, LH and HH detail sub-bands of the selected resolution levels. The selection criteria that allows us to perform the selection will be discussed Section 6.1.3. Next, the data is hidden during the TCQ quantization stage which is performed independently on each *code-block*. Afterward, EBCOT executes the entropy coding. Subsequently, rate-distortion optimization arranges the

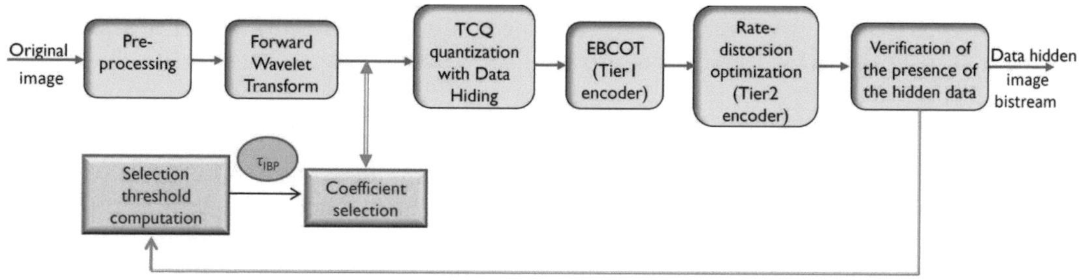

Fig. 5. The block diagram of the joint JPEG2000 codec and data hiding scheme.

code-blocks bitstreams into quality layers according to the target bitrate and proceeds to the formation of the JPEG2000 codestream.

Depending on the target compression ratio and on the information content of the processed image, some bits of the hidden data will be lost after rate-distortion optimization (bitstream truncation). To ensure the proper recovery of the hidden data, a verification process is performed after rate allocation to check if there is no data loss. This process consists of performing an EBCOT decoding and data extraction. If the embedded information is not perfectly recovered, a feedback process is employed to modify the value of the selection criteria for the considered *code-blocks* where erroneous bits were found. This allows us to select the coefficients that have survived the previous rate allocation stage and to exclude those who did not survive. In this way, we may tune the selection criteria recursively during the ongoing process of TCQ quantization, EBCOT, rate-distortion optimization and verification until there is no truncation to the hidden data during the JPEG2000 compression procedure. At each iteration of this feedback process, we make a new selection and embedding. The algorithm stops when the hidden bits are extracted correctly during the verification process. The payload is determined by the number of *selected coefficients*. So, we will have a different hiding payload for each bitrate. Basically, hiding payloads are smaller for images compressed at lower bitrates.

The following steps ensure the extraction of the hidden data during JPEG2000 decompression: the image bitstream is decoded by the EBCOT decoder. Then, the hidden data is extracted during the inverse TCQ quantization according to the previous positions of the *selected coefficients* respectively from each *code-block*. Next, the inverse DWT and the post-processing operations are performed to reconstruct the image.

6.1.3 Selection of the wavelet coefficients included in the data hiding process

Data is hidden in the least significant bits of the TCQ indices which represent the path through the trellis. We can represent the TCQ index q of the wavelet coefficient x in *sign magnitude form* as:

$$q = s, q_0 q_1 .... q_{L-1}, \tag{3}$$

where s is the sign, q_0 is the most significant bit (MSB), and q_{L-1} is the least significant bit (LSB) of q. L is the number of bits required to represent all quantization indices in the *code-block*. The calculation of the selection threshold τ_{IBP} (IBP: Intermediate Bit-Plane) for each *code-block* will allows us to select a sequence of significant coefficients **S**. Assuming that we have L bit-planes in the current *code-block* **C**, τ_{IBP} is computed as follows: $\tau_{IBP} = \lfloor \alpha * L \rfloor$, where α is a real factor between 0 and 1 initialized with a predefined value for each sub-band. The selection of coefficients included in the data hiding process is done as follows:

$$\text{if } \lceil \log_2(|\mathbf{q}[i]|+1) \rceil > \tau_{IBP}, \text{then add } \mathbf{x}[i] \text{ to } S_C, \quad (4)$$

where $\lceil \log_2(|\mathbf{q}[i]|+1) \rceil$ is the number of bits used to represent the TCQ index q of the ith wavelet coefficient x of the *code-block* **C**. We select coefficients whose TCQ indices have their number of bit planes greater than τ_{IBP}. In the case of a data loss after rate allocation, the value of τ_{IBP} is incremented during the backward process and we re-run selection and embedding until the hidden message is correclty recovered.

To be sure that the path will not be partially lost during the rate-distortion optimization stage, especially at low bitrates, we propose to move the LSBs of the TCQ indices of the *selected coefficients* to another position. The new position is located at q_1 (Eq. 3). It is the most higher position at which we can move the LSB without causing the loss of the MSB: indeed, if the LSB value is 0 and if it is moved at q_0, this will cause the loss of a bit plane because the MSB value will be 0.

The thresholds τ_{IBP} for each *code-block* are stored as side information and transmitted to the decoder. In this way, we are able to retrieve the right positions of the selected TCQ indices during the decompression. Thus, we do not need to save the localization of the selected quantization indices. The size of the transmitted file is very small compared to the hiding payload and to the JPEG2000 file size. This file can be encrypted to increase security.

6.1.4 Experimental results

To implement our joint JPEG2000 and data hiding scheme, we choose to use the OpenJPEG library [3] which is a JPEG2000 part 1 open-source codec written in C language. We replaced the scalar uniform quantization component by a JPEG2000 part 2 compliant TCQ quantization module. Simulations were run on 200 grayscale images of size 512 x 512 randomly chosen from the BOWS2 database [4]. The JPEG2000 compression parameters are the following: the source image is partitioned into a single tile and a five levels of irreversible DWT 9-7 is performed. The size of the *code-blocks* is: 64 x 64 for the first to the third level of resolution, 32 x 32 for the fourth level and 16 x 16 for the fifth level. We set the compression ratio from 2.5 bpp to 0.2 bpp. The data to hide is embedded in the HL, LH and HH detail sub-bands of the second, third, fourth and fifth resolution levels. We have a total of 21 *code-blocks* included in the data hiding process. The size of the side information file containing the 4-bit thresholds τ_{IBP} is equal to 84 bits (21 x 4 = 84). Performance evaluation of the proposed joint scheme covers two aspects: the compression performances and the data hiding performances.

6.1.4.1 Compression performances

We study the compression performances of the proposed joint scheme under various compression bitrates in terms of image quality and execution time. We seek to know if the embedding of the message leads to significant degradation of the JPEG2000 performances. We point out that there is no overhead in the JPEG2000 file format introduced by the data hiding process. In fact, the data is hidden during the quantization stage and is part of the TCQ indices within the JPEG2000 bitstream. The proposed joint scheme produces a JPEG2000 syntax compliant bitstream.

[3] The openjpeg library is available for download at http://www.openjpeg.org

[4] The BOWS2 database is located at http://bows2.gipsa-lab.inpg.fr

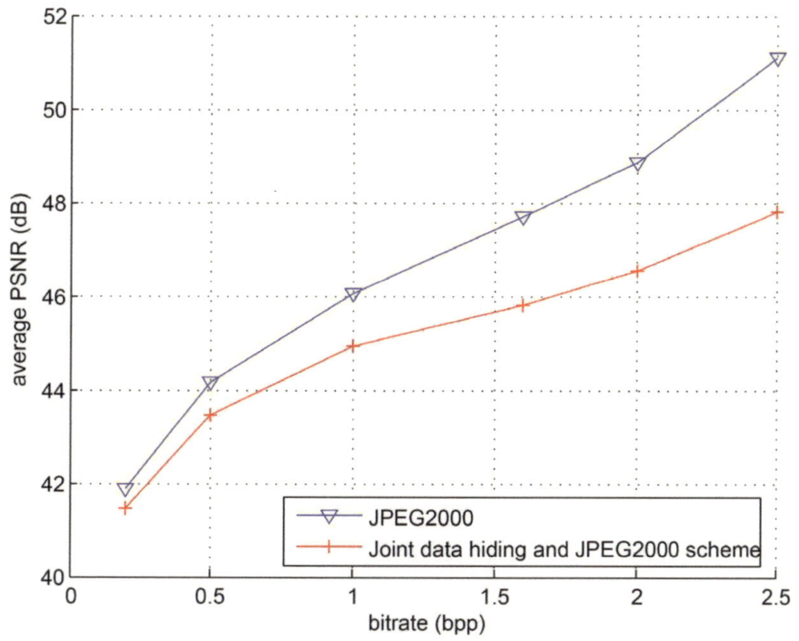

Fig. 6. Comparison between average PSNR results obtained by the proposed data hiding and JPEG2000 scheme and those obtained with JPEG2000 on 200 images of size 512 x 512.

Quality assessment was carried out using two objective evaluation criteria, PSNR [5] and SSIM [6]. For each bitrate, we compute the PSNR (respectively SSIM) of every image of the database. Next, the average PSNR (average SSIM) of all the tested images is computed. We compare respectively between the average PSNR (and the SSIM) computed for the JPEG2000 compressed images and those computed for the compressed and data hidden images. The fig. 6 and 7 show respectively the average PSNR curves and average SSIM curves obtained for the two coders. The average PSNR of the joint scheme is greater than 40 dB for all compression bitrates as shown in fig. 6. The quality degradation resulting from data hiding is relatively small when we compare between the joint scheme and JPEG2000 curves. At 2.5 dB, the difference between the two PSNR values is approximatively of 3 dB. When the bitrate decreases, this difference decreases to reach 0.4 dB at 0.2 bpp. When considering the SSIM results shown in fig. 7, we notice that the average SSIM provided by the joint scheme remains above 90% until 0.5 bpp. The difference between these values and those provided by JPEG2000 is relatively the same for all the tested bitrates (approximatively 1.6 %). Given the results, we can say that the proposed joint data hiding and JPEG2000 sheme exhibits relatively good quality performances in terms of PSNR and SSIM. An example of data hidden and compressed image at 1.6 bpp is presented in fig. 8 for the well known image test Lena.

The computational complexity of the proposed joint scheme is investigated. We first consider the encoding execution time. The joint scheme uses an iterative embedding algorithm during

[5] Pick Signal to Noise Ratio

[6] Structural SIMilarity. SSIM is a perceptual measure exploiting Human Visual System (HVS) properties. The SSIM values are real positive numbers in the range 0 to 1. Stronger is the degradation and lower is the SSIM measure.

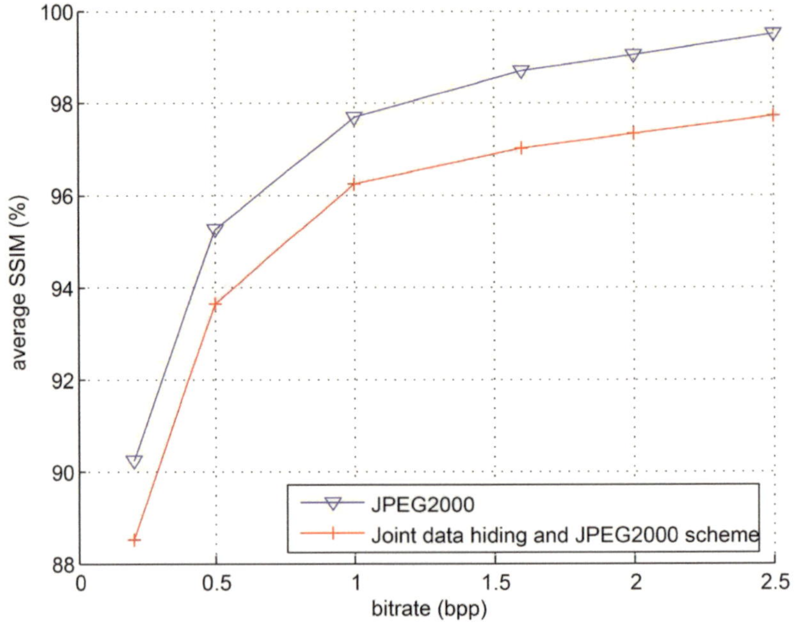

Fig. 7. Comparison between average SSIM results obtained by the proposed data hiding and JPEG2000 scheme and those obtained with JPEG2000 on 200 images of size 512 x 512.

JPEG2000 Joint data hiding and JPEG2000 scheme

Fig. 8. Comparison between Lena image data hidden and compressed with our joint scheme and the same image compressed with JPEG2000 at 1.6 bpp.

the compression stage. TCQ quantization, Tier 1 encoding and Tier 2 encoding steps are repeated until the message can be correctly extracted. The number of iterations depends on the target bitrate, the selection criteria and the content of the processed image. Execution time increases as the number of iterations increases. Table 1 gives the number of iterations and encoding execution times needed to achieve data hiding for the three test images Lena, Clown and Peppers. These execution times have been obtained on Intel dual core 2 GHZ processor with 3 GB of RAM. When the bitrate decreases, the number of iterations, and therefore, the execution time increases. The execution times obtained by the joint scheme are higher than those obtained with JPEG2000. The JPEG2000 average encoding execution time is 1.90 sec. for an image of size 512 x 512. JPEG2000 is faster than the proposed joint scheme during the compression stage. When considering the decoding execution time, we note that the two coders provide similar decoding times. The average decoding time is approximatively 0.55 sec for an image of size 512 x 512.

bitrate (bpp)	Test image	Number of iterations	Encoding execution time (sec.)
2.5	Lena	1	3.68
2		1	3.42
1.6		1	3.31
1		1	3.13
0.5		2	5.83
0.2		2	5.56
2.5	Clown	1	3.66
2		1	3.46
1.6		1	3.40
1		1	3.19
0.5		2	5.94
0.2		5	13.77
2.5	Peppers	1	3.57
2		1	3.43
1.6		1	3.34
1		1	3.13
0.5		2	6.06
0.2		2	5.78

Table 1. Encoding execution time and number of iterations of the iterative embedding algorithm.

6.1.4.2 Data hiding performances

Bitrate (bpp)	2.5	2	1.6	1	0.5	0.2
Average payload	11254	11203	11172	7384	4213	1573
Minimum payload	1266	1266	1266	1266	926	422
Maximum Payload	36718	26180	21903	13470	7530	2621

Table 2. Payloads obtained with the proposed joint scheme on 200 grayscale images of size 512 x 512.

We have noticed that the hidden message is imperceptible as seen in Section 6.1.4.1. We study now the data hiding performances of the proposed joint scheme in terms of data payload.

For each tested bitrate, the average, minimum and maximum payloads are computed. The results are summarized in Table 2 . We note that high average payloads are achieved at high bitrates. We can embed a message having a payload higher than 11000 bits until 1.6 bpp. The maximum payload is 36718 bits at 2.5 bpp and falls bellow 27000 bits for the remaining bitrates. The minimum payload is 1266 bits until 1 bpp and decreases up to 422 bits at 0.2 bpp. The large difference between the minimum and maximum payloads is due to the fact that the number of selected coefficients depends mainly on the content of the original image. Textured and complex shaped images give a great number of wavelet coefficients which are large and sparse. On the contrary, simple images with low constrast and poor textures give a limited number of significant wavelet coefficients. The hiding payload is also dependent on the compression bitrate. We note that from 1 bpp, we obtain lower payloads than those obtained at high bitrates. This is due to the bitstream truncation during the JPEG2000 rate allocation stage. The payload decreases as the bitrate decreases.

6.2 A joint TCQ watermarking and JPEG2000 scheme

The second joint scheme was designed to perform simultaneously watermarking and JPEG2000 coding (Goudia et al. (2011a)). We use a different TCQ-based watermark embedding method from the one used in the first joint scheme to embed the watermark. The watermark extraction is performed after JPEG2000 decompression.

6.2.1 The TCQ-based watermarking strategy

The watermarking strategy is based on the principles of the DM-QIM (Chen et al. (2010)) approach associated with a trellis. We replace the uniform scalar quantizers used in JPEG2000 part 2 by shifted scalar quantizers with the same step size Δ as for the original ones. We can also use a higher step size by multiplying the original step size by a constant. These quantizers differ from the previous quantizers by the introduction of a shift d which is randomly obtained with a uniform distribution over [-Δ/2,Δ/2] [7]. We propose the following principle: if the bit to embed is the bit 0 then the quantizer $D_j^0, j = 0, 1, 2, 3$ with the shift d_0 is used. If it is the bit 1 then we employ the quantizer D_j^1 with the shift d_1 satisfying the condition: $|d_0 - d_1| = \Delta/2$. For each transition i in the trellis, two shifts $\mathbf{d}_0[i]$ and $\mathbf{d}_1[i]$ and four union quantizers $A_{0,i}^0 = D_{0,i}^0 \cup D_{2,i}^0, A_{1,i}^0 = D_{1,i}^0 \cup D_{3,i}^0, A_{0,i}^1 = D_{0,i}^1 \cup D_{2,i}^1, A_{1,i}^1 = D_{1,i}^1 \cup D_{3,i}^1$ are constructed. Thus, we will have two groups of union quantizers for the trellis structure used in our approach: the group 0, which consists of all shifted union quantizers corresponding to the watermark embedded bit 0 and the group 1, which incorporates shifted union quantizers corresponding to the embedded bit 1. The trellis structure used in the proposed method has four branches leaving each state (Fig. 9.a). For each state of the trellis, two union quantizers instead of one are associated with branches exiting this state.

The watermark embedding process is split into two steps to perform watermarking within JPEG2000. The first step is achieved during the quantization stage of the JPEG2000 compression process. Let us consider a binary message $\mathbf{m}$ to embed and a host signal $\mathbf{x}$. The quantization stage produces the sequence of TCQ quantization indices $\mathbf{q}$. For each transition i in the trellis, the union quantizers are selected according to the value $\mathbf{m}$[i]. The trellis is thus

[7] Schuchman (1994) showed that the subtractive dithered quantization error does not depend on the quantizer input when the dither signal $\mathbf{d}$ has a uniform distribution within the range of one quantization bin ($d \in [-\Delta/2, \Delta/2]$) leading to an expected squared error of $E^2 = \Delta^2/12$.

modified in order to remove all the branches that are not labeled with the union quantizers that encode the message as illustrated in Fig. 9.b. The subsets $D_{j,i}^{m[i]}, j = 0, 1, 2, 3$ are associated to the branches of the modified trellis. The quantization index **q**[i] is given by:

$$\mathbf{q}[i] = Q_{D_{j,i}^{\mathbf{m}[i]}}(\mathbf{x}[i]), \tag{5}$$

where Q is the quantization function of JPEG2000, **m**[i] is the bit to embed at transition i and $D_{j,i}^{m[i]}$ is the shifted quantizer. For a given step size Δ, **q**[i] can be computed as:

$$\mathbf{q}[i] = sign(\mathbf{x}[i] - \mathbf{d}_{\mathbf{m}[i]}[i]) \left\lfloor \frac{|\mathbf{x}[i] - \mathbf{d}_{\mathbf{m}[i]}[i]|}{\Delta} \right\rfloor, \tag{6}$$

where $\mathbf{d}_{\mathbf{m}[i]}[i]$ is the shifting of the shifted quantizer $D_{j,i}^{m[i]}$. In addition to **q**, the sequence **l** is generated. It contains an extra information which ensures that the modified trellis structure is properly retrieved during the inverse quantization step.

The second step is performed during the inverse quantization stage of the JPEG2000 decompression process, yielding the watermarked signal $\hat{\mathbf{x}}$. The inverse quantization stage utilizes the same trellis employed in the quantization step. The reconstructed values $\hat{\mathbf{x}}$ are produced as:

$$\hat{\mathbf{x}}[i] = \bar{Q}^{-1}_{D_{j,i}^{\mathbf{m}[i]}}(\mathbf{q}[i]), \tag{7}$$

where $\bar{Q}^{-1}$ is the inverse quantization function of JPEG2000. For a given step size Δ, the reconstructed value $\hat{\mathbf{x}}$ can be computed as:

$$\hat{\mathbf{x}}[i] = sign(\mathbf{q}[i])(|\mathbf{q}[i]| + \delta)\Delta + \mathbf{d}_{\mathbf{m}[i]}[i], \tag{8}$$

where δ is a user selectable parameter within the range $0 < \delta < 1$.

6.2.1.1 Watermark embedding

The watermark embedding process is performed independently into each *code-block*.

Quantization

For each *code-block* **C**, the quantization/watermark embedding procedures are:

- **Computation of the shiftings $\mathbf{d}_0$ and $\mathbf{d}_1$**: we use a pseudo random generator initialized by the secret key k to compute the shiftings.
- **Generation of the group 0 and group 1 union quantizers**: for each transition i, we design shifted scalar quantizers. We label the branches of the trellis with these quantizers. Fig. 9.a. shows a three-stage of the trellis structure used in our joint scheme. The trellis is simplified so that all the branches through the trellis, and thus all the associated union quantizers, encode the message **m** as illustrated in Fig. 9.b.
- **Finding the optimal path**: the initial state of the given trellis structure is set to 0. The Viterbi Algorithm (Forney Jr (1973)) is applied in order to find the minimum distortion path (Fig. 9.b). The TCQ indices are produced (equation 6).

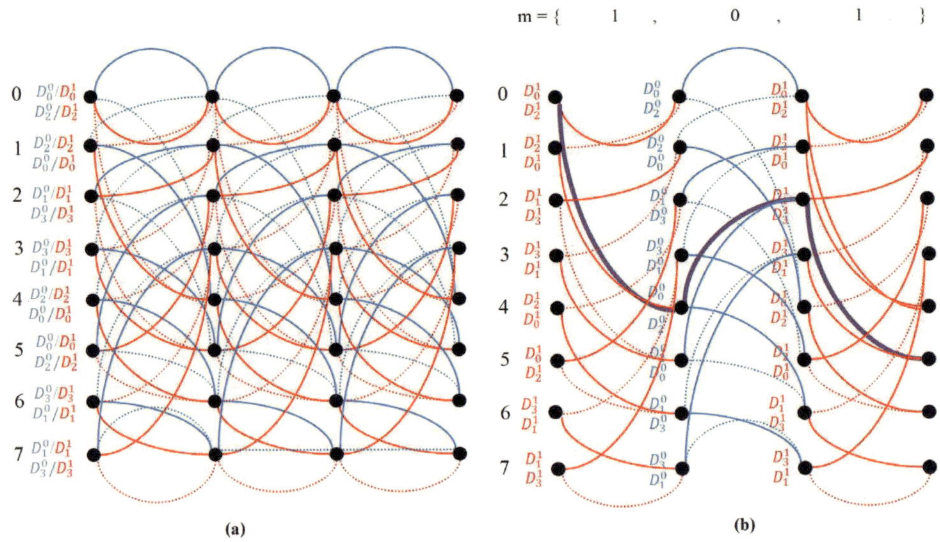

Fig. 9. a) A three-stage of the modified trellis structure, b) Insertion of the message m={1,0,1}: all the branches that are not labeled with the union quantizers that encode the message are removed. The bold branches represent the optimal path calculated by the Viterbi algorithm

Inverse quantization

The watermak embedding is completed during the inverse quantization of the JPEG2000 decompression stage. The image bitstream is decoded by the EBCOT decoder (Tier 2 and Tier 1 decoding) to obtain the sequence of decoded TCQ indices. For each *code-block* **C**, the inverse quantization steps are the following:

- **Computation of the shiftings $\mathbf{d}_0$ and $\mathbf{d}_1$.**
- **Generation of the group 0 and group 1 union quantizers.**
- **Inverse quantization**: the trellis structure with four branches leaving each state is generated. Each branch of the trellis is afterwards labeled with the shifted quantizers. The sequence **l** enables us to retrieve the pruned trellis used during the quantization stage. This trellis is used to reconstruct the wavelet coefficients. Given the TCQ indices, the embedding of the watermark is achieved during the computation of the reconstructed wavelet coefficients (equation 8).

6.2.1.2 Watermark extraction

The watermark recovery from the decompressed/watermarked image is a blind watermarking extraction process. In order to extract the embedded message within the decompressed image, we perform the following operations:

- **Apply the DWT**: we apply the DWT on the decompressed watermarked image. Each sub-band included in the watermarking process is partitionned into blocks of same size as the JPEG2000 code-blocks. The coefficients belonging to the current block are stored in the vector **y**. The following steps are repeated for each processed block.
- **Retrieve the shiftings $\mathbf{d}_0$ and $\mathbf{d}_1$**: we retrieve the shiftings by using the secret key k and we set the union quantizers group 0 and group 1.

- **Perform the TCQ quantization**: the decoder applies the Viterbi algorithm to the entire trellis (Fig. 9.a). The Viterbi algorithm identifies the path that yields the minimum quantization distortion between **y** and the output codewords. The hidden message is then decoded by looking at the TCQ codebook labeling associated to the branches in that path.

6.2.2 The proposed joint watermarking and JPEG2000 scheme

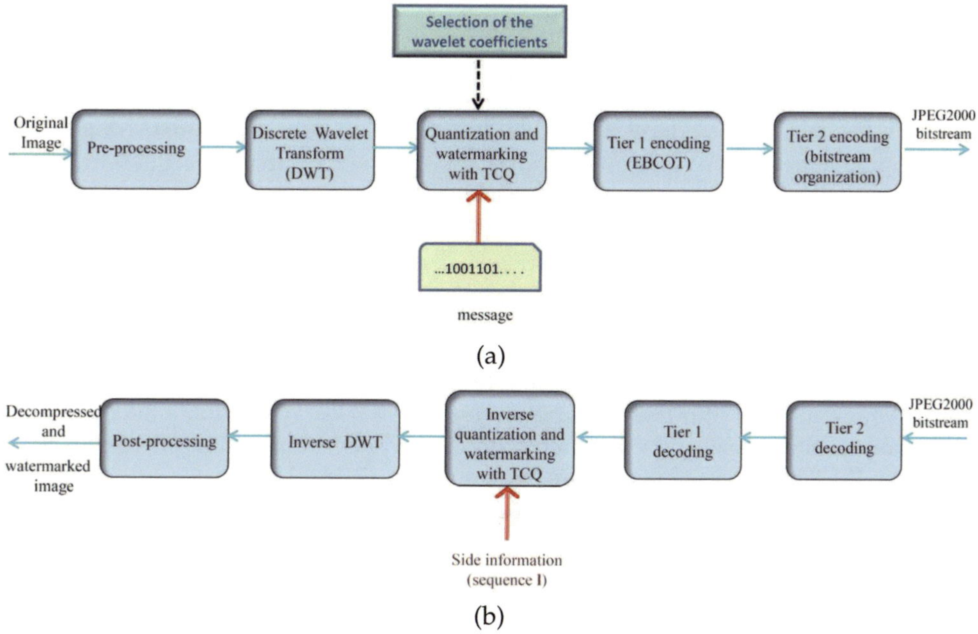

Fig. 10. The joint JPEG2000/watermarking scheme, a): compression process, b): decompression process

The block diagram of the joint JPEG2000 part 2 and watermark embedding scheme is illustrated in fig. 10. The classical TCQ quantization component of the JPEG2000 encoder and decoder is replaced by a hybrid TCQ module which can perform at the same time quantization and watermark embedding. One of the most important parameter to consider is the selection of the wavelet coefficients that must be included in the watermarking process. We chose to embed the watermark in the HL, LH and HH detail sub-bands of the selected resolution levels. All coefficients of these sub-bands are watermarked. Wavelet coefficients of the other sub-bands are quantized with the classical TCQ algorithm of JPEG2000 part 2. The watermarking payload is determined by the number of detail sub-bands included in the watermarking process. The payload increases when we add more detail sub-bands from a new selection of resolution levels. EBCOT and the rate-distortion optimisation stage are taken into account by the use of an error correcting code to add redundancy. The rate of this error correcting code must be low in order to allow reliable recovery of the watermark during the extraction stage. High watermarking payloads can be achieved by including as many detail sud-bands as necessary and by adjusting the rate of the error correcting code. Another important parameter to consider is the quantizer step size value of the selected sub-bands. The step size value of each selected sub-band should be large enough to obtain an acceptable watermarking power without affecting the quantization performances of JPEG2000.

6.2.3 Experimental results

The image database and the compression parameters used during the experimentations are the same as those used in the joint data hiding and JPEG2000 scheme (Section 6.1.4). The watermarking parameters are the following: binary logo of size 32 x 32 is used in the experiments (Fig. 14.(a)). The message of 1024 bits length is inserted in the detail sub-bands of the second to the fourth resolution level. The joint scheme embed one bit of the (non-coded) message for every 256 pixels in an image of size 512 x 512. The message is encoded with a very simple repetition code of 1/63-rate. We shuffle (scatter) pseudo randomly the bits of the coded message with a secret key. $\Delta_{sb}/4$ is the TCQ quantizer step size value of the sub-band sb used in JPEG2000 part 2. The selection of the step size value $\Delta_{sb,TCQ}$ for the sub-bands included in the watermarking process is done so that the best trade off between robustness and quality degradation is achieved. We select the value $\Delta_{sb,TCQ} = \Delta_{sb}$ after experimenting different step size values. We study the compression performances of the proposed joint scheme under various compression bitrates. We also evaluate the robustness of watermarked images against four attacks.

6.2.3.1 Compression performances

The compression performances and the impact of watermark embedding on the reconstructed image quality are investigated. An example of watermarked and compressed image at 1.6 bpp is presented in Fig. 11 for the well known test image Bike. We evaluate the image quality performances of the proposed joint scheme under various compression bitrates in terms of PSNR and SSIM. The obtained results are shown in Fig. 12 and 13.

(a) (b) (c)

Fig. 11. Comparison between : (a) Bike image compressed with JPEG2000 at 1.6 bp, and (c) the same image watermarked and compressed with our joint scheme at 1.6 bp. The extracted watermark is : (b) binary logo of size 32 x 32.

We first consider the PSNR results (Fig. 12). The curves representing the results obtained for JPEG2000 and the proposed joint scheme are quite far from each other. This is due to the use of a large step size value for the sub-bands included in the watermarking process. The step size value used for watermark embedding is four times higher than the JPEG2000 part 2 step size. The use of a large step size value allows a higher watermarking power. We obtain a lower fidelity in comparison with that obtained using the original TCQ quantizer step size while achieving better watermark robustness. We note that the average PSNR is greater than 40 dB until 0.5 bpp. At 2.5 bpp, the difference between the two PSNR values is approximatively of 4,7 dB. At 0.2 bpp, the difference is less (2.4 dB). When considering the SSIM results shown in

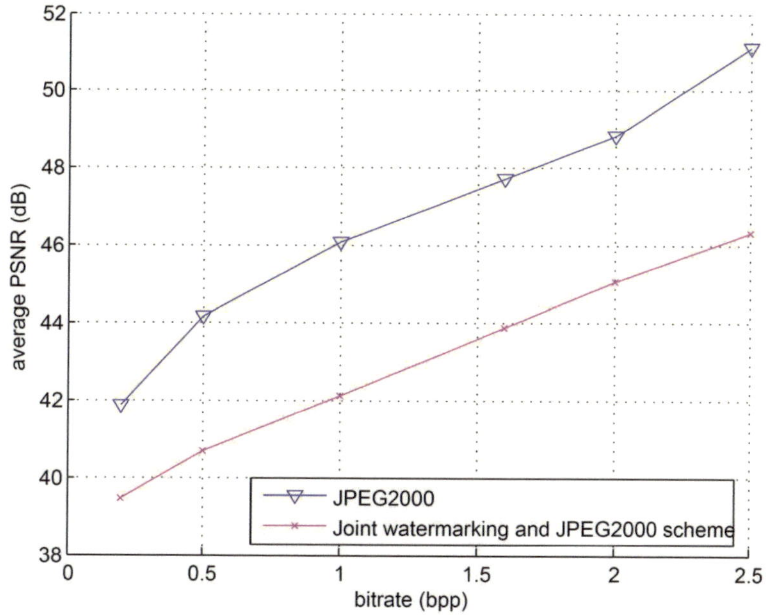

Fig. 12. Comparison between average PSNR results obtained by the proposed watermarking and JPEG2000 scheme and those obtained with JPEG2000 on 200 images of size 512 x 512.

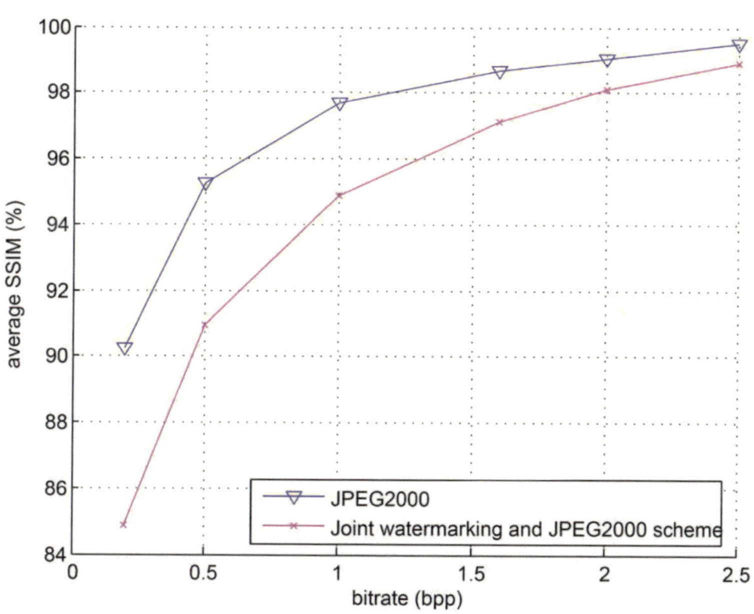

Fig. 13. Comparison between average SSIM results obtained by the proposed watermarking and JPEG2000 scheme and those obtained with JPEG2000 on 200 images of size 512 x 512.

fig. 13, we notice that the two curves are close to each other at high bitrates. The curves move away from each other from 1 bpp. The average SSIM provided by the joint scheme remains above 90% until 0.5 bpp. It drops below 86% at 0.2 bpp.

Image test	bitrate (bpp)	PSNR (dB)		SSIM	
		Joint decoder	JPEG2000 decoder	Joint decoder	JPEG2000 decoder
Lena	2.5	40.75	40.83	0.9612	0.9616
	2	39.45	39.57	0.9480	0.9484
	1.6	39.99	40.11	0.9407	0.9422
	1	38.25	38.22	0.9206	0.9221
	0.5	36.46	36.50	0.8886	0.8904
	0.2	33.58	33.59	0.8263	0.8283
Goldhill	2.5	40.93	40.94	0.9564	0.9558
	2	40.93	40.99	0.9394	0.9398
	1.6	39.32	39.27	0.9149	0.9154
	1	39.23	39.21	0.8761	0.8770
	0.5	38.19	38.14	0.7946	0.7956
	0.2	37.17	37.18	0.6987	0.6998
Bike	2.5	39.84	39.77	0.9610	0.9615
	2	38.70	38.59	0.9336	0.9343
	1.6	37.78	37.83	0.9064	0.9073
	1	34.59	34.62	0.8430	0.8439
	0.5	33.62	33.63	0.7316	0.7324
	0.2	34.67	34.77	0.5681	0.5690

Table 3. Comparison between the PSNR(dB) and SSIM of the images obtained from the watermarked bitstream with the proposed joint JPEG2000/watermarking decoder and the JPEG2000 part 2 decoder.

The computional complexity of the proposed joint scheme and JPEG2000 are similar. The encoding and decoding execution times of the two coders are nearly the same because, except the quantization stage, there are no additionnal processing to watermark the image.

The proposed joint scheme produces a JPEG2000 syntax compliant bitstream. This bitstream can be decoded by a classical JPEG2000 decoder. In this case, the two union quantizers A_0 and A_1 are used to dequantize the decoded wavelet coefficients instead of group 0 and 1 dithered union quantizers (the step size values are stored in the header of the JPEG2000 codestream). However, the JPEG2000 decoder produces an image which is close in quality to the one decoded with our joint scheme as shown in Table 3 . For the three test images Lena, Goldhill and Bike, the PSNR and SSIM results are similar and sometimes better than those obtained with the joint decoder.

6.2.3.2 Watermarking performances

In order to analyze the performance of the proposed joint system in terms of robustness, we compare its robustness with those of two conventional watermarking schemes: the dirty paper trellis codes (Miller et al. (2004)) and the TTCQ scheme (Le-Guelvouit (2009)). The two schemes use a trellis during watermark embedding and extraction stages. The TTCQ algorithm is a TCQ-based scheme which relies on the use of turbo codes to embed the watermark in the JPEG domain (Section 3.2). We use a specific protocol for the two

(a) (b) (c) (d) (e)

Fig. 14. Various examples of extracted watermarks after attacks: (a) original watermark, the extracted watermark with a BER of (b) 1.07%, (c) 3.34%, (d) 5.37%, and (e) 10.25%.

watermarking schemes to be able to make a valid comparison: we perform JPEG2000 compression attack after watermark embedding and before performing robustness attacks. The compression bitrate is fixed to 2 bpp. We fixed the degradation to an average PSNR value of 45 dB for the three schemes. The payload is the same as the one used in the experimentations (1 bit embedded in 256 pixels). We made a slight modification to the TTCQ algorithm to be able to use a payload of 1024 bits instead of 4096 bits (which is the fixed payload for an image of size 512 x 512 for this scheme). We use a very simple convolutional code 1/4-rate to code the message of 1024 bits.

The same database of 200 images has been considered to compare the watermark robustness of the joint scheme with those of DPTC and TTCQ. Four kinds of attacks have been performed: gaussian filtering attack, Gaussian noise attack, valumetric attack and JPEG attack. The Bit Error Rate (BER) is computed for each attack. The BER is the number of erroneous extracted bits divided by the total number of embedded bits. In Fig. 14, various examples of the extracted watermarks according to their BER are shown. As can be seen in the figure, an extracted watermark with a BER bigger than 10% is hard to recognize. The BER results for the four attacks are presented in Fig. 15 Fig. 16, Fig. 17 and Fig. 18 . The logarithmic (base 10) scale is used for the Y-axis (BER results).

The watermarked images are filtered by gaussian filter of width σ. The experiment was repeated for different values of σ, and the BER has been computed. The obtained results are reported in Fig. 15. We notice that the watermark robustness against this kind of attack is relatively the same for the three schemes but the BER values obtained by DPTC are much more lower than ours and TTCQ for low and middle power attack. The joint scheme gives better BER value than TTCQ until $\sigma = 0.9$. Fig. 16 shows the results obtained when the watermarked images are corrupted by additive gaussian noise with mean 0 and standard deviation σ. The experimental results shows that DPTC outperforms the two schemes. The proposed joint scheme is not robust to this kind of attack. The TTCQ scheme provides a better robustness than our joint scheme. The results against the valumetric scaling attack (each pixel is multiplied by a constant) are summarized in Fig. 17. The joint scheme gives better performances than TTCQ for this kind of attack. DPTC allows to obtain a null BER until a scaling factor value of 1.1. From this value, the joint scheme gives better BER than the two other approaches. Fig. 18 shows the BER results against JPEG attack. The two watermarking shemes provide better performances than the proposed joint scheme. The weak robustness to JPEG attack is inherent to the joint approach since the transformed domain is the wavelet domain and the coefficients included in the watermarking process are partly high frequency wavelet coefficients.

To sum up, the two watermarking schemes provide better watermark robustness than the proposed joint scheme facing gaussian noise attack and JPEG attack. The joint scheme is more

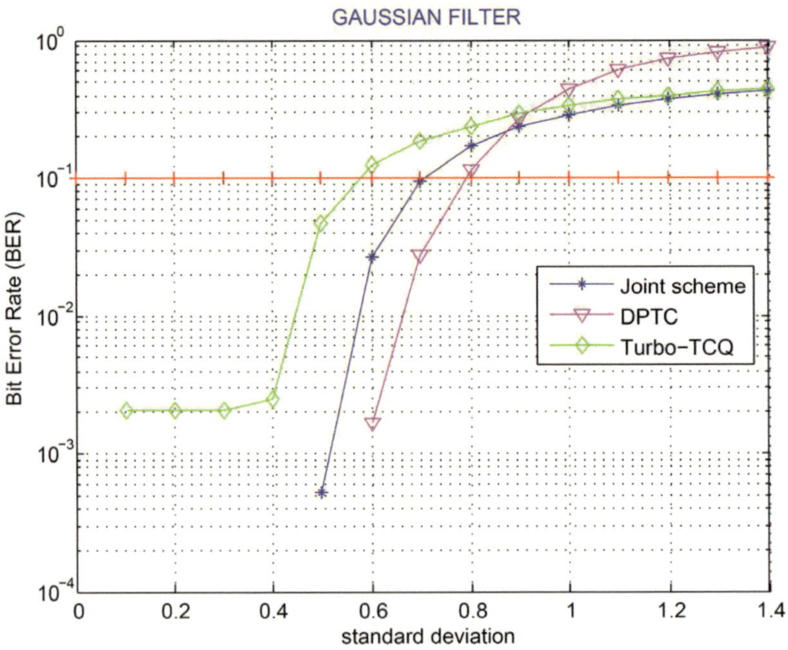

Fig. 15. BER results for Filtering attack

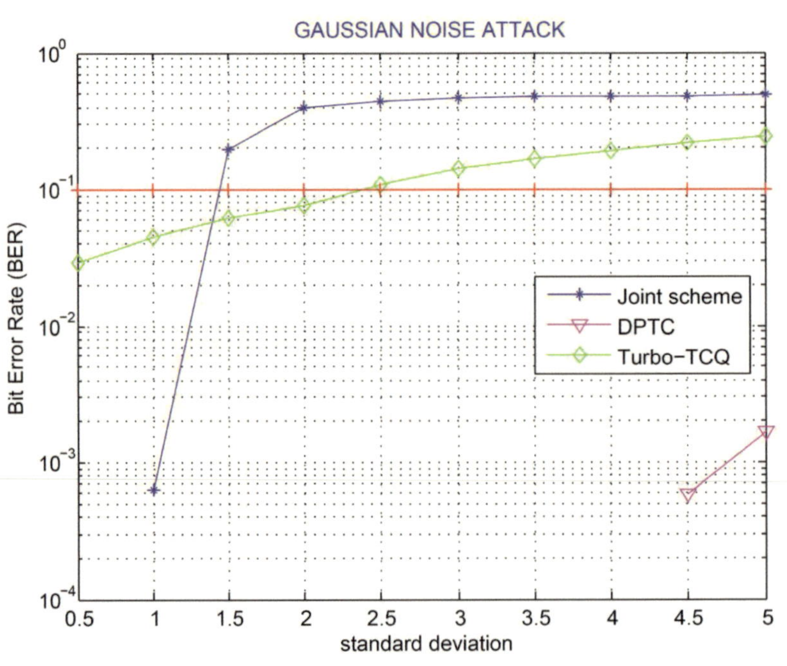

Fig. 16. BER results for Gaussian attack.

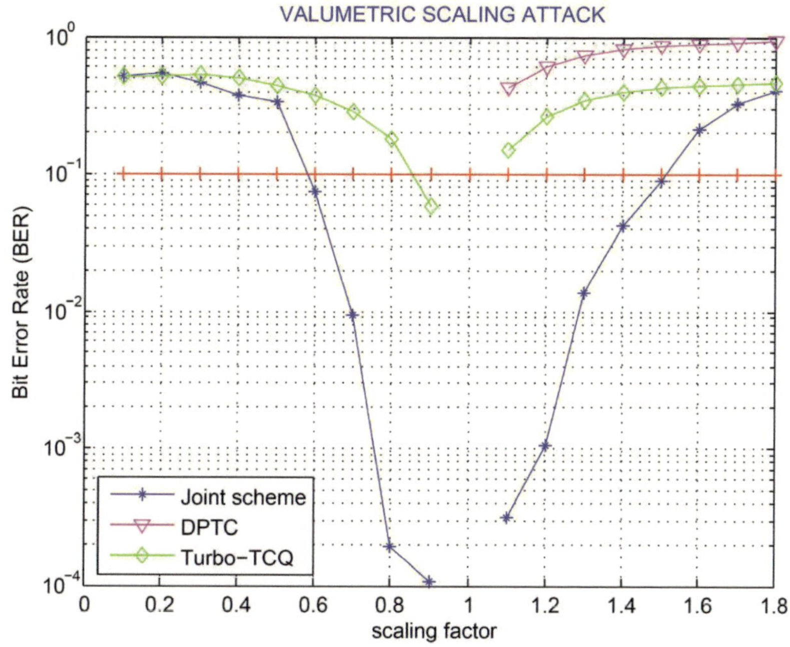

Fig. 17. BER results for Scaling attack

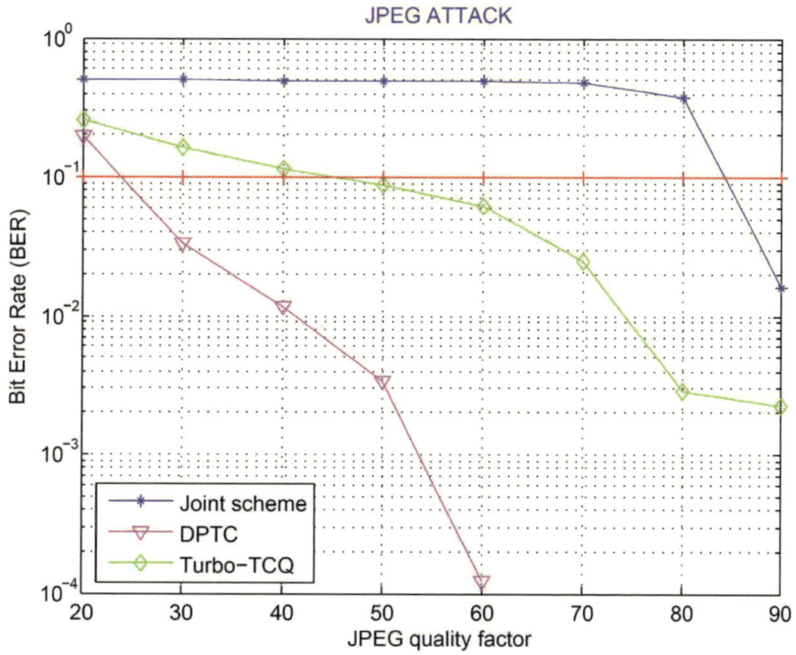

Fig. 18. BER results for JPEG attack.

resistant than TTCQ against the valumetric attack without exceeding DPTC performances. Finally, the robustness against gaussian filter is comparable for the three approaches.

We compare between the computational complexity of the joint scheme and those of watermarking schemes and separate JPEG2000 compression. DPTC achieve high performances with respect to robustness. However, this watermarking scheme suffers from its CPU computational complexity. Three hours are necessary to watermark an 512 x 512 image with the DPTC algorithm on an Intel dual core 2 GHZ processor while it requires only 2 seconds to watermark and compress the same image with our joint scheme. The TTCQ watermark embedding / JPEG2000 compression / TTCQ watermark extraction operations need 15 seconds to be performed. So, the joint scheme is much more faster than the two other schemes.

7. Conclusion

In this chapter, the use of quantization watermarking in the design of joint compression and data hiding schemes is investigated in the JPEG2000 still image compression standard framework. Instead of treating data hiding and compression separately, it is interesting and beneficial to look at the joint design of data hiding and compression systems. We have proposed two TCQ quantization strategies in the coding pipeline of JPEG2000 part 2, leading to the design of two joint schemes. We exploit the characteristics of the TCQ quantization as defined in the part 2 of the standard to perform information hiding. The main contribution of this work is that the proposed schemes allows both quantization of wavelet coefficients and data hiding by using the same quantization module.

In the first joint data hiding and JPEG2000 scheme, we propose to hide the message by quantizing selected wavelet coefficients with specific codebooks from the JPEG2000 union quantizers. These codebooks are associated with the values of the data to be inserted. The wavelet coefficients included in the data hiding process are selected carefully in order to survive the entropy coding stage and the rate control stage of JPEG2000 compression. In the second joint watermarking and JPEG2000 scheme, we propose to watermark the image during JPEG2000 compression and decompression stages by using two groups of dithered union quantizers. We replace the uniform scalar quantizers used in JPEG2000 part 2 by shifted scalar quantizers. The trellis structure used during quantization is modified in order to add branches labeled by these dithered quantizers. The trellis is afterwards pruned so that all the branches through the trellis, and thus all the associated union quantizers, encode the message to embed.

Experimental inverstigations covered both the compression efficiency and the data hiding performances of the proposed schemes. The properties of our joint schemes are the following:

- robustness to JPEG2000 compression for all tested bitrates,
- good image quality,
- high payloads,
- lower complexity in comparison to the separate approach.

The work presented in this chapter suggests that it is possible to design joint data hiding and compression coders in the JPEG2000 domain with smaller complexity and relatively good performances. The proposed joint schemes can be used in enrichment and management applications.

8. References

Braci, S., Boyer, R. & Delpha, C. (2009). Security evaluation of informed watermarking schemes, *Proc. International Conference on Image Processing, ICIP 2009* pp. 117–120.

Chaumont, M. (2010). A novel embedding technique for dirty paper trellis codes watermarking, *Visual Information Processing and Communication, VIPC 2010, Part of IS&T/SPIE 22th Annual Symposium on Electronic Imaging, SPIE 2010*, Vol. 7543, paper 7543-38, San Jose, California, USA.

Chen, B. & Wornell, G. W. (2001). Quantization index modulation: A class of provably good methods for digital watermarking and information embedding, *IEEE Transactions on Information Theory* 47(4): 1423 –1443.

Chen, J., Chen, T. S., Lin, C. N. & Cheng, C. Y. (2010). A bitrate controlled data hiding scheme for JPEG2000, *International Journal of Computers and Applications* 32(2): 238–241.

Chou, J., Pradhan, S. S. & Ramchandran, K. (1999). On the duality between distributed source coding and data hiding, *Proc. of the Thirty-third Asilomar Conference on Signals, Systems, and Computers*, Vol. 2, Pacific Grove, CA , USA, pp. 1503–1507.

Costa, M. (1983). Writing on dirty paper, *IEEE Transactions on Information Theory* 29(3): 439–441.

Cox, I. J., Miller, M. L., Bloom, J. A., Fridrich, J. & Kalker, T. (2008). *Digital watermarking and steganography*, second edn, Morgan Kaufmann.

Eggers, J., Bauml, R., Tzschoppe, R. & Girod, B. (2003). Scalar costa scheme for information embedding, *IEEE Transactions on Signal Processing* 51(4): 1003–1019.

Esen, E. & Alatan, A. A. (2004). Data hiding using trellis coded quantization, *Proc. of the IEEE International Conference on Image Processing, ICIP2004*, Vol. 1 of *Proc. ICIP 2004*, Singapore, pp. 59–62.

Fan, Y.-C. & Tsao, H. (2007). A dual pyramid watermarking for JPEG2000, *International Journal of High Performance Computing and Networking* 5: 84–96.

Fan, Y., Chiang, A. & Shen, J. (2008). ROI-based watermarking scheme for JPEG 2000, *Springer journal of Circuits, Systems, and Signal Processing* 27(5): 763–774.

Forney Jr, G. D. (1973). The viterbi algorithm, *IEEE Transaction on Information Theory* 61: 268–278.

Goudia, D., Chaumont, M., Puech, W. & Said, N. H. (2011a). A joint JPEG2000 compression and watermarking system using a TCQ-based quantization scheme, *VIPC 2011, SPIE 2011, Visual Information Processing and Communication II, Part of SPIE 23th Annual Symposium on Electronic Imaging*, Vol. 7882-11, San Francisco, California, USA.

Goudia, D., Chaumont, M., Puech, W. & Said, N. H. (2011b). A Joint Trellis Coded Quantization (TCQ) Data Hiding Scheme in the JPEG2000 Part 2 Coding Framework, *The 19th European Signal Processing Conference, EUSIPCO 2011*, Barcelona, Spain.

ISO/IEC JTCI/SC29 WG1 (2000). JPEG2000 part II final committee draft version 1.0.

Le-Guelvouit, G. (2005). Trellis-coded quantization for public-key watermarking, accepted for IEEE International Conference on Acoustics, Speech and Signal Processing (ICASSP 2005), 2005, see the website http://www.gleguelv.org/pub/index.html.

Le-Guelvouit, G. (2009). Tatouage robuste d'images par turbo tcq, *Traitement du Signal* 25(6).

Li, Q. & Cox, I. (2007). Using perceptual models to improve fidelity and provide resistance to valumetric scaling for quantization index modulation watermarking, *IEEE Transactions on Information Forensics and Security* 2(2): 127–139.

Lin, L., Cox, I. J., Doërr, G. & Miller, M. L. (2005). An efficient algorithm for informed embedding of dirty paper trellis codes for watermarking, *Proc. of the IEEE International Conference on Image Processing, ICIP 2005*, Vol. 1, Genova, Italy, pp. 697–700.

Marcellin, M. & Fischer, T. (1990). Trellis coded quantization of memoryless and gauss-markov sources, *IEEE Transaction on communication* 38: 82–93.

Meerwald, P. (2001). Quantization watermarking in the JPEG2000 coding pipeline, *Proc. of the 5th joint working Conference on Communications and Multimedia Security, Communications and Multimedia Security Issues of the new century, IFIP TC6/TC11*, Darmstadt, Germany, pp. 69–79.

Miller, M., Doerr, G. & Cox, I. (2004). Applying Informed Coding and Embedding to Design a Robust High Capacity Watermark, *IEEE Transactions on Image Processing* 13(2): 792–807.

Ouled-Zaid, A., Makhloufi, A. & Bouallegue, A. (2007). Wavelet Domain Watermark Embedding Strategy using TTCQ Quantization, *International Journal of Computer Science and Network Security (IJCSNS)* 7(6): 165–170.

Ouled-Zaid, A., Makhloufi, A. & Olivier, C. (2009). Improved QIM-Based Watermarking Integrated to JPEG2000 Coding Scheme, *Springer journal of Signal, Image and Video Processing* 3: 197–207.

Pérez-Gonzàlez, F., Mosquera, F., Barni, M. & Abrardo, A. (2005). Rational dither modulation: A high-rate data-hiding method invariant to gain attacks, *IEEE Transactions on Signal Processing, Supplement on Secure Media* 53(10): 3960–3975.

Schlauweg, M., Profrock, D. & Muller, E. (2006). JPEG2000-based secure image authentication, *Proc. of the 8th ACM Multimedia and Security Workshop*, Proc. MM&Sec 2006, Geneva, Switzerland, pp. 62–67.

Schuchman, L. (1994). Dither signals and their effect on quantization noise, *IEEE Transaction on Communication Technology (COM)* 12: 162–165.

Su, P. C. & Kuo, C. J. (2003). Steganography in JPEG2000 compressed images, *IEEE Transaction on Consumer Electronics* 49(4): 824–832.

Taubman, D. & Marcellin, M. (2001). *JPEG2000: Image Compression Fundamentals, Standards, and Practice*, Kluwer Academic Publishers, Dordrecht.

Thomos, N., Boulgouris, N. V., Kokkinou, E. & Strintzis, M. G. (2002). Efficient data hiding in JPEG2000 images using sequential decoding of convolutional codes, *Proc. of the International Conference in Digital Signal Processing 2002*, Vol. 2, pp. 710–720.

Ungerboeck, G. (1982). Channel coding with multilevel/phase signals, *IEEE Transaction on Information Theory* 28: 55–67.

Wang, X. & Zhang, X. P. (2007). Generalized trellis coded quantization for data hiding, *Proc. of the IEEE International Conference on Acoustics, Speech, and Signal Processing, ICASSP 2007* pp. 269–272.

2

Application of ICA in Watermarking

Abolfazl Hajisami and S. N. Hosseini
Sharif University of Technology
Iran

1. Introduction

Data embedding in an image may be carried out in different domains, including spatial and transform domains. Early image watermarking schemes operated directly in spatial domain, which were mostly associated with poor robustness properties. Accordingly, different transform domains have been studied in the last decade to improve the efficiency and the robustness of watermarking methods (Bounkong et al., 2003; Cox et al., 1997; Langelaar et al., 1997; M.Wang et al., 1998). One of the most effective transform in this area is ICA transform.

Independent Component Analysis (ICA) is a statistical and computational technique for revealing hidden factors that underlie sets of random variables, measurements, or signals (Comon, 1994). The ICA is typically known as a method for Blind Source Separation (BSS) and can be used in watermarking. It is studied in (Bounkong et al., 2003) that the ICA allows the maximization of the information content and minimization of the induced distortion by decomposing the original signal into statistically independent sources used for data embedding.

The idea of applying ICA to image watermarking has been presented in quite a handful of studies, such as in the works of (Bounkong et al., 2003; Gonzalez-Serrano et al., 2001; Hajisami et al., 2011; Shen et al., 2003; Yu et al., 2002; Zhang & Rajan, 2002). The similarity between ICA and watermarking schemes and the blind separation ability of ICA are the reasons that make ICA an attractive approach for watermarking (Nguyen et al., 2008).

Watermarking methods can be categorized into three major groups: blind, semi-blind, and non-blind (Lu, 2004). In the blind methods, there is no need for the original signal or the watermark for watermark extraction. In semi-blind methods, some features of the original signal are to be known a priori, where the original signal should be available for extracting the watermark in non-blind methods.

Firstly, in this chapter we investigate the problem of decomposition of a signal into multiple scales with a different point of view. More accurately, we propose an algorithm that contains two steps. At the first step, we decompose our signal by the use of a blocking method in which we divide the original signal into the blocks of the same size. By putting the corresponding components of each block into a vector, we can extract a number of observation signals from the original signal. At the second step, we apply a linear transform on these extracted signals. In addition, we need to find a suitable transform to analyze the original signal into multiples scales. Therefore, we see our problem as a blind source separation (BSS) problem in which the above extracted signals from different blocks are the observations in the source separation problem. Indeed, by the use of our blocking technique the extracted signals contain adjacent components of the original signal which are similar to each other, because of the fact that neighboring components of an ordinary signal are so close to each other in the sense of magnitude. Hence, by extracting the independent components of these observations by the use of ICA, one can expect that one of the resulting sources will be an approximation of the original signal while the others, will stand for details. In addition, this method of decomposing, which is called MRICA, has the advantage that it results in statistically independent components which may have applications in some signal processing areas such as watermarking (Hajisami & Ghaemmaghami, Oct. 2010).

It is reported in (Bounkong et al., 2003) that in the context of watermarking, ICA allows the maximization of the information content and minimization of the induced distortion by decomposing the cover signal into statistically independent components. Embedding information in one of these independent components minimizes the emerging cross-channel interference. In fact, for a broad class of attacks and fixed capacity values, one can show that distortion is minimized when the message is embedded in statistically independent components. Information theoretical analysis also shows that the information hiding capacity of statistically independent components is maximal (Moulin & O'Sullivan, 2003). Also as we mentioned above, MRICA can decompose the original signal into approximation and details that are statistically independent. Hence, we can exploit MRICA to improve the watermarking schemes.

This chapter is organized as follows. In the next section, some preliminary issues around the subject of BSS and ICA will be provided. Following by that, in Section 3, we will introduce MRICA and its multi-scale decomposition property. After that, in Section 4 and Section 5,two watermarking schemes are presented based on MRICA. Finally, The conclusion is drawn in Section 6.

2. Blind source separation and independent component analysis

In the BSS, a set of mixtures of different source signals is available and the goal is to separate the source signals, when we have no information about the mixing system or the source signals (hence the name blind). The mixing and separating systems are shown in Fig. 1 that can be represented mathematically as:

$$\begin{aligned} \mathbf{x}(t) &= \mathbf{A}\mathbf{s}(t) \\ \mathbf{y}(t) &= \mathbf{B}\mathbf{x}(t) \end{aligned} \tag{1}$$

in which $\mathbf{s}(t) = [s_1(t), \ldots, s_N(t)]^T$ is the vector of sources that are mixed by the mixing matrix $\mathbf{A}$ and create the observations vector $\mathbf{x}(t) = [x_1(t), \ldots, x_N(t)]^T$. Let also $\mathbf{A}$ be a the square matrix $(N \times N)$ of full column rank that means number of sources are equal to the number of observations and observations are linearly independent. The goal is to achieve the separating matrix $\mathbf{B}$ such that the $\mathbf{y}(t) = [y_1(t), \ldots, y_N(t)]^T$ is an estimation of the sources. The ICA, as a method for the BSS, exploits the assumption of source independence and estimates $\mathbf{B}$ such that the outputs y_i's are statistically independent. It has been shown (Comon, 1994) that this leads to retrieving the source signals provided that there are at most one Gaussian source.

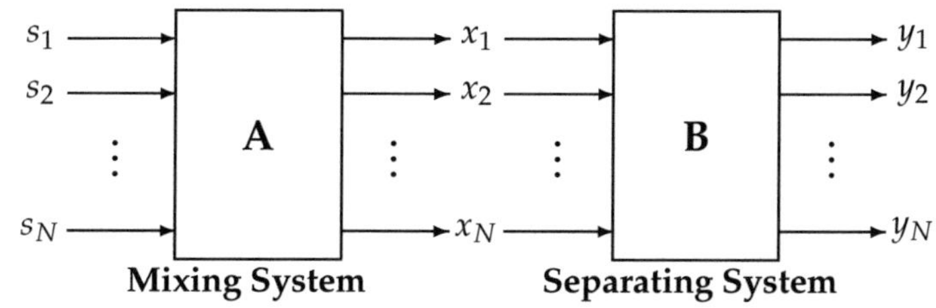

Fig. 1. Mixing and separating systems in BSS.

3. Multi Resolution by Independent Component Analysis (MRICA)

In this section we propose a new idea for multi-scale decomposition based on ICA called MRICA. Our method has two steps: 1) blocking the original signal and extracting our observation signals. 2) decomposing the original signal by a linear transform. Henceforth, we describe the motivation of our idea. Suppose that $s_1(t)$ and $s_2(t)$ are two independent signals which $s_1(t)$ has much more energy than $s_2(t)$. Also, suppose that $x_1(t)$ and $x_2(t)$ are two linear mixture of $s_1(t)$ and $s_2(t)$ which are presented as:

$$\begin{bmatrix} x_1(t) \\ x_2(t) \end{bmatrix} = \begin{bmatrix} 1 & 1 \\ 1 & 0.9 \end{bmatrix} \begin{bmatrix} s_1(t) \\ s_2(t) \end{bmatrix} \tag{2}$$

In this case the shape of $x_1(t)$ and $x_2(t)$ is completely similar to the $s_1(t)$ (the signal with the more energy). Now, if we consider $x_1(t)$ and $x_2(t)$ as observations of the ICA algorithm, outputs will consist of two parts: 1) $s_1(t)$ that is the signal with the more energy and is similar to the mixtures of $x_1(t)$ and $x_2(t)$, and 2) $s_2(t)$ that is the signal with lower energy. Therefore, we expect that if we extract two **similar** signals from the $x(t)$ and consider them as $x_1(t)$ and $x_2(t)$, by applying ICA algorithm to these two signals, we must have two signals in the output, as one of them is the approximation signal and must be similar to $x_1(t)$ and $x_2(t)$ and the other one is the detail signal.

Generally, for decomposing the one-dimensional signal into k level approximation and details, it is sufficient to divide it into blocks of length k and consider the corresponding components of the blocks as an observation of the ICA algorithm. On the other hand for decomposing the two-dimensional signal into k^2 level of approximation and details it is sufficient to divide it into blocks of size $k \times k$ and consider the corresponding components of these blocks as an observation of the ICA algorithm. Procedure of blocking for one-dimensional and two-dimensional signals is shown in Fig. 2, in which $x_j(i)$ is ith sample of jth observation. Therefore, we will get k and k^2 observation signals for one-dimensional and two dimensional signals, respectively. Fig. 3 and Fig. 4 show the observation signals which are obtained from the blocking process. Then, by applying the ICA into these observation signals, for one-dimensional signals we can get one approximation signal and $k-1$ detail signals and for two-dimensional signals we can get one approximation signal and k^2-1 detail signals. Hence, a new transform (MRICA), which is able to decompose signals into statistically independent approximation and details, is available.

To show the performance of the MRICA, a sinusoidal wave which is added to the white gaussian noise with zero mean and variance of 0.01, shown in Fig. 5, is supposed. Odd and even samples of this noisy signal are depicted in Fig. 6. By applying the ICA algorithm to these signals, we can decompose the noisy signal into the approximation and the detail

$x_1(1)$	$x_2(1)$	$x_3(1)$	$x_4(1)$	$x_1(2)$	$x_2(2)$	$x_3(2)$	$x_4(2)$	$x_1(3)$	$x_2(3)$	$x_3(3)$	$x_4(3)$	$x_1(4)$	$x_2(4)$	$x_3(4)$	$x_4(4)$

(a) Blocking procedure for one-dimensional signals ($k = 4$)

$x_1(1)$	$x_3(1)$	$x_1(4)$	$x_3(4)$	$x_1(7)$	$x_3(7)$
$x_2(1)$	$x_4(1)$	$x_2(4)$	$x_4(4)$	$x_2(7)$	$x_4(7)$
$x_1(2)$	$x_3(2)$	$x_1(5)$	$x_3(5)$	$x_1(8)$	$x_3(8)$
$x_2(2)$	$x_4(2)$	$x_2(5)$	$x_4(5)$	$x_2(8)$	$x_4(8)$
$x_1(3)$	$x_3(3)$	$x_1(6)$	$x_3(6)$	$x_1(9)$	$x_3(9)$
$x_2(3)$	$x_4(3)$	$x_2(6)$	$x_4(6)$	$x_2(9)$	$x_4(9)$

(b) Blocking procedure for two-dimensional signals ($k = 2$)

Fig. 2. Procedure of blocking

$x_1(1)$	$x_1(2)$	$x_1(3)$	$x_1(4)$

(a)

$x_2(1)$	$x_2(2)$	$x_2(3)$	$x_2(4)$

(b)

$x_3(1)$	$x_3(2)$	$x_3(3)$	$x_3(4)$

(c)

$x_4(1)$	$x_4(2)$	$x_4(3)$	$x_4(4)$

(d)

Fig. 3. Observation signals obtained from one-dimensional signal for $k = 4$

$x_1(1)$	$x_1(4)$	$x_1(7)$
$x_1(2)$	$x_1(5)$	$x_1(8)$
$x_1(3)$	$x_1(6)$	$x_1(9)$

(a)

$x_3(1)$	$x_3(4)$	$x_3(7)$
$x_3(2)$	$x_3(5)$	$x_3(8)$
$x_3(3)$	$x_3(6)$	$x_3(9)$

(b)

$x_2(1)$	$x_2(4)$	$x_2(7)$
$x_2(2)$	$x_2(5)$	$x_2(8)$
$x_2(3)$	$x_2(6)$	$x_2(9)$

(c)

$x_4(1)$	$x_4(4)$	$x_4(7)$
$x_4(2)$	$x_4(5)$	$x_4(8)$
$x_4(3)$	$x_4(6)$	$x_4(9)$

(d)

Fig. 4. Observation signals obtained from two-dimensional signal for $k = 2$

signals as shown in Fig. 7. Moreover, to demonstrate the performance of the MRICA for two-dimensional signals, we consider the *Lena* image which is shown in Fig. 8. If we suppose $k = 3$, then 9 observation signals will be obtained, which are exhibited in Fig. 9. Next, by applying the ICA to these 9 images, the *Lena* image can be decomposed into one approximation and 8 detail signals, which are depicted in Fig. 10.

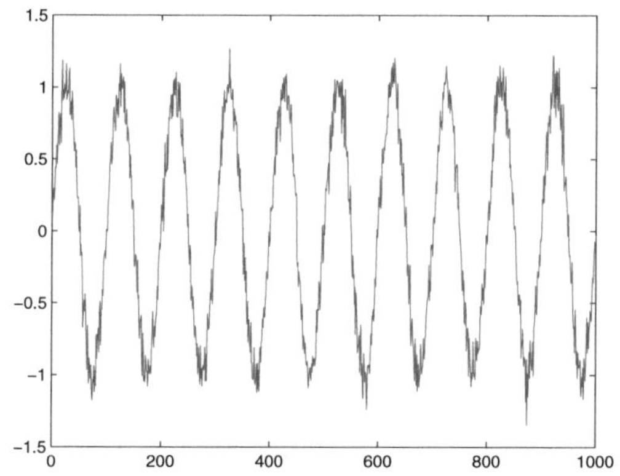

Fig. 5. Sinusoidal wave which is added to the white gaussian noise with zero mean and variance of 0.01.

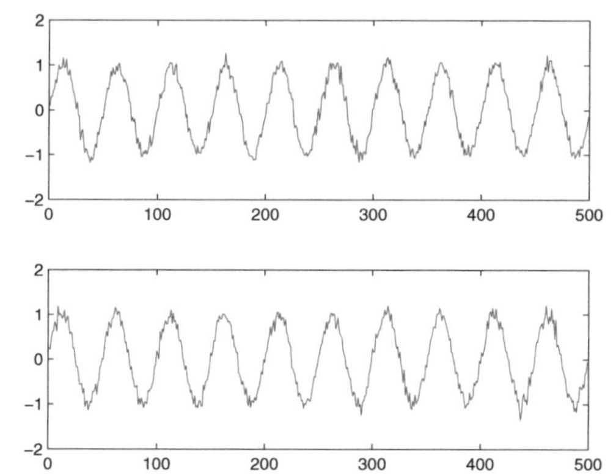

Fig. 6. Observation signals (from up to down odd samples and even samples, respectively).

4. First proposed watermarking algorithm based on MRICA

In this section, the main idea is to employ the MRICA properties in order to improve the robustness, imperceptibility, and embedding rate of the watermarking. In this method, we divide the original image into blocks of size $k \times k$ and consider the corresponding components of these blocks as an observation signal, so we will have k^2 observation signals. Then we apply the ICA to these observation signals to obtain k^2 independent signals that build our ICA bases (As we previously mentioned in Section 3). In other words, if I is an intensity image of size $n \times m$, we divide I into blocks $D_{i,j}$ of size $k \times k$, where $i = 1, \cdots, n/k$ and $j = 1, \cdots, m/k$, then

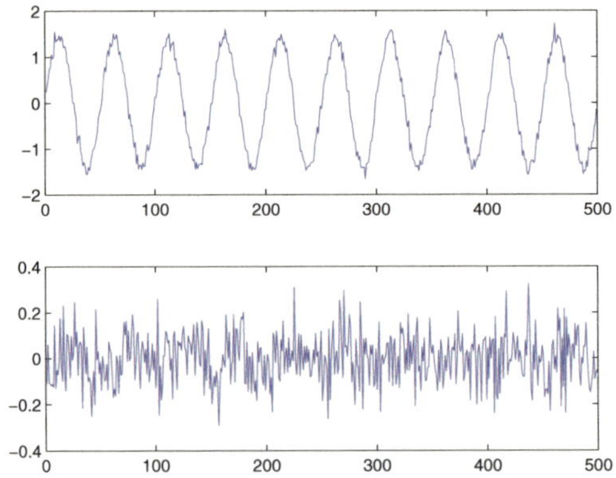

Fig. 7. Outputs of ICA algorithm (from up to down approximation and detail, respectively).

Fig. 8. Image of Lena

we place entries of each block on vector $\mathbf{x}_l$ of size $k^2 \times 1$, where l is the index of block number $l = 1, \cdots, nm/k^2$. The ICA problem consists of finding a $k^2 \times k^2$ matrix $\mathbf{B}$, as:

$$\mathbf{y}_l = \mathbf{B}\mathbf{x}_l \tag{3}$$

such that entries of $\mathbf{y}_l$ are statistically independent. Now, by placing each vector $\mathbf{x}_l$ on the lth column of matrix $\mathbf{X}$ of size $k^2 \times nm/k^2$, we can obtain matrix $\mathbf{Y}$, as:

$$\mathbf{Y} = \mathbf{B}\mathbf{X} \tag{4}$$

The rows of $\mathbf{Y}$ are statistically independent and are taken as our ICA bases. From (Lewicki et al., 1999) we know the ICA basis with highest energy has more information of image (see Fig. 13(a)), so it is expected to achieve higher robustness if we embed in this basis. Also, as mentioned in Section 1, maximization of the information content and minimization of the induced distortion will be attained by embedding information across independent sources obtained from the original signal through the decomposition process. Therefore, in our proposed method, we embed in the ICA basis of the highest energy:

$$IC_W = IC_H + \alpha W \tag{5}$$

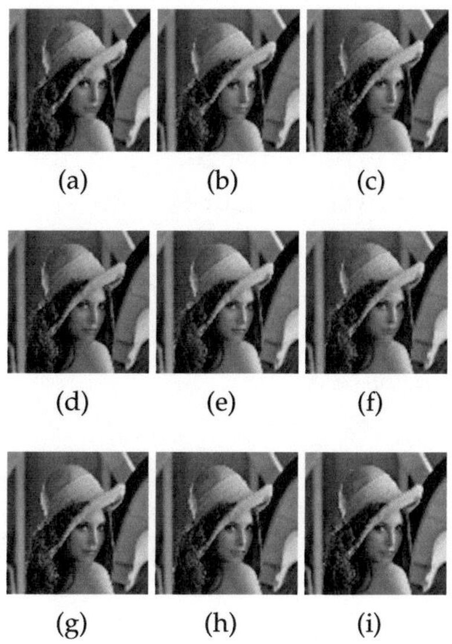

Fig. 9. Observation signals which are obtained from image of Lena for $k = 3$.

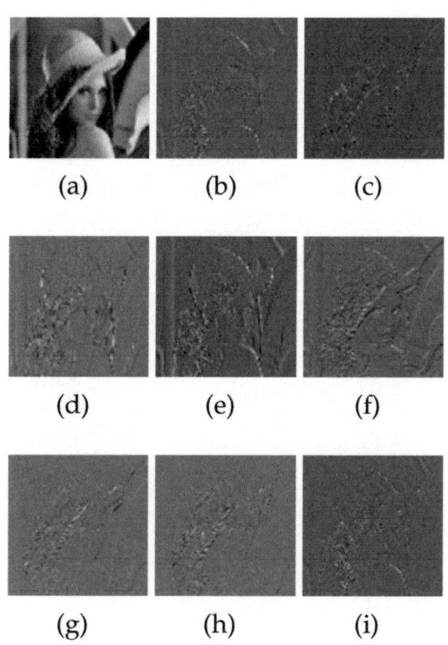

Fig. 10. Approximation and detail signals which are obtained from image of Lena for $k = 3$.

where IC_H is the ICA basis of the highest energy, W is the watermark and α denotes the embedding strength. The watermarking process outlined above can be summarized in the following algorithm:

1. Divide the original image into blocks of size $k \times k$ and compute the components $\mathbf{x}_l$.
2. Compute the ICA components $\mathbf{y}_l$ of the image.
3. Compute the ICA bases by constructing matrix $\mathbf{Y}$.
4. Embed the watermark in the ICA basis of highest energy, as described in (5).
5. Restore the matrix $\mathbf{X} = \mathbf{B}^{-1}\mathbf{Y}$.
6. Quantize entries of matrix $\mathbf{X}$ to obtain integer elements.
7. Restore the blocks from columns of $\mathbf{X}$.
8. Restore the image from the blocks.

We take the watermarking problem as a BSS problem, where the original image and the watermark are the statistically independent sources to be separated. Accordingly, the watermarked image is assumed to be the observation in the BSS model that undergoes the ICA based extracting process.

The extraction algorithm can be described as:

1. Divide both the original image and the watermarked one into blocks of size $k \times k$ and compute the components $\mathbf{x}_l$.
2. Use the ICA to obtain matrices $\mathbf{Y}$ and $\mathbf{Y}'$ of both watermarked and original images.
3. Obtain $IC_H + \alpha W$ and IC_H' of watermarked and original images, respectively.
4. Apply ICA to $IC_H + \alpha W$ and IC_H' to obtain W.

4.1 Condition of blind extraction

In this part, we will show that the watermark extraction in the proposed scheme can be treated as blind, if multiple copies of an image contain the watermark at different strengths. In this situation, IC_W's that are obtained from (5) become linearly independent. Assuming we have got N copies of an image to watermark, the embedding is carried out as:

$$\begin{bmatrix} IC_{W_1} \\ IC_{W_2} \\ \vdots \\ IC_{W_N} \end{bmatrix} = \begin{bmatrix} 1 & \alpha_1 \\ 1 & \alpha_2 \\ \vdots & \vdots \\ 1 & \alpha_N \end{bmatrix} \begin{bmatrix} C \\ W \end{bmatrix} \quad \text{and } \alpha_i \neq \alpha_j \text{ for } i \neq j \ , \tag{6}$$

To extract the watermark, it is sufficient to have two different copies of the watermarked images and follow the procedure given below.

1. Divide both the watermarked images into blocks of size $k \times k$ and compute the components $\mathbf{x}_l$ for each one.
2. Use the ICA to obtain matrices $\mathbf{Y}$ and $\mathbf{Y}'$ of both watermarked images.
3. Obtain $IC_H + \alpha W$ and $IC_H' + \alpha' W$ from the two watermarked images.
4. Apply ICA to linearly independent $IC_H + \alpha W$ and $IC_H' + \alpha' W$ to extract W.

4.2 Experimental results

In this section, we experimentally study the robustness of the suggested method against adding noise, resizing, lowpass filtering, multiple marks embedding, JPEG compression, gray-scale reduction, and cropping parts of the image. The results of these experiments show that this method is robust against the above attacks. Moreover, we show superiority of the proposed method over some well-known embedding methods, by comparing our results to those of the methods given in (Cox et al., 1997; Langelaar et al., 1997; M.Wang et al., 1998) that embed the watermark in different domains. It is to be noted that we have used FastICA algorithm (Hyvärinen, 1999) in our simulations.

4.2.1 Simulation setup

In our simulation, we have used a database of 200 natural images as the original images and 50 various logos as the watermarks. Fig. 11 illustrates a sample of a binary watermark image (Sharif university logo) of size 128×128 and original image (cameraman) of size 256×256. To embed the watermark, first we divide the original signal into blocks of size 2×2, so, four observation signals will be obtained, as shown in Fig. 12. Then, by applying the ICA to these signals, one approximation and tree detail signals will be acquired which are our ICA bases (see Fig. 13). In Fig. 14(a), the watermarked image that is created by (5) for $\alpha = \frac{3}{255}$ is shown. Figure 14(b) represents the extracted watermark from the watermarked image using the ICA. To measure the quality of the watermarked image, we use Peak Signal-to-Noise Ratio (PSNR). The PSNR between an image X and its perturbed version $\hat{X}$ is defined as:

$$\text{PSNR} = 20 \log_{10} \left(\frac{255}{\sqrt{1/(MN) \sum_{i=1}^{M} \sum_{j=1}^{N} (X_{(i,j)} - \hat{X}_{(i,j)})^2}} \right), \tag{7}$$

where $M \times N$ is the size of the two images. In the watermarked image that is shown in Fig. 14(a), PSNR is equal to $52.87dB$, whereas the PSNR in the methods of (Cox et al., 1997), (Langelaar et al., 1997) and (M.Wang et al., 1998) are equal to $38.4dB$, $36.7dB$ and $34.2dB$, respectively. To study the extraction process, we use Bite Error Rate (BER) that is defined as:

$$\text{BER} = \frac{\text{Number of error bits}}{\text{Number of total embedded bits}} . \tag{8}$$

In our experiments over the given original and watermark databases, we had $\text{BER} = 0.004$, as the average error rate.

4.2.2 Robustness against different attacks

In this section, we study the performance of the suggested method against different types of attacks.

Experiment 1 (Noise addition): In this experiment, we added a Gaussian noise of zero mean and variance 0.25 and a Salt & Pepper noise of density 0.5% to the watermarked image. It was observed that FastICA could still extract the watermark as shown in Fig. 15(b) and 16(b). This is because, after adding the Gaussian noise, Equation (5) changes to $IC_W = IC_H + \alpha W + n$, where n denotes the Gaussian noise. In this case, the two sources are IC_H and $\alpha W + n$ and, following the extraction process, we retrieve $\alpha W + n$ as the watermark. In case of additive

(a) Original image (b) Watermark

Fig. 11. Exhibition of original and watermark images

(a) (b)

(c) (d)

Fig. 12. Observation signals which are obtained from image of Cameraman for $k = 2$

(a) (b)

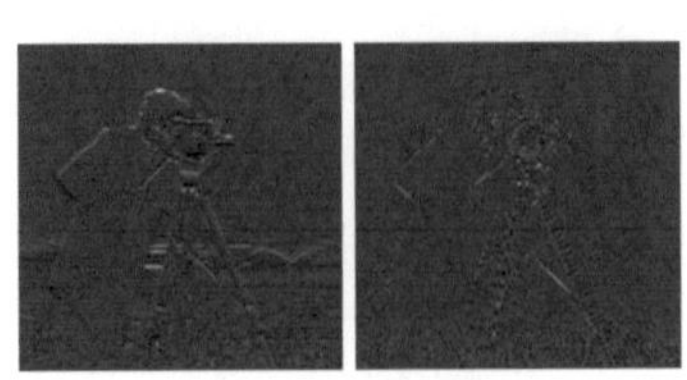

(c) (d)

Fig. 13. Approximation detail signals which are obtained from image of Cameraman for $k = 2$

(a) Watermarked image (b) Extracted watermark

Fig. 14. Exhibition of watermarked image and extracted watermark

Salt & Pepper noise, instantaneous mixture model might be destroyed for a number of pixels, but the ICA could still retrieve the sources.

(a) Watermarked image by applying Gaussian noise (b) Extracted watermark

Fig. 15. Exhibition of robustness against Gaussian noise

(a) Watermarked image by applying salt & pepper noise (b) Extracted watermark

Fig. 16. Exhibition of robustness against salt & pepper noise

Experiment 2 **(Lowpass filtering)**: we applied a lowpass filter to the watermarked image by averaging each pixel with its neighbors. The result of this filtering process is illustrated in Fig. 17(a). Our extraction algorithm was quite successful to detect the watermark, as shown in Fig. 17(b).

(a) Watermarked image by applying LPF filter

(b) Extracted watermark

Fig. 17. Exhibition of robustness against Lowpass filtering attack

Experiment 3 **(Resizing)**: We scaled down watermarked image by factor 2 using the *bilinear* method. To examine the extraction performance in this case, we used the resized version of the original image due to the ICA requirement. However, because we might not be aware of the resizing procedure employed by the attacker, we used the *bicubic* method to resize the original image. Our mark extraction method was again found successful in all such resizing attacks applied to the images in our database. An example is shown in Fig. 18.

(a) Watermarked image after resizing

(b) Extracted watermark

Fig. 18. Exhibition of robustness against resizing attack

Experiment 4 **(Multiple marks embedding)**: In order to study the performance of our method when another watermark is embedded in the genuine watermarked image, we added another watermark randomly selected from our watermark database. An example is shown in Fig. 19(a) that is the second watermark embedded into the watermarked cameraman image. It is observed from Fig. 19(b) that the original watermark can still be retrieved from the attacked image. This is because in this case, Equation (5) changes to $IC_W = IC_H + \alpha W + \beta W'$ and our two sources become IC_H and $\alpha W + \beta W'$, where $\alpha W + \beta W'$ is retrieved by the ICA as the watermark.

(a) Another watermark added to the watermarked image (b) Extracted watermark

Fig. 19. Exhibition of robustness against multiple marks embedding

Experiment 5 **(Cropping)**: Here, we cropped 25% of the image, and then applied our method to extract the watermark. Fig. 20 illustrates performance of the method in this case, where the instantaneous mixture model still holds for remainder pixels.

(a) Cropped watermarked image (b) Extracted watermark

Fig. 20. Exhibition of robustness against cropping attack

Experiment 6 **(Gray-scale reduction)**: In this experiment the gray-scale of watermarked image is reduced from 256 down to 64. In this case, the pixel value of new image is almost 1/4 times of the older one. Because the ICA is not sensitive to multiplying the observation by a constant, the watermark can still be retrieved, as illustrated in Fig. 21(b).

Experiment 7 **(JPEG compression)**: In the last experiment, we JPEG compressed the watermarked image by the quality factor of 80%. The result of our watermark retrieval method is displayed in Fig. 22(c) for the case of the cameraman. Results of a brief comparison made with two other well-known watermarking methods (Langelaar et al., 1997; M.Wang et al., 1998) are shown in Fig.22(b) against different JPEG quality factors.

(a) Watermarked image after gray-scale reduction (b) Extracted watermark

Fig. 21. Exhibition of robustness against Gray-scale reduction

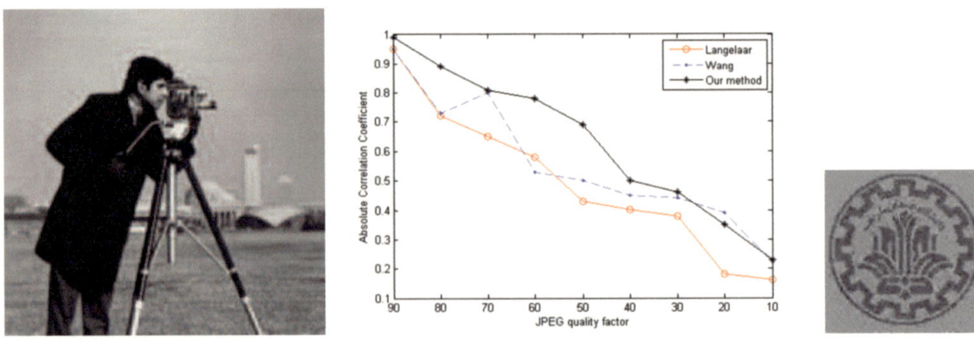

(a) Watermarked image after JPEG compression (b) Performance of this method against JPEG compression (c) Extracted watermark

Fig. 22. Exhibition of robustness against JPEG compression

5. Second proposed watermarking algorithm based on MRICA

In this part, a blind method for image watermarking is proposed which is robust against different type of attacks including noise addition, gray-scale reduction, cropping, and JPEG compression.

As mentioned in the Section. 3, MRICA is able to decompose the original signal into the approximation and the details that are statistically independent. In MRICA, detail signals with less energy are not valuable parts of the original signal and replacing them with the watermark will not have tangible impact on the quality of the original signal. Therefore, we decompose the original image into k^2 independent signals by means of MRICA. Accordingly, we will have one approximation and $k^2 - 1$ details. In order to embed the watermark, we eliminate the detail with the lowest energy and replace it with the watermark and then we convert the watermarked image into spatial domain. It should be noted that after converting the watermarked image into spatial domain, it is necessary to quantize the pixel values to obtain integer elements as image format. Also to extract the watermark, we decompose the watermarked image into k^2 independent signals by means of MRICA and extract the signal with lowest energy that is the watermark. Detailed procedures are explained as follows:

Suppose I is an intensity image of size $n \times m$, we divide I into blocks $D_{i,j}$ of size $k \times k$, where $i = 1, \cdots, n/k$ and $j = 1, \cdots, m/k$. Next, we construct matrix $\mathbf{Y}$, as explained in Section 4. The rows of matrix $\mathbf{Y}$ (approximation and detail signals) are statistically independent and are taken as our ICA bases. According to what we mentioned in Section. 1, the detail signal with lowest energy is not valuable part of image. Moreover, maximization of the information content and minimization of the induced distortion will be attained by embedding information across independent signals obtained from the original signal through the decomposition process. Therefore, in our proposed method, we replace the secret massage with the ICA basis of lowest energy:

$$IC_L = \alpha W \tag{9}$$

where IC_L is the ICA basis of the lowest energy, W is watermark and α denotes the embedding strength. The embedding process outlined above can be summarized as follows:

1. Divide the original image into blocks of size $k \times k$ and compute the components $\mathbf{x}_l$.
2. Compute the ICA components $\mathbf{y}_l$ of the image.
3. Compute the ICA basis (approximation and detail signals) by constructing matrix $\mathbf{Y}$.
4. Replace the watermark with the ICA basis of lowest energy, as described in (9).
5. Restore the matrix $\mathbf{X} = \mathbf{B}^{-1}\mathbf{Y}$.
6. Quantize entries of matrix $\mathbf{X}$ to obtain integer elements.
7. Restore the blocks from columns of $\mathbf{X}$.
8. Restore the image from blocks.

In order to extract the watermark, it is sufficient to apply MRICA to the image and get k^2 approximation and detail signals then the watermark is obvious between the detail signals.

5.1 Experimental results

In this section, we experimentally study the robustness of the suggested method against adding noise, gray-scale reduction, cropping parts of the image, and JPEG compression. The results of these experiments show that this method is robust against the above attacks. Moreover, we will show superiority of the MRICA over some well-known wavelet transforms.

5.1.1 Simulation setup

In our simulation, we have used a database of 200 natural images as the original images and 50 various binary logos as the watermark. Fig. 23 illustrates a sample of a binary watermark image (Sharif university logo) of size 128×128 and an original image (picture of ship) of size 256×256. To embed the watermark, first we divide the original signal into blocks of size 2×2, so 4 observation signals will be obtained, as shown in Fig. 24. Then by applying the ICA algorithm to these observations, one approximation and three detail signals can be obtained, shown in Fig. 25. After that, we replace the watermark with the detail signal of lowest energy (Fig. 25(d)). Finally, we convert the image into spatial domain and quantize pixel values to obtain integer elements. In Fig. 26(a), the watermarked image that is created by (9) for $\alpha = \frac{4}{255}$ is shown. To measure the quality of the watermarked image, we use Peak Signal-to-Noise Ratio (PSNR). In the watermarked image that is shown in Fig. 26(a), PSNR is equal to 41.87dB, whereas the PSNR in the methods of (Cox et al., 1997), (Langelaar et al., 1997) and (M.Wang et al., 1998) are equal to 38.4dB, 36.7dB and 34.2dB, respectively. After extraction process, the watermark will be obtained as shown in Fig. 26(b). In our experiments over the given original and watermark databases, we had BER = 0.007, as the average error rate. Moreover, in Figures 26(c) and 26(d), MRICA has been compared with Haar and db5 wavelet transforms as embedding is carried out by replacing the watermark with diagonal detail coefficients matrix of these wavelet transforms. BER = 0.233 and BER = 0.164 are obtained for Haar and db5 wavelet transforms, respectively.

(a) Original image (b) Watermark

Fig. 23. Exhibition of original and watermark images

(a) (b)

(c) (d)

Fig. 24. The observation signals that have been obtained through the blocking process.

5.2 Robustness against different attacks

In this section, we study the performance of the suggested method against different types of attacks.

Experiment 1 **(Noise addition)**: In this experiment, we added a Gaussian noise of zero mean and variance 0.25 and a Salt & Pepper noise of density 0.5% to the watermarked image. It was observed that MRICA could still extract the watermark as shown in Fig. 27(b) and 28(b).

(a) Approximation signal

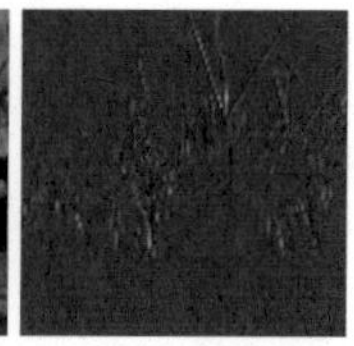

(b) Vertical detail signal

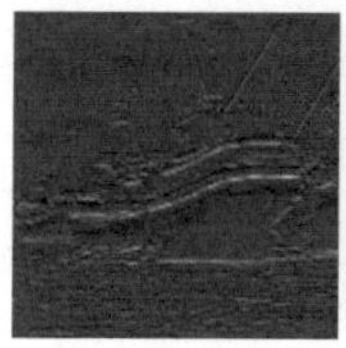

(c) Horizontal detail signal

(d) Diagonal detail signal

Fig. 25. Decomposing of the *ship* image into approximation and details by means of MRICA.

(a) Watermarked image

(b) Extracted watermark by means of MRICA

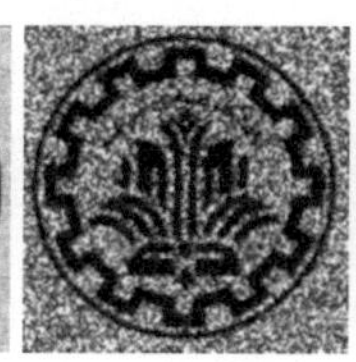

(c) Extracted watermark by means of Haar wavelet transform

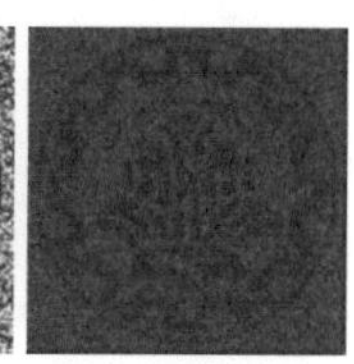

(d) Extracted watermark by means of db5 wavelet transform

Fig. 26. Watermark Extraction.

Also, watermarks that have been extracted by Haar and db5 wavelet transforms are shown in Fig. 27(c) and 27(d). The average error rates obtained for Fig. 27(b), 27(c), and 27(d) are BER = 0.011, BER = 0.291, and BER = 0.185, respectively.

Experiment 2 **(Gray-scale reduction)**: In this experiment, the gray-scale of the watermarked image is reduced from 256 down to 64. In this case, the pixel value of new image is almost 1/4 times of the older one. Because ICA is not sensitive to multiplying the observation by a constant, the watermark still can be retrieved, as illustrated in Fig. 29(b). Moreover, Fig. 29(c) and 29(d) exhibit that MRICA is more successful than Haar and db5 wavelet transforms.

(a) Watermarked image by applying Gaussian noise of mean 0 and variance 0.25

(b) Extracted watermark by means of MRICA

(c) Extracted watermark by means of Haar wavelet transform

(d) Extracted watermark by means of db5 wavelet transform

Fig. 27. Exhibition of robustness against Gaussian noise

(a) Watermarked image by applying Salt & Pepper noise

(b) Extracted watermark by means of MRICA

(c) Extracted watermark by means of Haar wavelet transform

(d) Extracted watermark by means of db5 wavelet transform

Fig. 28. Exhibition of robustness against salt & pepper noise

Experiment 3 **(Cropping)**: Here, we cropped 25% of the watermarked image, and then applied our method to extract the watermark. Fig. 30 illustrates performance of the method in this case, where the instantaneous mixture model still holds for remainder pixels.

Experiment 4 **(JPEG compression)**: In the last experiment, we JPEG compressed the watermarked image by the quality factor of 80%. The result of our watermark retrieval method is displayed in Fig. 31(b). Moreover, Fig. 31(c) and 31(d) demonstrate performance improvement of MRICA compared with Haar and db5 wavelet transforms. In addition, results of a brief comparison made with two other well-known methods (Langelaar et al., 1997; M.Wang et al., 1998) are shown in Fig.32 against different JPEG quality factors.

(a) Watermarked image after gray-scale reduction

(b) Extracted watermark by means of MRICA

(c) Extracted watermark by means of Haar wavelet transform

(d) Extracted watermark by means of db5 wavelet transform

Fig. 29. Exhibition of robustness against Gray-scale reduction

(a) Cropped watermarked image

(b) Extracted watermark by means of MRICA

(c) Extracted watermark by means of Haar wavelet transform

(d) Extracted watermark by means of db5 wavelet transform

Fig. 30. Exhibition of robustness against cropping attack

(a) Watermarked image after JPEG compression

(b) Extracted watermark by means of MRICA

(c) Extracted watermark by means of Haar wavelet transform

(d) Extracted watermark by means of db5 wavelet transform

Fig. 31. Exhibition of robustness against JPEG compression

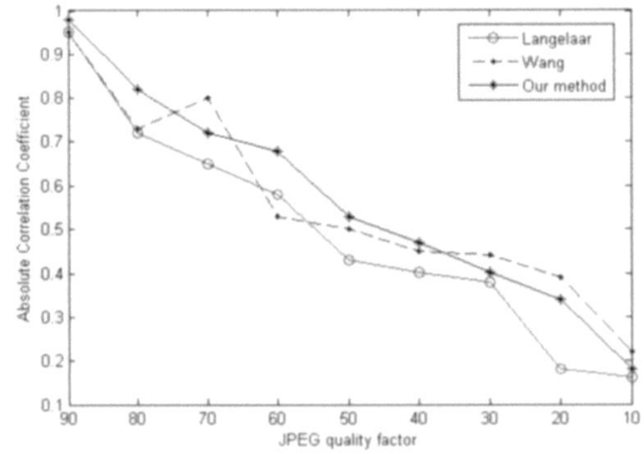

Fig. 32. Performance of our method against JPEG compression.

6. Conclusion

In this chapter, a new basis, which is based on ICA, for watermarking was introduced. For constructing the ICA basis, at first a new method for multi-scale decomposition called MRICA was presented. For MRICA, we divided the original image into blocks of same size. Then, we considered the corresponding components of these blocks as the observation signals. After that, by applying the ICA algorithm to these observation signals, we projected the original signal into a basis with its components as statistically independent as possible. Next, two watermarking algorithms were proposed in which data embedding was carried out in the ICA basis and the MRICA was used for watermark extraction. Experimental results showed that the MRICA outperforms wavelet transform in our watermarking schemes. Also, it was shown that our watermarking schemes has better performance than some well-known methods (Cox et al., 1997; Langelaar et al., 1997; M.Wang et al., 1998) and is robust against various attacks, including noise addition, gray-scale reduction, cropping parts of image, and JPEG compression.

7. References

Bounkong, S., Toch, B., Saad, D. & Lowe, D. (2003). ICA for watermarking digital images, *Journal of Machine Learning Research* 4(7): 1471–1498.

Comon, P. (1994). Independent component analysis, a new concept?, *Signal Processing* 36(3): 287Ű–314.

Cox, I. J., Kilian, J., Leighton, F. T. & Shamoon, T. (1997). Secure spread spectrum watermarking for multimedia, *IEEE Transactions on Image Processing* 6(12): 1673–1687.

Gonzalez-Serrano, F. J., Molina-Bulla, H. Y. & Murillo-Fuentes, J. J. (2001). Independent component analysis applied to digital image watermarking, *Proceedings of the IEEE International Conference on Acoustics, Speech, and Signal Processing (ICASSP '01)* 3: 1997–2000.

Hajisami, A. & Ghaemmaghami, S. (Oct. 2010). Robust Image Watermarking Using Independent Component Analysis, *Third International Symposium on Information Processing*, pp. 363–367.

Hajisami, A., Rahmati, A. & Babaie-Zadeh, M. (2011). Watermarking based on independent component analysis in spatial domain, *2011 UKSim 13th International Conference on Modelling and Simulation*, IEEE, pp. 299–303.

Hyvärinen, A. (1999). Fast and robust fixed-point algorithms for independent component analysis, *IEEE Transactions on Neural Networks* 10(3): 626–634.

Langelaar, G. C., van der Lubbe, J. C. A. & Lagendijk, R. L. (1997). Robust labeling methods for copy protection of images, *Proceedings of SPIE* 3022: 298–309.

Lewicki, M., Lee, T. & Sejnowski, T. (1999). Unsupervised classification with non-gaussian mixture models using ica, 11.

Lu, C. (2004). *Multimedia security: steganography and digital watermarking techniques for protection of intellectual property*, Idea Group Publishing.

Moulin, P. & O'Sullivan, J. (2003). Information-theoretic analysis of information hiding, *Information Theory, IEEE Transactions on* 49(3): 563–593.

M.Wang, H.-J., Su, P.-C. & Kuo, C.-C. J. (1998). Wavelet-based digital image watermarking, *Optics Express* 3(12): 491–496.

Nguyen, T. V., Patra, J. C. & Meher, P. K. (2008). A new digital watermarking technique using independent component analysis, *EURASIP Journal on Advances in Signal Processing* 2008.

Shen, M., Zhang, X., Sun, L., Beadle, P. J., & Chan, F. H. Y. (2003). A method for digital image watermarking using ICA, *Proceedings of the 4th International Symposium on Independent Component Analysis and Blind Signal Separation (ICA '03)* pp. 209–214.

Yu, D., Sattar, F. & Ma, K.-K. (2002). Watermark detection and extraction using independent component analysis method, *EURASIP Journal on Applied Signal Processing* 2002(1): 92–104.

Zhang, S. & Rajan, P. K. (2002). Independent component analysis of digital image watermarking, *Proceedings of the IEEE International Symposium on Circuits and Systems (ISCAS '02)* 3: 217–220.

3

Pixel Value Adjustment for Digital Watermarking Using Uniform Color Space

Motoi Iwata, Takao Ikemoto, Akira Shiozaki and Akio Ogihara
Osaka Prefecture University
Japan

1. Introduction

In this chapter, we propose a pixel adjustment procedure for digital watermarking methods using uniform color space. Many digital watermarking methods use uniform color space due to the convenience of controlling image quality (Yoshiura & Echizen, 2006). However, there is the problem that watermarked RGB integer pixel values in such methods are not quite corresponding to the watermarked real-number pixel values in uniform color space because the color transform between RGB space and uniform color space is non-linear, where we assume that the watermarked RGB integer pixel values are obtained by rounding off the RGB real pixel values transformed from the real pixel values in uniform color space. Note that RGB space means sRGB color space in this chapter. In sRGB color space, each color component is stored as an integer value and the range of pixel values is [0, 255]. This problem often causes erroneous extraction.

We have already found that the simple rounding off procedure used in many existing watermarking methods is not enough to control robustness. Then we didn't use the simple rounding off procedure but used RGB neighboring search procedure for calculating watermarked RGB integer pixel values in our watermarking method for uniform color space (Iwata et al., 2010). In RGB neighboring search, firstly we obtain watermarked RGB real-number pixel values from the watermarked real pixel values in uniform color space. Next we obtain eight ($= 2^3$) candidates by rounding up or rounding down each pixel value in R, G and B components. Finally we select suitable one for extracting correct watermark bits. We confirmed that we could improve the robustness by using RGB neighboring search procedure. In fact, RGB neighboring search procedure is the most suitable for watermarking methods using linear color transformations such as YCbCr.

In case of watermarking methods using uniform color space, the most suitable pixel value for extracting correct watermark bits is not always in the eight candidates in RGB neighboring search because color transformation between RGB space and uniform color space is non-linear. Therefore we propose a new pixel value adjustment procedure based on a color transformation table. The color transformation table represents the relationship between RGB integer pixel values and the corresponding real pixel values in uniform color space. It is the advantage by using the color transformation table that we can select the most suitable real-number pixel values in uniform color space from the candidates which correspond to RGB integer pixel values. Note that each candidate can be extracted as the same value as the original value even after transforming it into RGB space and then transforming it into uniform color space again. Therefore we can obtain the selected real-number pixel values in uniform color space from watermarked images. We adopt two approaches to use the color transformation table. One is that the color transformation table is applied to watermarked real pixel values in uniform color space after embedding. In this approach, we search the pixel value nearest to the watermarked real pixel value. The other is that the color transformation table is applied to original pixel values in uniform color space before embedding. In this approach, we select the most suitable pixel value for embedding from the set of colors near the original pixel value, where original pixel value means the pixel value of an image which is going to be watermarked but has not yet.

In experiments, we demonstrate the advantage of the proposed pixel value adjustment based on color transformation table by comparing with the simple rounding off procedure and RGB neighboring search procedure. Moreover we demonstrate the advantage of the latter approach described above.

The rest of this chapter consists of six sections. Firstly We describe color spaces in Sec. 2. Next we introduce existing pixel value adjustments and propose a new pixel value adjustment procedure based on color transformation table in Sec. 3. Then we describe two approaches utilizing pixel value adjustments in Sec. 4. Moreover we describe watermarking procedure for evaluating pixel value adjustments in Sec. 5. Then we show and discuss the performance of the proposed pixel value adjustment and the proposed approach in Sec. 6. Finally we conclude this chapter in Sec. 7.

2. Color spaces

In this section, we describe sRGB color space, XYZ color space and L*a*b*color space in Sec. 2.1, Sec. 2.2 and Sec. 2.3 respectively.

2.1 sRGB color space

sRGB color space is a standard RGB color space used for general monitors and so on. In sRGB, one color is composed of red, green and blue components. Each component is represented by an integer value of size 8 bits. The range of each component is [0, 255]. Then one color is represented by 24 bits.

2.2 XYZ color space

XYZ color space is a color space established by CIE (Commission Internationale de l'Eclairage) in 1931. The transformation of sRGB color space into XYZ color space is as follows (JSA, 2007):

2.2.1 sRGB to XYZ

First we obtain gamma-transformed sRGB color space by the following equations.

$$R_{\bullet} = \begin{cases} \dfrac{\hat{R}}{12.92}, & \hat{R} \leq 0.04045 \\ \left(\dfrac{\hat{R}+0.055}{1.055}\right)^{2.4}, & \text{otherwise} \end{cases} \tag{1}$$

$$G_{\bullet} = \begin{cases} \dfrac{\hat{G}}{12.92}, & \hat{G} \leq 0.04045 \\ \left(\dfrac{\hat{G}+0.055}{1.055}\right)^{2.4}, & \text{otherwise} \end{cases} \tag{2}$$

$$B_{\bullet} = \begin{cases} \dfrac{\hat{B}}{12.92}, & \hat{B} \leq 0.04045 \\ \left(\dfrac{\hat{B}+0.055}{1.055}\right)^{2.4}, & \text{otherwise} \end{cases} \tag{3}$$

$$\hat{R} = \frac{R}{255} \tag{4}$$

$$\hat{G} = \frac{G}{255} \tag{5}$$

$$\hat{B} = \frac{B}{255} \tag{6}$$

where $R_{\bullet}$, $G_{\bullet}$ and $B_{\bullet}$ are the values in gamma-transformed sRGB color space, and R, G and B are the values in sRGB color space.

Then we obtain XYZ color space from gamma-transformed sRGB color space by the following equations.

$$\begin{pmatrix} X \\ Y \\ Z \end{pmatrix} = \begin{pmatrix} 0.412453 & 0.35758 & 0.180423 \\ 0.212671 & 0.71516 & 0.072169 \\ 0.019334 & 0.119193 & 0.950227 \end{pmatrix} \begin{pmatrix} R_{\bullet} \\ G_{\bullet} \\ B_{\bullet} \end{pmatrix} \tag{7}$$

where X, Y, Z represents the value of X component, Y component and Z component respectively.

2.2.2 XYZ to sRGB as real-number

The pixel value (X, Y, Z) in XYZ color space can be transformed into the corresponding pixel value (R, G, B) in sRGB color space by the following equations. Note that R, G and B in Eqs.(9) $\sim$ (11) are not integers but real-numbers.

$$\begin{pmatrix} R_{\bullet} \\ G_{\bullet} \\ B_{\bullet} \end{pmatrix} = \begin{pmatrix} 3.2406 & -1.5372 & -0.4986 \\ -0.9689 & 1.8758 & 0.415 \\ 0.0557 & -0.2040 & 1.0570 \end{pmatrix} \begin{pmatrix} X \\ Y \\ Z \end{pmatrix} \tag{8}$$

$$R = \begin{cases} 255 \times 1.055 R_{\bullet}^{\frac{1}{2.4}} - 0.055, & R_{\bullet} > 0.0031308 \\ 255 \times 12.92 R_{\bullet}, & \text{otherwise} \end{cases} \tag{9}$$

$$G = \begin{cases} 255 \times 1.055 G_{\bullet}^{\frac{1}{2.4}} - 0.055, & G_{\bullet} > 0.0031308 \\ 255 \times 12.92 G_{\bullet}, & \text{otherwise} \end{cases} \quad (10)$$

$$B = \begin{cases} 255 \times 1.055 B_{\bullet}^{\frac{1}{2.4}} - 0.055, & B_{\bullet} > 0.0031308 \\ 255 \times 12.92 B_{\bullet}, & \text{otherwise} \end{cases} \quad (11)$$

2.3 L*a*b*color space

L*a*b*color space is one of uniform color spaces established by CIE in 1976 (*Lab color space*, n.d.). In a uniform color space, the distances between colors are fixed based on the perceptual differences between the colors (JSA, 2007; Oyama, 2000).

2.3.1 XYZ to L*a*b*

The pixel value (X, Y, Z) in XYZ color space can be transformed into the corresponding pixel value (L^*, a^*, b^*) in L*a*b*color space by the following equations.

$$L^* = 116 f\left(\frac{Y}{Y_n}\right) - 16 \quad (12)$$

$$a^* = 500\left\{f\left(\frac{X}{X_n}\right) - f\left(\frac{Y}{Y_n}\right)\right\} \quad (13)$$

$$b^* = 200\left\{f\left(\frac{Y}{Y_n}\right) - f\left(\frac{Z}{Z_n}\right)\right\} \quad (14)$$

where

$$f(t) = \begin{cases} t^{\frac{1}{3}}, & \text{if } t > \left(\frac{6}{29}\right)^3 \\ \frac{1}{3}\left(\frac{29}{6}\right)^2 t + \frac{16}{116}, & \text{otherwise} \end{cases} \quad (15)$$

where X_n, Y_n and Z_n are coefficients which depend upon the illuminant (for daylight illuminant D65, $X_n = 95.045$, $Y_n = 100$ and $Z_n = 108.892$).

2.3.2 L*a*b*to XYZ

The reverse transformation is as follows:

$$Y = Y_n f^{-1}\left(\frac{1}{116}(L^* + 16)\right) \quad (16)$$

$$X = X_n f^{-1}\left(\frac{1}{116}(L^* + 16) + \frac{1}{500}a^*\right) \quad (17)$$

$$Z = Z_n f^{-1}\left(\frac{1}{116}(L^* + 16) - \frac{1}{200}b^*\right) \quad (18)$$

where

$$f(t) = \begin{cases} t^3, & \text{if } t > \frac{6}{29} \\ 3\left(\frac{6}{29}\right)^2\left(t - \frac{4}{29}\right), & \text{otherwise} \end{cases} \tag{19}$$

3. Pixel value adjustment

In this section, we use L*a*b*color space and RGB color space as pre-transform color space and transformed color space respectively. Let (L^*, a^*, b^*) be a pixel value in L*a*b*color space and let (R, G, B) be the corresponding pixel value in RGB color space, where the pixel values of pre-transformed color space are real numbers and those of transformed color space are integers. Pixel value adjustments transform (L^*, a^*, b^*) to (R, G, B) in each manner described in the following sections.

3.1 Simple adjustment

Firstly (L^*, a^*, b^*) is transformed to (R', G', B') by the equations described in Sec. 2, where R', G' and B' are real numbers calculated by the equations. Then R, G and B are obtained by rounding R', G' and B' off to integers respectively.

3.2 Adjustment by RGB neighboring search

Firstly (L^*, a^*, b^*) is transformed to (R', G', B') by the equations described in Sec. 2 as same as simple adjustment. Next the candidates $\bullet_i (0 \leq i < 8)$ are calculated as the following:

$$\bullet_1 = (\lfloor R' \rfloor, \lfloor G' \rfloor, \lfloor B' \rfloor) \tag{20}$$

$$\bullet_2 = (\lfloor R' \rfloor, \lfloor G' \rfloor, \lceil B' \rceil) \tag{21}$$

$$\bullet_3 = (\lfloor R' \rfloor, \lceil G' \rceil, \lfloor B' \rfloor) \tag{22}$$

$$\bullet_4 = (\lfloor R' \rfloor, \lceil G' \rceil, \lceil B' \rceil) \tag{23}$$

$$\bullet_5 = (\lceil R' \rceil, \lfloor G' \rfloor, \lfloor B' \rfloor) \tag{24}$$

$$\bullet_6 = (\lceil R' \rceil, \lfloor G' \rfloor, \lceil B' \rceil) \tag{25}$$

$$\bullet_7 = (\lceil R' \rceil, \lceil G' \rceil, \lfloor B' \rfloor) \tag{26}$$

$$\bullet_8 = (\lceil R' \rceil, \lceil G' \rceil, \lceil B' \rceil) \tag{27}$$

where $\lfloor R' \rfloor$ represents the maximum integer which is less than R', and $\lceil R' \rceil$ represents the minimum integer which is larger than R'. Finally one of the above eight candidates is selected as (R, G, B). The general criterion of this selection is the Euclidean distance between (L^*, a^*, b^*) and (L_i^*, a_i^*, b_i^*), where L_i^*, a_i^* and b_i^* are the corresponding pixel value in L*a*b*color space to $\bullet_i$.

3.3 Adjustment based on color transformation table

3.3.1 Color transformation table

Color transformation table represents the relationship between RGB integer pixel values and the corresponding real pixel values in uniform color space. In this chapter, we use color transformation table to transform real-number pixel values in uniform color space into the corresponding integer pixel values in RGB color space. The output of color transformation table is the set of real-number pixel values in uniform color space which are near to the input pixel value. Note that all pixels in the set can be transformed without loss into RGB color space because they have the integer pixel values corresponding to themselves in RGB color space.

3.3.2 Adjustment procedure

Firstly (L^*, a^*, b^*) is transformed to $Z = \{\bullet_i\}$, where $\bullet_i$ represents a color in uniform color space near to the input (L^*, a^*, b^*). In the set Z, the nearest color to the input is $\bullet_0$, followed in order by $\bullet_1, \bullet_2, \ldots$. Then one of the colors in the set is selected, and is transformed without loss into the corresponding (R, G, B).

3.3.3 Approximate search

Exhaustive search to obtain Z requires extraordinary computational cost. Thus we use the approximate search to obtain Z as follows:

step1 The input (L^*, a^*, b^*) is given. Z is initialized to $Z = \emptyset$. The parameters $\bullet$ and n are fixed, where $\bullet$ represents the range of approximate search around the input, and T_Z represents the minimum number of $|Z|$.

step2 Add the colors $\bullet$ satisfying $|L^* - L^*(\bullet)| \leq \bullet$ to Z, where $L^*(\bullet)$ represents the L^* component at $\bullet$.

step3 Remove the colors $\bullet$ satisfying $|a^* - a^*(\bullet)| > \bullet$ from Z, where $a^*(\bullet)$ represents the a^* component at $\bullet$.

step4 Remove the colors $\bullet$ satisfying $|b^* - b^*(\bullet)| > \bullet$ from Z, where $b^*(\bullet)$ represents the b^* component at $\bullet$.

step5 If $|Z| \geq T_Z$, go to step6. Otherwise, increase $\bullet = \bullet + \mathrm{d}\bullet$, initialize $Z = \emptyset$, and go to step2, where $\mathrm{d}\bullet$ is a pre-determined constant value.

step6 Sort $\bullet_i$ in Z so that the Euclidean distance between the input (L^*, a^*, b^*) and $\bullet_0$ is the shortest, followed in order by $\bullet_1, \bullet_2, \ldots$.

Finally we obtain the set Z of colors which are near to the input (L^*, a^*, b^*). All colors $\bullet_i$ in Z calculated by this approximate search satisfy $|L^* - L^*(\bullet_i)| \leq \bullet$, $|a^* - a^*(\bullet_i)| \leq \bullet$, $|b^* - b^*(\bullet_i)| \leq \bullet$ and $|Z| \geq T_Z$.

4. Approaches to use pixel value adjustment procedures

We adopt two approaches to use the color transformation table. One is that the color transformation table is applied to watermarked real-number pixel values in uniform color

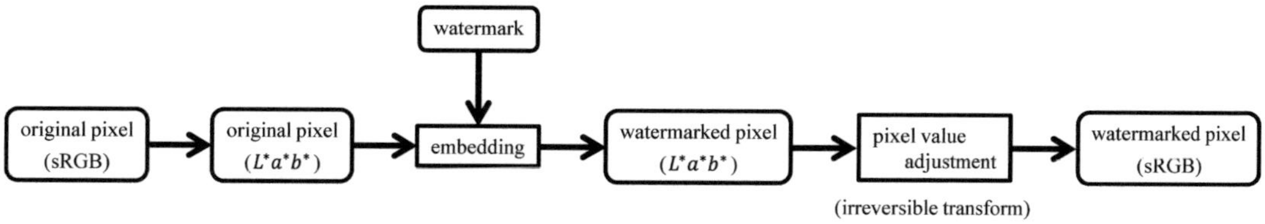

Fig. 1. Former approach : Adjustment after embedding

space after embedding. In this approach, we search the pixel value nearest to the watermarked real-number pixel value. Generally, simple adjustment and adjustment by RGB neighboring search are also adopt this approach. The other is that the color transformation table is applied to original pixel values in uniform color space before embedding. In this approach, we select the most suitable pixel value for embedding from the set of colors near the original pixel value, where original pixel value means the pixel value of an image which is going to be watermarked but has not yet. The former approach is existing one, and the latter approach is new one we proposed.

4.1 Adjustment after embedding

Figure 1 shows the flow of the former approach described here. This approach is generally used for many existing methods using a uniform color space.

step1 Original pixels in sRGB color space are transformed into the corresponding original pixels in L*a*b*color space by using the equations in Sec. 2.

step2 Watermarks are embedded into the original pixels in L*a*b*color space. Then the watermarked pixels in L*a*b*color space are obtained.

step3 The watermarked pixels in L*a*b*color space are transformed into the real-number watermarked pixels in sRGB color space by using the equations in Sec. 2.

step4 The real-number watermarked pixels in sRGB color space are adjusted to integers by using the adjustment procedure described in Sec. 3.

Note that the pixel value adjustment used in step4 is irreversible because the real-number watermarked pixels in sRGB color space have difference of maximum size 0.5 from integers. This fact sometimes causes erroneous extraction. The origin of this problem is that the watermarked pixels in L*a*b*color space are calculated without consideration of the existence of the corresponding integer pixels in sRGB color space. Moreover the influence of adjustments from real-number sRGB pixels to integer sRGB pixels on the corresponding pixel values in L*a*b*is not constant because the transformation between L*a*b*and sRGB is non-linear.

4.2 Fusion of adjustment and embedding

Figure 2 shows the flow of the latter approach described here. It is a new approach we describe in this chapter.

step1 Original pixels in sRGB color space are transformed into the corresponding original pixels in L*a*b*color space by using the equations in Sec. 2.

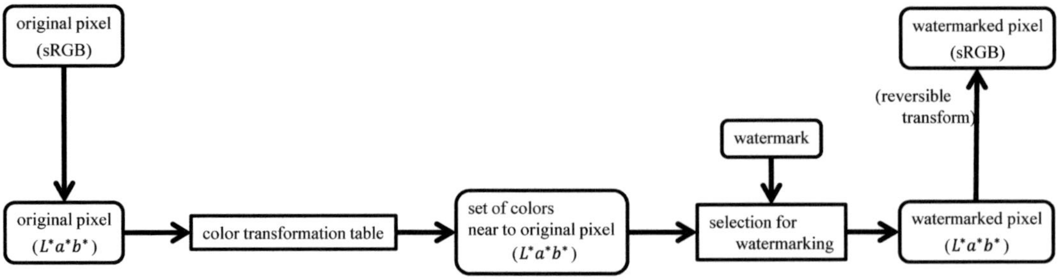

Fig. 2. Latter approach : Fusion of adjustment and embedding

step2 The original pixels in L*a*b*color space are transformed into the sets of colors near to themselves by using color transformation table in the way described in Sec. 3.3

step3 Each watermarked pixel in L*a*b*color space is selected from the set of colors near to the corresponding original pixel in L*a*b*color space so that the watermarked pixel satisfies the watermarking condition according to the watermark.

step4 The watermarked pixels obtained in step3 are transformed without loss into the watermarked pixels in sRGB color space.

Note that the transformation in step4 is reversible because the watermarked pixel selected from the set in step3 has the corresponding pixel in integer sRGB color space. This fact causes correct extraction because extractors can obtain the very same watermarked pixel values as embedders produce in L*a*b*color space although the pixels have been transformed into integer sRGB color space.

5. Watermarking procedure for evaluation

We use the watermarking method proposed by Chou and Wu (Chou & Wu, 2003) to evaluate each pixel value adjustment procedure. In this section, we briefly describe the method. The method proposed by Chou and Wu embeds 3 bits into a pixel in L*a*b*color space.

5.1 Embedding procedure

We describe how to embed the i-th watermark vector $\boldsymbol{W_i} = (w_i^L, w_i^a, w_i^b)$ into the i-th pixel value $\boldsymbol{P_i} = (L_i, a_i, b_i)$ in the following, where $w_i^L \in \{0,1\}$ and $w_i^a \in \{0,1\}$ and $w_i^b \in \{0,1\}$ and L_i, a_i and b_i represent the pixel values of L^*, a^* and b^* components respectively.

step1 The quantization index $\boldsymbol{q_i}$ is calculated from $\boldsymbol{P_i}$ by the following equation.

$$\boldsymbol{q_i} = \left(\frac{L_i}{Q_L}, \frac{a_i}{Q_a}, \frac{b_i}{Q_b} \right) \tag{28}$$

where Q_L, Q_a and Q_b represent the quantizer stepsizes of L^*, a^* and b^* components respectively. Note that this quantization adopts rounding off.

step2 The watermarked quantization index $\boldsymbol{q_i^W}$ is obtained by the following equation.

$$\boldsymbol{q_i^W} = \boldsymbol{q_i} + (\boldsymbol{\nu_i} \times (\boldsymbol{\hat{q}_i} \oplus \boldsymbol{W_i})) \tag{29}$$

where

$$\boldsymbol{\hat{q}_i} = \boldsymbol{q_i} \bmod 2 \tag{30}$$

Here $\boldsymbol{\nu_i} = (\bullet_i^L, \bullet_i^a, \bullet_i^b)$ is a random sequence, where $\bullet_i^L \in \{-1, 1\}$, $\bullet_i^a \in \{-1, 1\}$ and $\bullet_i^b \in \{-1, 1\}$. Note that $\boldsymbol{q_i^W} = \boldsymbol{q_i}$ when $\boldsymbol{\hat{q}_i} = \boldsymbol{W_i}$.

step3 The watermarked pixel value $\boldsymbol{P_i^W} = (L_i^W, a_i^W, b_i^W)$ is calculated from $\boldsymbol{q_i^W}$ by inverse quantization as follows:

$$\begin{aligned} \boldsymbol{P_i^W} &= (Q_L, Q_a, Q_b) \times \boldsymbol{q_i^W} \\ &= (Q_L q_i^{LW}, Q_a q_i^{aW}, Q_b q_i^{bW}) \end{aligned} \tag{31}$$

5.2 Extracting procedure

We describe how to extract the i-th watermark vector $\boldsymbol{W_i'}$ from the i-th watermarked pixel value $\boldsymbol{P_i'}$ as follows:

step1 The quantization index $\boldsymbol{q_i'}$ is calculated from $\boldsymbol{P_i'}$ with the same quantizer stepsizes used for embedding by the following equation.

$$\boldsymbol{q_i'} = \left(\frac{L_i'}{Q_L}, \frac{a_i'}{Q_a}, \frac{b_i'}{Q_b} \right) \tag{32}$$

step2 The i-th watermark vector is extracted by the following equation.

$$\boldsymbol{W_i'} = \boldsymbol{q_i'} \bmod 2 \tag{33}$$

5.3 Watermarking condition for latter approach

At step3 in Sec. 4.2, the watermarking condition to select watermarked pixels from the set of colors is arbitrarily decided. Then we decide the watermarking condition based on the watermarking procedure for evaluation as the following equation.

$$\boldsymbol{q}(\bullet_i) \equiv \boldsymbol{W_i} \pmod 2 \tag{34}$$

where

$$\boldsymbol{q}(\bullet_i) = \left(\frac{L^*(\bullet_i)}{Q_L}, \frac{a^*(\bullet_i)}{Q_a}, \frac{b^*(\bullet_i)}{Q_b} \right) \tag{35}$$

Here $\bullet_i$ represents the i-th color in the set of colors near to the original pixel in L*a*b*color space, and $L^*(\bullet_i)$, $a^*(\bullet_i)$ and $b^*(\bullet_i)$ represent the pixel values of $\bullet_i$ in L^*, a^* and b^* components respectively.

We select $\bullet_i$ which has minimum index i and satisfy Eq.(34) as the watermarked pixel.

6. Experiments

6.1 Environments

Firstly we investigated the image quality of watermarked images for each pixel value adjustment, that is, simple adjustment, adjustment by using RGB neighboring search, adjustment based on color transformation table after embedding and fusion of adjustment and embedding. In this section, adjustment by using RGB neighboring search, adjustment based on color transformation table after embedding and adjustment based on color transformation with fusion of adjustment and embedding are represented by "RGB neighboring search," "former approach" and "latter approach." Then we confirmed the number of error bits in each pixel value adjustment. Finally we investigated the computational time for former approach and latter approach.

Shown in Fig. 3 we used twelve color bitmap images "aerial," "airplane," "balloon," "couple," "earth," "girl," "lena," "mandrill," "milkdrop," "parrots," "pepper" and "sailboat" as original images. They were standard images widely used for experiments. The size of all original images was 256 × 256 pixels. They are mainly in standard image database (SIDBA) (*The USC-SIPI Image Database*, n.d.), and all of them are often used for experiments in technical papers.

In watermarking procedure, we used $Q_L = 1.5$, $Q_a = 2$ and $Q_b = 2$ as the quantizer stepsizes. The watermark is pseudo-random vector sequence of length 65536 (= 256 × 256), where the element of the watermark is 3-dimensional vector as described in Sec. 5. Thus the length of watermark bits is 196608 (= 65536 × 3) bits.

In the proposed adjustment based on color transformation table, we used • $= 2.25$, $T_Z = 1000$ and d• $= 0.25$. In ideal manner, • gradually increases for the appropriately fixed T_Z and then the appropriate • is fixed. However this manner requires great computational cost. Thus we fixed • so that the computational cost is convenient.

We used PSNR for the metric of the amount of change of pixel values in RGB space. PSNR was calculated by the following equation.

$$\mathrm{PSNR} = 10\log_{10}\frac{255^2}{\mathrm{MSE}} \tag{36}$$

$$\mathrm{MSE} = \frac{1}{3N_xN_y}\sum_{i=1}^{3N_xN_y}(\mathrm{img}_i - \mathrm{oimg}_i)^2 \tag{37}$$

where img_i and oimg_i represent the pixels in one image and the other image respectively.

The CPUs of the personal computer used for this experiment are two Xeon E5520(2.27GHz). We used Java for implementation. The size of the memory of Java Virtual Machine is 4.0GB.

6.2 Image quality

Figures 4∼6 show the watermarked images by using RGB neighboring search, former approach and latter approach. We omitted the watermarked images by simple adjustment because they are similar to those by RGB neighboring search. This fact can be confirmed by

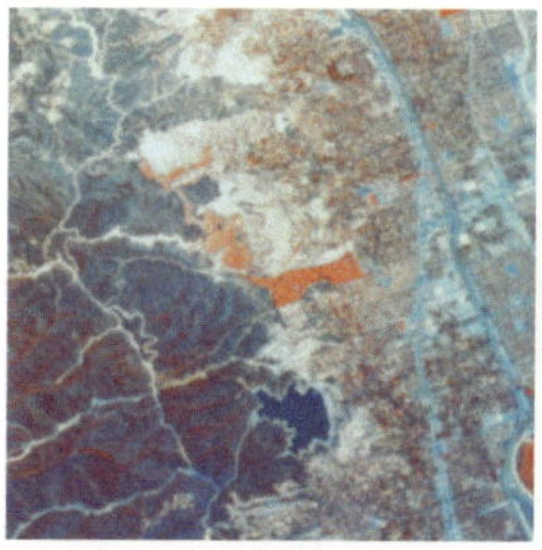
(a) Aerial

(b) Airplane

(c) Balloon

(d) Couple

(e) Earth

(f) Girl

(g) Lena

(h) Mandrill

(i) Milkdrop

(j) Parrots

(k) Pepper

(l) Sailboat

Fig. 3. Original images

the PSNRs described below. Shown in Figs. 4∼6, the degradation of the watermarked images is imperceptible.

Table 1 shows the PSNRs in each pixel value adjustment. The PSNRs of latter approach are the highest in all PSNRs.

original images	simple adjustment	RGB neighboring search	color transformation table (former approach)	color transformation table (latter approach)
Aerial	34.16	34.16	34.16	44.71
Airplane	33.95	33.88	33.84	44.52
Balloon	35.44	35.42	35.42	45.10
Couple	36.34	36.35	36.32	44.64
Earth	35.37	35.37	35.38	45.06
Girl	36.89	36.89	35.40	45.24
Lena	36.39	36.38	36.36	45.24
Mandrill	34.60	34.59	34.55	44.90
Milkdrop	35.68	35.69	35.01	44.47
Parrots	34.95	34.94	33.57	43.89
Pepper	35.21	35.20	33.58	43.93
Sailboat	34.98	34.97	34.97	45.14

Table 1. The PSNRs in each pixel value adjustment.

6.3 Number of error bits

Table 2 shows the number of error bits from the watermarked images in each pixel adjustment. The number of error bits of latter approach is the least for all original images, followed in order by that of former approach, RGB neighboring search and simple adjustment.

The number of error bits of latter approach is theoretically zero. However, there are some cases that there is no color satisfying the watermarking condition in the set of colors near to original pixels in "Aerial," "Airplane," "Parrots" and "Pepper" when • = 2.25. In such cases, • should be larger so that there is a color satisfying the watermarking condition in the set for all original pixels, although the computational cost becomes greater.

6.4 Computational time

Table 3 shows the computational time [ms] for pixel value adjustment in former approach and latter approach when • = 2.25. The computational time for simple adjustment and RGB neighboring search is omitted because it is extremely fast compared with that for former approach and latter approach.

Compared the computational time of former approach with that of latter approach, former approach is slightly faster than latter approach. However the performance of former approach is almost same as that of simple adjustment and RGB neighboring search. Then it is desirable that the pixel value adjustment based on color transformation table is used by latter approach.

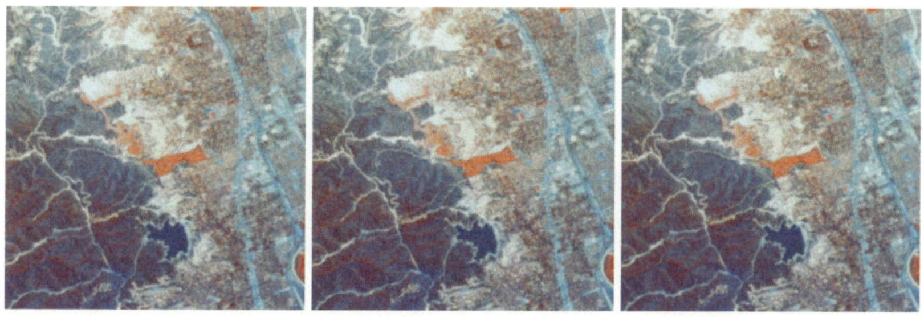

(a) Aerial : RGB neighboring search, former approach, latter approach

(b) Airplane : RGB neighboring search, former approach, latter approach

(c) Balloon : RGB neighboring search, former approach, latter approach

(d) Couple : RGB neighboring search, former approach, latter approach

Fig. 4. Experimental results(Aerial, Airplane, Balloon, Couple)

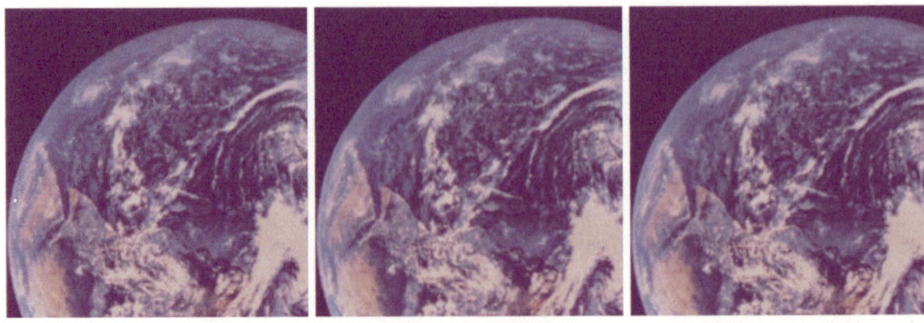

(a) Earth : RGB neighboring search, former approach, latter approach

(b) Girl : RGB neighboring search, former approach, latter approach

(c) Lena : RGB neighboring search, former approach, latter approach

(d) Mandrill : RGB neighboring search, former approach, latter approach

Fig. 5. Experimental results(Earth, Girl, Lena, Mandrill)

(a) Milkdrop : RGB neighboring search, former approach, latter approach

(b) Parrots : RGB neighboring search, former approach, latter approach

(c) Pepper : RGB neighboring search, former approach, latter approach

(d) Sailboat : RGB neighboring search, former approach, latter approach

Fig. 6. Experimental results(Milkdrop, Parrots, Pepper, Sailboat)

original images	simple adjustment	RGB neighboring search	color transformation table (former approach)	color transformation table (latter approach)
Aerial	195	196	104	3
Airplane	181	166	57	7
Balloon	0	0	0	0
Couple	4237	3839	4215	0
Earth	0	0	0	0
Girl	2516	2424	1347	0
Lena	83	79	42	0
Mandrill	119	118	36	0
Milkdrop	2163	2050	837	0
Parrots	1911	1899	1352	3
Pepper	2674	2569	1427	2
Sailboat	15	15	6	0

Table 2. The number of error bits from watermarked images in each pixel value adjustment.

original images	former approach	latter approach
Aerial	3893365	5173605
Airplane	3371501	4443929
Balloon	4403430	5759862
Couple	1224645	1534407
Earth	3536644	4889056
Girl	1947603	2319508
Lena	3648970	5725525
Mandrill	4180504	5310248
Milkdrop	3779653	5622682
Parrots	3699138	4604142
Pepper	3666946	4965765
Sailboat	2921615	3673465

Table 3. Computational time in the pixel value adjustment based on color transformation table of former approach and latter approach when • = 2.25.

6.5 Discussion

Shown in Tab. 1, the PSNRs of latter approach are the highest in all PSNRs. The PSNRs of other three pixel adjustments are similar to each other because they modify pixel values only around the corresponding watermarked pixel values (real-number). From this fact, we guess that the original pixel values in $L^*a^*b^*$color space are often modified to the watermarked pixel values far from the pixel values which have the corresponding integer pixel values in sRGB color space. Moreover latter approach is more suitable than other pixel value adjustments from viewpoint of less change in $L^*a^*b^*$color space because the modification of latter approach for watermarking in $L^*a^*b^*$color space is the least under condition of satisfying the watermarking condition. Then Human Visual System is hard to perceive the degradation by watermarking method adopting latter approach.

Shown in Tab. 2, the number of error bits of latter approach is the least in all pixel value adjustments. In case of "Aerial," "Airplane," "Parrots" and "Pepper," the number of error bits is not zero. Even in such cases, the number of error bits must be zero by increasing • although the computational time also increases. This result confirms the contribution of fusion of pixel value adjustment and watermarking toward the reduction of erroneous extraction.

Shown in Tab. 3, the computational time for the pixel value adjustment based on color transformation table is very long. Thus the proposed adjustment of latter approach reduces error bits and improves image quality at a computational cost. Note that the computational time for extraction is independent from the pixel value adjustment for watermarking. The computational time for extraction is usual even if the proposed adjustment of latter approach is used for watermarking.

The discussion demonstrates that the proposed adjustment of latter approach contributes to both of few error bits and high PSNRs although the long computational time for watermarking is required.

7. Conclusion

We have proposed a new pixel value adjustment based on color transformation table for watermarking methods using a uniform color space. The proposed adjustment fuses a pixel value adjustment into a watermarking procedure. This fusion produces both of few erroneous extraction from watermarked images and high PSNRs. We have investigated the image quality of watermarked images and the number of error bits from watermarked images for all pixel value adjustments. Moreover we have investigated the computational time of the pixel value adjustment based on color transformation table. We have confirmed the contribution of the fusion of a pixel value adjustment and a watermarking procedure toward the property of watermarking method using a uniform color space through the experiments and the discussion.

Our future works should be to reduce the computational cost of using color transformation table and to expand color transformation table so as to be able to apply watermarking method using frequency transform.

8. References

Chou, C. H. & Wu, T. L. (2003). Embedding color watermarks in color images, *EURASIP Journal on Applied Signal Processing* Vol.1: 32–40.

Iwata, M., Kanaya, T., Shiozaki, A. & Ogihara, A. (2010). Digital watermarking method warranting the lower limit of image quality of watermarked images, *EURASIP Journal on Advances in Signal Processing* Vol.2010: Article ID 426085, doi:10.1155/2010/426085.
URL: *http://www.hindawi.com/journals/asp/2010/426085/*

JSA (2007). *JIS handbook 61 Color 2007*, Japanese Standards Association.

Lab color space (n.d.). Wikipedia.
URL: *http://en.wikipedia.org/wiki/Lab_color_space*

Oyama, T. (2000). *Invitation to visual psycology*, Saiensu-sha Co., Ltd.

The USC-SIPI Image Database (n.d.). University of Southern California.
URL: *http://sipi.usc.edu/database/database.php*

Yoshiura, H. & Echizen, I. (2006). Maintaining picture quality and improving robustness of color watermarking by using human vision models, *IEICE Trans. Inf.&Syst.* Vol.E89-D: 256–270.

4

Watermarking on Compressed Image: A New Perspective

Santi P. Maity[1] and Claude Delpha[2]
[1]*Bengal Engineering and Science University, Shibpur*
[2]*Laboratoire des Signaux et Systemes, Universite Paris, SUPELEC,CNRS*
[1]*India*
[2]*France*

1. Introduction

Watermarking is highly demanding in recent times for the protection of multimedia data in network environment from illegal copying, violation of copyright, authentication etc (Hartung & Kutter,1999), while compression of multimedia signals is essential to save storage space and transmission time. Hence, it is needless to mention the importance of watermarking on compressed data. However, the working principles of watermarking and compression seem to be different as perceptual data coding removes inherent redundancy during compression. On the other hand, watermarking uses this redundancy space for making data embedding imperceptible. As a matter of fact, watermarking on compressed data becomes more challenging, and many solutions come out as an optimization problem in the form of joint watermarking and compression (JWC). Moreover, the other requirement is that watermarking process should not increase bit rate for the compressed data to a large extent while satisfying high value of document-to-watermark ratio (DWR) and watermark decoding reliability. Over and above, it is desirable that watermarking algorithm must be compatible with ease of integration with the existing compression framework, for example, JPEG and JPEG 2000 compression for digital images.

The objective of this chapter is to first look into the fundamental problems in watermarking on compressed data followed by robust and efficient algorithm design. The readers would understand stepwise movement for the choice of different tools and techniques to develop an integrated algorithm to meet certain well-defined objectives. One such objective considered here is to develop high DWR and low bit error rate (BER) watermarking system with moderate payload and without much increase in file size of the compressed watermarked data. This can be accomplished by using error correction code (ECC) intelligently through the creation of virtual redundancy space. In other words, the flexibility for data embedding lost due to quantization operation may be regenerated by applying channel coding scheme directly on the host compressed data, instead of applying it on watermark signal as is done in the conventional watermarking system. It should also be considered that the so called created redundancy should not increase much the file size of the compressed watermarked data which is the primary goal of compression operation.

The rest of the chapter is organized as follows: Section 2 makes a brief literature review on related works and their limitations followed by the scope of the present work. A general outline for new algorithm design of watermarking on compressed data is then highlighted in Section 3. Section 4 presents proposed watermarking method, while performance analysis is done in Section 5. Finally conclusions are drawn in Section 6 along with scope of the future works.

2. Review of related works, limitations and scope of the work

In this section, we present a brief literature review for watermarking on compressed data with an objective to discuss their merits, limitations and finally scope of the proposed work.

2.1 Related works and limitations

Some watermarking algorithms work entirely on the compressed domain such as JPEG-to-JPEG (J2J) watermarking (Wong, 2000; Wong2001). Robust watermarking scheme is proposed in (Wong & Au, 2002) using iterative spread spectrum technique (SST) in JPEG images. These methods embed different amount of watermark bits into JPEG images while maintaining good visual quality of the watermarked JPEG images. Huang et al (Huang et al., 2007) propose an effective watermark embedding method for JPEG image which can resist high compression attack and retains a good image quality. The algorithm consists of three parts, searching for the optimal embedding position, proper embedded value and the embedded/extracted processing based on quantization index modulation (QIM). Elbasi (Elbasi, 2007) propose a robust MPEG video watermarking in wavelet domain by embedding a pseudo random sequence in MPEG-1 using two bands (LL-low low and HH-high high). They show experimentally that for one group of attacks (i.e. JPEG compression, Gaussian noise, resizing, lowpass filtering, rotation and frame dropping), the correlation with the real watermark is higher than the threshold in the LL band, and for another group of attacks (i.e. cropping, histogram equalization, contrast adjustment and gamma correction), the correlation with real watermark is higher than the threshold in the HH band.

Taniguchi (Taniguchi, 2005) proposes a method that provides robustness against scaling for watermarked MPEG content using a pseudo-random sequence of block patterns and a tiled structure. Detection of the watermark information is based on a cross-correlation between the watermarked content and the watermark pattern. Basically the scaling change is detected by observing the auto-correlation peaks generated by the tiled structure. Allatar etal (Allatar at el., 2003) propose a novel watermarking method for low bit rate video that is compressed according to the advanced simple profile of MPEG-4. A simple spread spectrum watermark was embedded directly to the MPEG-4 bit-streams. A synchronization template was employed to combat cropping, scaling, and rotation. A gain control algorithm adjusts the local strength of the watermark depending on local image characteristics, in order to maximize watermark robustness and to minimize the impact on the quality of the video. He et al (He et al., 2002) propose an object based watermarking solution for MPEG4 video authentication. Nakajima et al. (Nakajima et al.,2005) proposed a high capacity data hiding method in MPEG domain utilizing the idea of zero run-level encoding.

Embedding of watermark information on compressed data needs partial or full decoding depending on the domain where the watermark would be embedded in least significant bits

(LSB) of the levels of variable-length codes (VLC) in MPEG stream (Langelaar, 2000), and the same for the appended bits of certain pairs of AC coefficients of JPEG data (Fridrich, 2004), are made to match the watermark bit. The approach in (Langelaar, 2000) is effective but is lossy, too predictable and requires Huffman decoding of the JPEG file, while (Fridrich, 2004) is an adaption of (Langelaar, 2000) to JPEG. A fragile but lossless and file preserving watermarking algorithm is proposed in (Mobasseri, 2005) that is applicable to any entropy coded compression stream, provided that the total code space is not used. Inter-block correlation of the selected DCT coefficients for JPEG compressed data, by adding or subtracting an off-set to the mean value of the neighboring DCT coefficients, are also used in (Choi, 2000) and in (Luo, 2002) to embed watermark.

An achievable region of quantization (or compression) rate and embedding rate was developed in (Karakos, 2003) in the case of private watermarking, Gaussian host signals, and a fixed Gaussian attack. In (Maor,2004), the attack-free public version of the problem was treated, both for the finite and continuous alphabet cases. In (Maor,2005) the best trade-offs among the embedding rate, compression rate, and quantization distortion were studied from an information theoretic perspective for public watermarking in the case of a finite alphabet and a fixed memoryless attack channel. Wu et al (Wu et al.,2005) maximizes robustness of watermark decoding against additive white Gaussian noise (AWGN) in the context of JWC. They first investigate optimum decoding of a binary JWC system, and demonstrate by experiments the distortion-to-noise (DNR) region of practical interest. The minimum distance (MD) decoder achieves performance comparable to that of the maximum likelihood decoder. In addition, it offers advantages of low computation complexity and is also independent of the statistics of the host signal.

On summarization of the review works, it is observed that watermark embedding in the bitstream domain (Mobasseri, 2005) is fragile and requires re-encoding at alternate bit rates. On the other hand, JWC works reported in (Wu, 2005) are mostly ad hoc and put primary focus on quantization (or compression) rate and embedding rate. The other J2J works reported in (Langelaar, 2000; Fridrich, 2004; Choi, 2000; Luo, 2002) show much performance degradation both in DWR and the reliability of the watermark decoding against AWGN, with the increase of the compression rate. Works reported in (Karakos, 2003; Maor, 2004; Maor, 2005) consider trade-off aspects of embedding rate, compression rate, quantization distortion but suffer from overhead problem, large size in code book, lack of involvement of real life host data. These drawbacks create a pressing demand for practical implementation of watermarking algorithm on real life compressed host image. Another important aspect of watermarking on the compressed data, to the best of our knowledge, is possibly unexplored; how to increase simultaneously DWR and watermark decoding reliability i.e. low bit error rate (BER) for the given compression rate (determines the size of the embedding space) with moderate watermark payload and at the same time the size (bit rate) of the compressed watermarked data does not change much.

2.2 Scope of the work

The objective here is to develop an algorithm for watermarking on compressed host data integrating channel coding and lifting based integer wavelet (Maity, 2009a). To achieve relative gain in DWR and BER performance with compression rate, we exploit the benefits of memory system, both from mathematical structure of lifting based implementation and convolution coding. The objective is to improve simultaneously DWR and BER performance for watermark decoding against AWGN. It is also important to meet the condition that the file size of the compressed watermarked data should not increase much due to watermarking. Convolution coded compressed host data is decomposed by discrete wavelet transform using lifting to generate lossless integer wavelet coefficients. Watermark information is casted using dither modulation (DM) based QIM for ease of implementation. Experimentation is carried out on JPEG compressed data at different compression rates. The relative gain on imperceptibility and robustness performance are reported for direct watermark embedding on entropy decoded host, using repetition code, convolution code, and finally the combined use of convolution code and lifting.

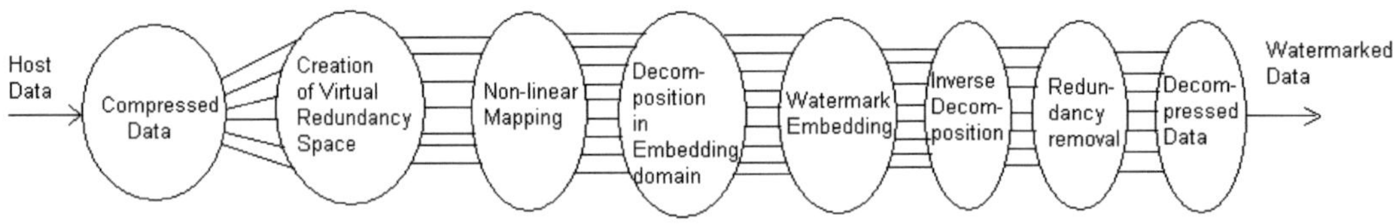

Fig. 1. Basic outline for algorithm development

3. Outline for algorithm development

The first step would be to recreate the virtual redundancy (lost due to quantization operation in compression) space on compressed data so that flexibility in data embedding is possible to regain to a certain extent. This needs the use of ECC in an intelligent way so that so called created redundancy (virtual redundancy) would not increase much the file size of the data. The other important requirement is to choose proper embedding space i.e. choice of transforms for the host image so that further data loss in QIM is protected. The choice of discrete cosine transform (DCT) and discrete wavelet transform (DWT) for decomposition of host is preferable as popular image compression of recent times like JPEG and JPEG 2000 are based on these two transforms. At the same time, one drawback for the two transforms is the results of floating-point numbers. In QIM based data embedding, it would be rounded to integer values and small values may be set to zero. Hence perfect invertibility is lost and the original input data cannot be regenerated. Another important aspect is that DCT based watermarking algorithms are robust against JPEG but not equally robust for JPEG 2000; similar argument is also valid for DWT based watermarking methods. It is seen that lifting based wavelet transform maps an integer data set into another integer data set. This transform is perfectly invertible, yields exactly the original data set and may be a potential choice for QIM watermarking on JPEG compressed data.

3.1 Integration of channel coding with integer wavelets

The convolution code is chosen here to apply on the entropy decoded compressed host data as this error-correcting code (ECC) operates on serial data and uses memory system. The use of memory system in turn creates the correlation among the sample coefficients. The Viterbi decoding is used because of highly satisfactory bit error performance, high speed of operation, ease of implementation, low cost, and fixed decoding time (Bose,2002). Again Viterbi decoding works on a bit based on either soft-decision or hard-decision. It is also reported in the digital communication literature that soft-decision decoding outperforms over hard-decision decoding by a margin of roughly 3 dB in AWGN channels. The convolution coded data is further operated by lifting based integer wavelet transform to reduce data loss due to quantization operation for information hiding. Lifting based filtering consists of a sequence of very simple operations for which alternately odd sample values of the signal are updated with a weighted sum of even sample values and even sample values are updated with a weighted sum of odd sample values. This mathematical structure of lifting operation after applying on compressed convolution coded data creates correlation among the sample values and leads to better visual quality of watermark data. Fig. 1 shows the outline of different steps for developing general watermarking algorithm.

4. Proposed watermarking method on compressed data

The proposed watermark embedding scheme is based on the creation of virtual redundancy space on compressed data through convolution coding followed by signal decomposition through lifting based integer wavelet transform to obtain embedding space.

4.1 Watermark embedding process

Fig. 2 shows the block diagram representation of the proposed watermarking scheme. The steps are described briefly as follows:

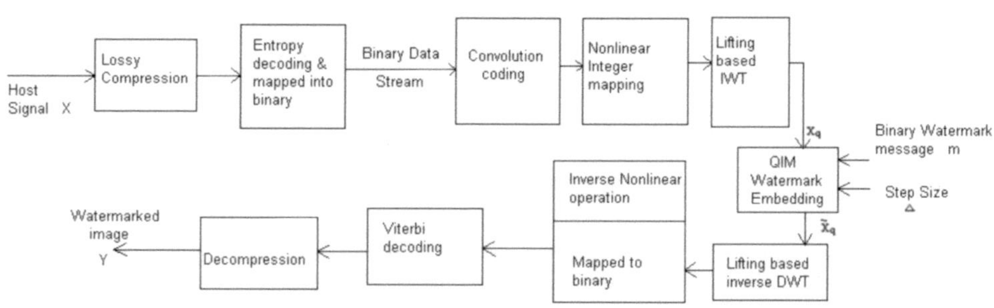

Fig. 2. Block diagram representation of watermark embedding scheme

Step 1. Entropy decoding and binary mapping

The lossy JPEG compressed host signal is first entropy decoded. The non-zero quantized DCT coefficients are then mapped to the binary data.

Step 2. Convolution coding

The binary data obtained in step 1 is then encoded using convolution coding so that each `k' bits are mapped to `t' bits where $t \leq k$.

Step 3. Non-linear mapping of encoded data

The channel coded binary data is not suitable for direct application of QIM watermarking. To create suitable quantization based embedding space, convolution coded data is then converted to integer coefficients through non-linear mapping. A simple, easily implementable and reversible such nonlinear mapping may be binary-to-decimal conversion and is used here. The binary to decimal conversion would be restricted to 8 bits/sample so that sample values remain like the pixel values of a gray scale image.

Step 4. Decomposition using Lifting based IWT

The integer signal obtained in step 3 undergoes IWT using 5-tap/3-tap filter coefficients, however, other lifting based DWT filters can also be used. The channel coded DCT coefficients are decomposed using lifting based DWT so that watermarked signal can be simultaneously compatible to JPEG and JPEG 2000 compression operations. It is reported in watermarking literature that most wavelet-based embedding schemes are very robust against low quality JPEG 2000 compression, but are not similarly resilient against low quality JPEG compression. Similarly, DCT based digital watermarking methods are having exactly inverse characteristics for compression operations. To this aim, this method would offer certain degree of robustness against JPEG 2000 due to IWT operation applied on DCT compressed watermarked data.

Step 5. QIM watermarking

A binary message `W' is used as watermark and two dither sequences, with length L, are generated pseudo randomly with step size (Δ) as follows:

$$d_q(0) = \{R(key) * \Delta\} - \Delta/2, 0 \le q \le L\text{-}1 \tag{1}$$

$$d_q(1) = \begin{cases} d_q(0) + \Delta/2 \text{ if } d_q(0) < 0 \\ d_q(0) - \Delta/2 \text{ if } d_q(0) \ge 0 \end{cases} \tag{2}$$

Where R (*key*) is a random generator. The q-th watermarked wavelet coefficients S_q is obtained as follows:

$$S_q = \begin{cases} Q\{X_q - d_q(0), \Delta\} + d_q(0) \text{ if } W'(i,j) = 0 \\ Q\{X_q + d_q(1), \Delta\} - d_q(1) \text{ if } W'(i,j) = 1 \end{cases} \tag{3}$$

where X_q is the convolution coded q-th IWT coefficients of the compressed host data, Q is a uniform quantizer (and dequantizer) with step Δ, and W(i,j) is the (i,j) -th pixel of the watermark.

Step 6. Watermarked image formation

Inverse integer wavelet transform (IIWT) is then applied on the watermarked coefficients. Inverse non-linear operation i.e decimal to binary conversion maps each integer signal into binary data. The Viterbi decoding is then applied on the binary data to map each t-bits into k bits. This operation is done for the inverse operation of channel coding used as convolution codes i.e. for redundancy removal and not for watermark decoding. Thus entropy decoded watermarked data is obtained. This watermarking process may be analogous to `hidden QIM' as the information embedding process shown in Fig. 1 and Fig. 2 consists of (i) preprocessing of the compressed host data using convolution coding, non-linear mapping, IWT operation (2) QIM embedding, and (3) post processing using convolution decoding, inverse non-linear mapping, and IIWT to form the composite signal (Chen & Wornell, 2001).

4.2 Watermark decoding process

The watermark decoding is done from the compressed watermarked image. Entropy decoding of compressed watermarked data is done first followed by binary mapping. Then again convolution coding with proper code rate followed by non-linear mapping are done as it was performed during watermark embedding. Integer wavelet coefficients for watermarked data are then used for watermark extraction. Fig. 3 shows block diagram representation of watermark decoding process.

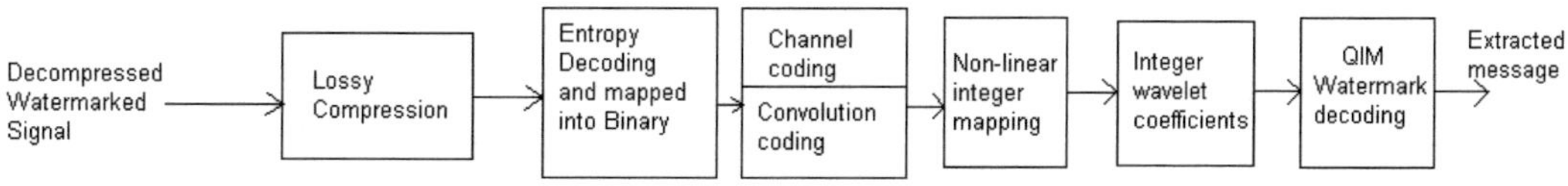

Fig. 3. Block diagram representation of watermark decoding scheme

The watermark information can be extracted from the compressed data using the following rule.

$$A = \sum_{q=0}^{L-1} (| Q(Y_q - d_q(0), \Delta) + d_q(0) - Y_q |)$$

$$B = \sum_{q=0}^{L-1} (| Q(Y_q + d_q(1), \Delta) - d_q(1) - Y_q |) \quad (4)$$

where Yq is the q-th IWT coefficient (possibly noisy due to transmission channel or any attack operation applied on the watermarked data) of the watermarked data. The symbols A and B are the decision variables used for extraction of watermark bits. A watermark bit W'(i,j) is decoded using the rule: where Yq is the q-th IWT coefficient (possibly noisy due to transmission channel or any attack operation applied on the watermarked data) of the watermarked data. The symbols A and B are the decision variables used for extraction of watermark bits. A watermark bit W'(i,j) is decoded using the rule:

$$W'(i,j) = \begin{cases} 0 \text{ if } A < B \\ 1, \text{ otherwise} \end{cases} \quad (5)$$

5. Performance evaluation

Performance of the proposed watermarking method is studied in terms of change in DWR with the change in watermark power as well as robustness performance as measure of BER for watermark decoding against AWGN. We have extensively studied the performance for direct watermarking on entropy decoded DCT coefficients, using repetition codes and convolution codes with code rate R=1/2, 1/4, 1/6. The experimentation has been carried out for large number of JPEG compressed images with different compression rates, however, we report here results for quality factor 60.

Fig. 4 (a)-(c) show some benchmark test images (petitcolas) Lena, Boat and Perrer of size (256x 256), 8 bit/pixel gray scale image and Fig. 4(d) shows a visually recognizable binary watermark of size (32x 32). The binary watermark size so chosen would allow embedding of single watermark bit in each (8x 8) block of the host image. The present study uses peak-signal-to-noise-ratio (PSNR) (Gonzalez & Woods, 2005) and mean structural similarity index measure (MSSIM)(Wang et al., 2004) to quantify the visual quality of the watermarked image with respect to the host image.

(a) (b) (c) (d)

Fig. 4. Original or host image (a)Lena (b) Boat (c) Pepper (d) Binary watermark

First of all we would present the effect of different watermark powers on relative quality of the watermarked images. Fig. 5 (a)-(e) show the watermarked images obtained after data embedding on entropy decoded DCT coefficients at various watermark powers determined by the different step sizes of the quantization operation used for QIM. The watermark powers are set at 12.73 dB, 14.31 dB, 15.22 dB, 16.05 dB and 16.81 dB for Fig. 5(a), 5(b), 5(c), 5(d) and 5(e), respectively. The corresponding PSNR values for the watermarked images are 36.89 dB, 35.59 dB, 34.84 dB, 34.09 dB and 33.42 dB, respectively, while corresponding MSSIM values for them are 0.9388, 0.9197, 0.9068, 0.8920 and 0.8767, respectively. The watermark power (Boyer et al, 2006) is defined as:

$$WP = 10 \ \log_{10} \frac{\Delta^2}{12} \ dB \tag{6}$$

(a) (b) (c) (d) (e)

Fig. 5. Watermarked images after embedding on entropy decoded DCT coefficients at watermark power (a) 12.73 dB, (b) 14.31dB (c) 15.22 dB (d) 16.05dB (e) 16.81dB

Fig. 6(a)-(e), Fig. 7(a)-(e), and Fig. 8(a)-(e) show the different watermarked images with watermark powers at 12.73 dB, 14.31 dB, 15.22 dB, 16.05 dB and 16.81 dB, respectively and with convolution coding rate R=1/2, 1/4 and 1/ 6, respectively. The symbols P and M associated with each figure indicate PSNR values in dB and MSSIM values, respectively. Similarly, Fig. 9(a)-(e), Fig. 10(a)-(e) and Fig. 11(a)-(e), show the different watermarked images with watermark powers at 12.73 dB, 14.31 dB, 15.22 dB, 16.05 dB and 16.81 dB, respectively and with the combined use of IWT and convolution coding on entropy decoded DCT coefficients at coding rate R=1/ 2, 1/ 4 and 1/ 6, respectively.

Fig. 6. Watermarked images after embedding on entropy decoded DCT coefficients with convolution coding rate 1/2 at watermark power (a) 12.73dB (b)14.31 dB, (c) 15.22 dB, (d) 16.05 dB, (e)16.81 dB

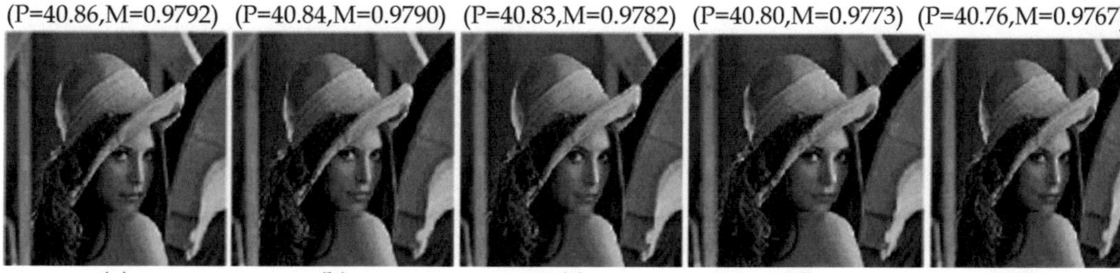

Fig. 7. Watermarked images after embedding on entropy decoded DCT coefficients with convolution coding rate 1/4 at watermark power (a) 12.73dB (b)14.31 dB, (c) 15.22 dB, (d) 16.05 dB, (e)16.81 dB

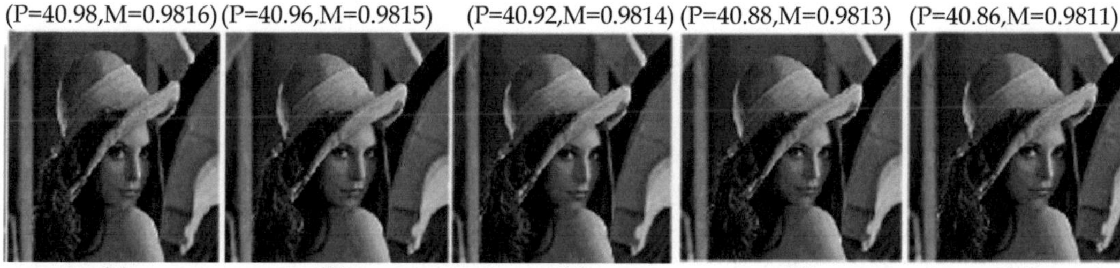

Fig. 8. Watermarked images after embedding on entropy decoded DCT coefficients with convolution coding rate 1/6 at watermark power (a) 12.73dB (b)14.31 dB, (c) 15.22 dB, (d) 16.05 dB, (e)16.81 dB

(P=41.23,M=0.9851) (P=41.20,M=0.9847) (P=41.19,M=0.9825) (P=41.16,M=0.9823) (P=41.12,M=0.9821)

(a) (b) (c) (d) (e)

Fig. 9. Watermarked images after embedding on entropy decoded DCT coefficients with integer wavelets and convolution coding rate 1/2 at watermark power (a) 12.73dB (b)14.31 dB, (c) 15.22 dB, (d) 16.05 dB, (e)16.81 dB

(P=42.67,M=0.9815) (P=42.61,M=0.9814) (P=42.58,M=0.9812) (P=42.53,M=0.9811) (P=42.52,M=0.9811)

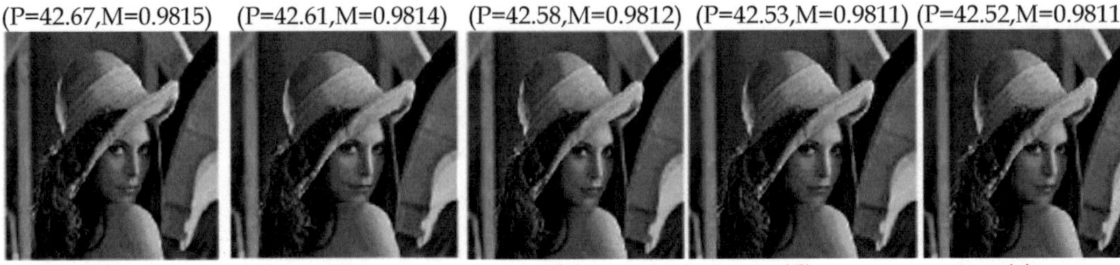

(a) (b) (c) (d) (e)

Fig. 10. Watermarked images after embedding on entropy decoded DCT coefficients with integer wavelets and convolution coding rate 1/4 at watermark power (a) 12.73dB (b)14.31 dB, (c) 15.22 dB, (d) 16.05 dB, (e)16.81 dB

(P=43.12,M=0.9856) (P=43.10,M=0.9847) (P=43.09,M=0.9845) (P=43.06,M=0.9843) (P=43.02,M=0.9839)

(a) (b) (c) (d) (e)

Fig. 11. Watermarked images after embedding on entropy decoded DCT coefficients with integer wavelets and convolution coding rate 1/6 at watermark power (a) 12.73dB (b)14.31 dB, (c) 15.22 dB, (d) 16.05 dB, (e)16.81 dB

We have also studied DWR vs watermark power performance for the repetition code at different coding rates and performance comparison for convolution code and repetition codes are shown graphically in Fig. 11. In the figure, repetition codes is denoted as Rep. and convolution codes as Con. with different code rates. Fig.13 shows the similar comparison of DWR using channel coding and IWT coefficients using lifting (denoted as Lift. in the graphs as it is generated by lifting scheme). It is quite clear from both the graphs that significant improvement in DWR is achieved due to the use of convolution coding compared to the direct embedding of watermark information on the entropy decoded coefficients. The improvement is found to be higher in case of convolution codes compared to the repetition codes. The use of integer wavelet coefficients in both cases show relative improvement in DWR of the order of ~ 0.75 dB but benefits in other way. A careful inspection on Fig. 12 and Fig. 13 show that the use of integer wavelet coefficients with channel coding, particularly for convolution coding, maintains high DWR values even with large increase in watermark power leading to a significant improvement in BER performance against AWGN attack. The overall high DWR value is achieved due to convolution coding which is further augmented through the correlations among the sample coefficients due to the use of lifting. In other words, large value of step sizes (Δ) can be selected even with maintaining high DWR. This large watermark power improves BER performance greatly against AWGN attack leading to better robustness.

The above observation for robustness improvement is further supported by BER performance shown in Fig. 14 and is also explained mathematically by Eq. (7). BER is mathematically indicated by probability of bit error P_b in watermark detection. The more general expression for P_b in case of M-PAM (M-pulse amplitude modulation) signaling (Voloshynovskiy& Pun, 2002), is expressed as

$$P_b = \frac{2(M-1)}{M}\,\gamma\left(\sqrt{\frac{Nd_0^2}{4\sigma_x^2}}\right) \qquad (7)$$

where M corresponds to M-PAM (for the present case M=2), N is the gain in code rate in terms of the number of host sample points over which each watermark bit is embedded, d_0^2 indicates the watermark power, γ *(.)* indicates the complementary error function and σ_x^2 is

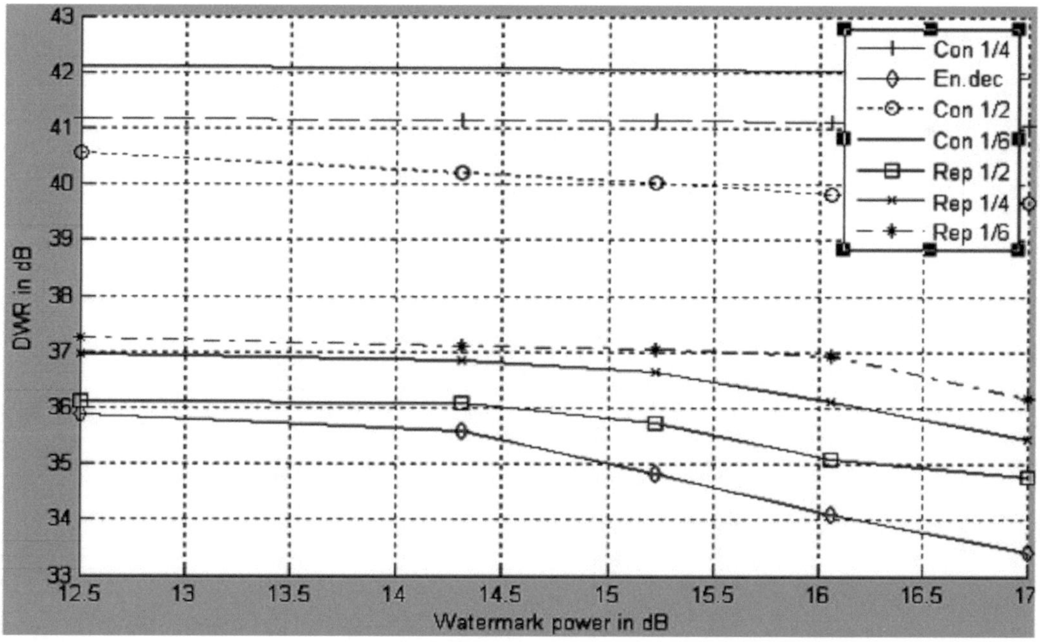

Fig. 12. DWR vs watermark power for direct embedding on entropy decoded data and using channel coding, namely convolution coding and repetition coding

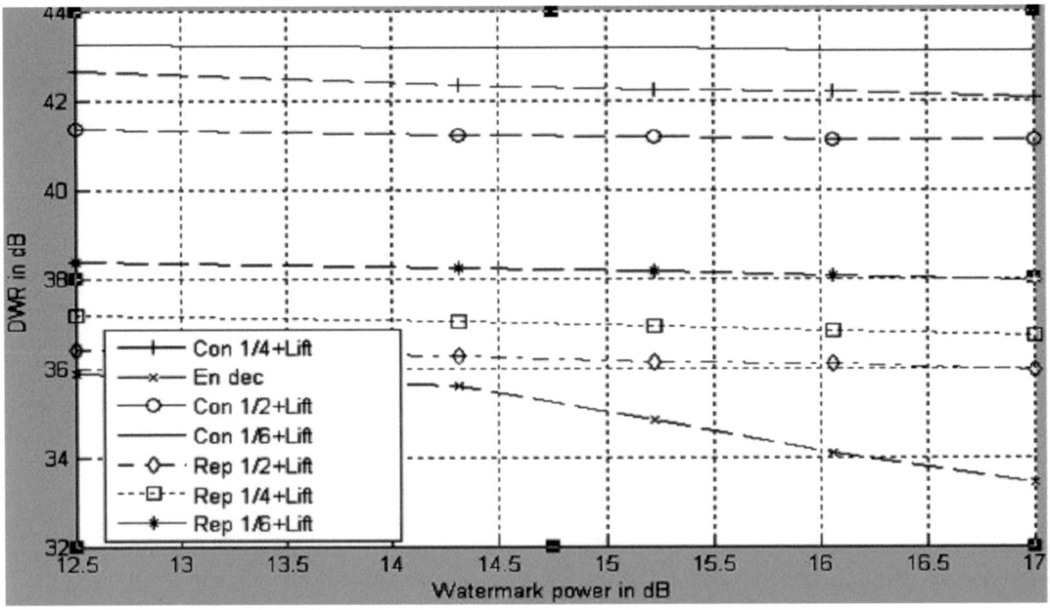

Fig. 13. DWR vs watermark power for direct embedding on entropy decoded data and using both channel coding and lifting

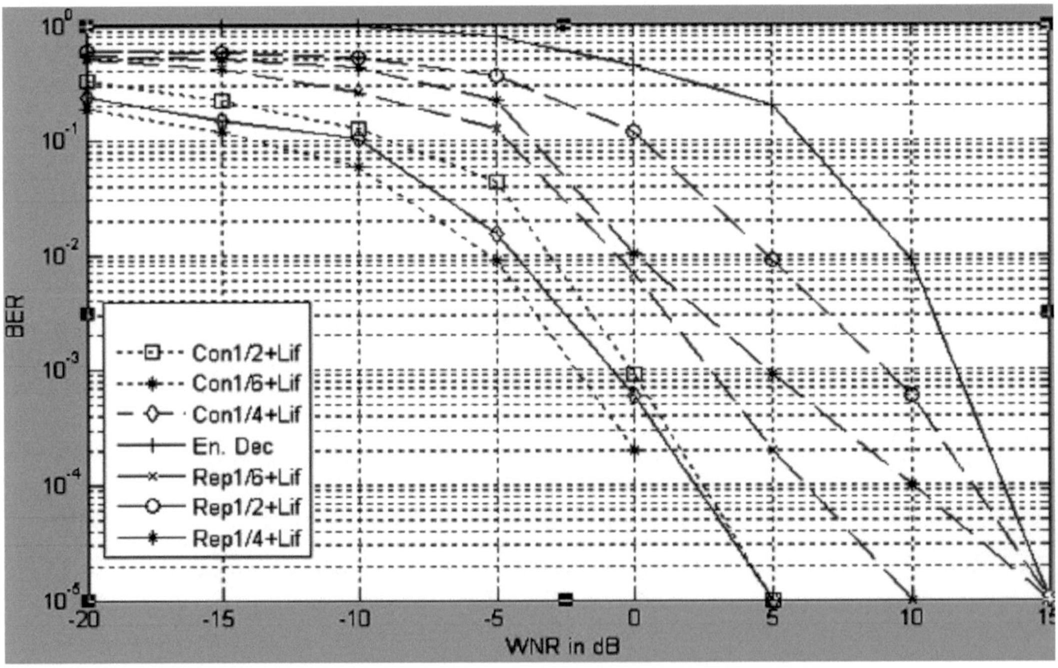

Fig. 14. BER performance at different watermark- to-noise (WNR) in dB

the variance of the embedding coefficients. It is seen from the simulation results over large number of images and shown in Table 3 that the variance values of the IWT coefficients are much lower than the similar for DWT coefficients. This low variance in turn leads to the reduction in P_b values for the former compared to the latter. BER Performance for watermarking on entropy coded data is poor as in such case N=1 and σ_x^2 is high. On the other hand, low P_b value for the decoded watermark in the proposed system is achieved due to two-fold advantages, namely large N-values due to code rates and low σ_x^2 value compared to normal DWT coefficients.

To test the robustness of the proposed scheme, some typical signal processing operations, such as filtering, sampling, histogram equalization, various noise addition, dynamic range change, and lossy JPEG compression are performed on watermarked image. Robustness performance is also tested against shifts, different rotations, and other geometric attacks like affine transformation, since QIM-based schemes reported in the literature show relatively inferior performance for such kind of operations. The subsequent simulation results are reported here after applying various operations over watermarked images obtained by combined use of convolution coding at rate R=1/ 6 and integer wavelets, at quality factor 60 and watermark power 12.73 dB. The associated quantitative measures for the watermarked images are ~ 40.98 dB (PSNR) and ~ 0.9816 (MSSIM) before applying any attack operation. For image scaling operation, before watermark extraction, the attacked images are rescaled to the original size. For rotation operation, the rotation angles undergone by the watermarked images are estimated by control point selection method with the help of the original images. The rotated watermarked images are then inverse rotated and are corrected by linear interpolation. Now those corrected watermarked images are used for watermark detection. This is done to compensate for the effect of loss in data due to the rotation operation. The experimental results of robustness against various image processing operations are shown in Table 1. It is seen that proposed algorithm can successfully resist attacks like filtering, scaling, cropping, random removal of some rows and columns, combination of scaling and small rotation. The visual quality of the extracted watermark is quantified by normalized cross correlation (NCC) as defined below

$$NCC = \frac{\sum_i \sum_j w_{ij} w'_{ij}}{\sum_i \sum_j w_{ij}^2} \tag{8}$$

Where, $1 \le (i,j) \le n$ and w_{ij} and w'_{ij} are the binary pixel values at the position (i,j) of the embedded and extracted watermarks, respectively.

Fig. 15(a) and Fig. 15(c) show the watermarked images with DWR 21.41 dB and 24.03 dB, respectively obtained after spatial mean and median filtering operations using window sizes (11x11). The corresponding extracted watermark images are shown in Fig. 15(b) and 15(d), respectively with NCC values 0.9816 and 0.9911, respectively. Fig. 15(e) shows significantly improved robustness performance for the present scheme compared to (Huang, 2007;Wu et al., 2005) method against JPEG compression operation. In all three cases, watermark power is set to 12.73 dB and watermark size is (32 x 32).

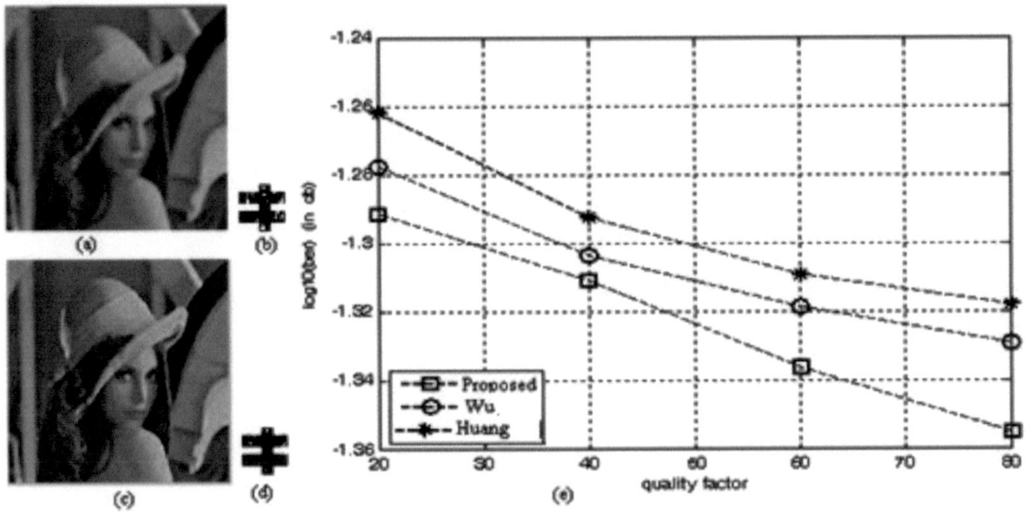

Fig. 15. (a), (c): Watermarked images after mean and median filtering, respectively, (b)and(d): Extracted watermarks from (a), and (c), respectively, (e) Robustness performance comparison against JPEG compression

Name of attack	Strength	PSNR in dB	MSSIM value	NCCvalue
Lowpassfiltering	3x3	28.70	0.89	0.98
Highpassfiltering	3x3	20.36	0.95	1.00
Down and upsampling	0.9	35.45	0.96	1.00
	0.75	34.12	0.95	1.00
	0.5	30.32	0.95	0.87
Cropping	13%	11.09	0.75	1.00
	52%	8.32	0.51	1.00
Rotation	90	45.21	0.98	1.00
	17	15.66	0.86	0.95
	60	14.01	0.82	0.87
Dyn. range change	(50-200)	22.23	0.85	1.00
Salt & Peppre Noise	0.01	24.42	0.75	0.96
	0.03	19.67	0.47	0.92
	0.05	17.44	0.32	0.87
Speckle Noise	0.01	25.31	0.54	0.97
	0.03	20.10	0.36	0.89
	0.05	17.50	0.28	0.83
Gaussian Noise	0.01	19.00	0.25	0.94
	0.03	18.70	0.24	0.83
	0.05	18.08	0.24	0.79

Table 1. Robustness performance against various image processing operations for the proposed method at quality factor 60; PSNR and MSSIM values for the watermarked images are ~ 40.98 dB and ~ 0.9816 (MSSIM), respectively before applying any attack operation

Performance of the proposed algorithm is also studied for gray scale watermark image. We consider a 4-bits/pixel gray image of size (16×16) as watermark and (512×512), 8 bits/pixel gray images, as host image. The gray scale watermark image is now converted into bit string. An extended binary string is then developed by employing variable redundancy in different bit planes of the gray scale watermark image. The variable redundancy is accomplished by incorporating more number of bits in higher order bit plane and less or no redundancy for lower order bit plane. The reason is that the higher order bit planes contain the majority of the visually significant data and needs more protection in watermarking. On the other hand, lower bit planes contribute to more subtle details in the image. In the present case, MSB i.e. 4th bit of pixel value is repeated nine (9) times, 3rd bit five (5) times, and no redundancy for the remaining two LSBs. Thus a single 4bits/ pixel now becomes as 16 bits. The length of the 4bits/pixel (16x16) gray scale watermark image thus becomes an equivalent binary watermark of size (64x64). The host image of size (512x512) then embeds (64x64) watermark, where each (8x8) block would embed one watermark bit. The binary watermark is first extracted. Then each watermark substring of length 16 is partitioned into four segments of length 9, 5, 1 and 1. A decision of bit '1' or '0' is made for both sub strings of length nine (9) and five (5), based on majority decision, in accordance with the watermark image encoding rule. The scheme is identical to the use of error correction code controlled by Hamming distance.

Fig. 16(a) shows (512x512) Lena image and Fig. 16(b) is a (16x16), 4bits/pixel gray scale watermark image (although looks binary but it is a gray scale watermark image of 4bits/pixel) and Fig. 16(c) shows watermarked images after embedding on entropy decoded

(a) (b) (c)

Fig. 16. (a) Host image Lena (512 x512) (b)4 bits/pixel gray scale watermark of size (16x16) (d): Watermarked image

(a) (b) (c) (d) (e) (f)

Fig. 17. (a), (c): Watermarked images after mean and median filtering, respectively, (b) and (d): Extracted watermarks from (a), and (c), respectively, (e) watermarked image after histogram equalization, (f) extracted watermark from Fig. (e).

DCT coefficients with integer wavelets and convolution coding rate 1/6 at watermark power 12.73dB. The PSNR and MSSIM values for the watermarked image are 37.25 dB and 0.93, respectively. Fig. 17 (a) and (b) show the watermarked image after mean filtering (21.41dB) with size (11x11) and extarcted watermark, respectively. Fig. 17(c) and (d) show the watermarked image after median filtering (24.03 dB) with window size (9 x9) and the extracted watermark, respectiley. Finally, Fig. 17(e) and (f) shows the watermarked image (19.42 dB) after histogram equalization and the corresponding extracted watermark, respectively. In all cases, extracted watermark images are visually recognizable and indicate the robustness of the proposed scheme.

The proposed algorithm, although presented for gray scale images, can easily be extended for color images by considering each color channel as a gray-scale image. There are several ways to represent color images numerically, for example: RGB, YC_bC_r, CMY. The symbolsR, G, B, Y, C_b and C_r denote the red, the green, the blue, the luminance, the chrominance-blue and the chrominance-red, respectively while C, M and Y indicate cyan, magenta, and yellow, respectively. The CMY format is preferably used in printing industry and color images are most commonly represented in RGB format. In RGB format, the image is composed of three component planes; red, green, and blue color components. When the discrete cosine transformation is applied, each color component is transformed independently. Researchers have reported that for some typical applications, such as image compression, the RGB color space is not optimal. It turns out the human brain is more attuned to small changes in terms of luminance and chrominance (i.e. chrominance blue and chrominance red). A luminance channel carries information regarding the brightness of a pixel. Chrominance is the difference between a color and a reference channel at the same brightness. The most common of these spaces and the one used by JPEG2000 is the YC_bC_r space. The Y channel is luminance, while C_b and C_r are chrominance channels. Moreover, Y, C_r and C_b color components are less statistically dependent than R, G and B color components, and hence, they can be processed independently leading to better compression. The watermarks can then be embedded in appropriate color channels.

Finally, we also like to highlight simplicity of digital circuit design for the implementation of IWT of the filter coefficients, which is one of our future research work for the proposed algorithm. The multiplication operations may be carried out using simple shift-and-add multiplier blocks. Since multiplicands are signed, 2's complement arithmetic can be used in all mathematical operations. It is observed that the denominators of the coefficients are expressed in power of 2. Hence the division operation can easily be accomplished using parameterized right shifter blocks. Thus a right shifter block tailing every multiplier unit would be used in the filter bank design. The circuit of decimation (down-sampling) and interpolation (up-sampling) can be realized using D type flip-flop. In the decimator, a D flip-flop would be used and the clock rate of the input must be equal to half the clock rate of the D flip-flop so that only every alternate input to the decimator is fed to the interpolator unit. The clock rate of the input to the latter must be equal to twice that of the clock for the D flip-flop so that a zero would be inserted between every two successive inputs to the up-sampling block. This simplicity in hardware design makes this algorithm attractive for application specific integrated circuit (ASIC) or field programmable gate array(FPGA) based real-time implementation (Maity et al, 2009b).

6. Conclusions and scope of future works

A novel QIM watermarking is proposed using channel coding and lifting while channel coding is applied on host compressed data unlike conventional encoding of the watermark itself. Channel coding essentially creates a virtual redundancy space on compressed data to obtain flexibility in watermarking without increasing the file size of the compressed data. Channel coding offers improvement both for imperceptibility as well as BER performance while lifting contributes much on BER performance. Simulation results show that 6.24 dB (9.50 dB) improvement in DWR for watermark power at 12.73 dB (16.81 dB) and 15 dB gain in noise power for watermark decoding at BER of 10^{-2} are achieved, respectively over direct watermarking on entropy decoded data.

Future works may be carried out to design capacity optimized hidden watermarking scheme on the compressed data using non-zero and zero coefficients, as the latter may easily be mapped to non-zero coefficients using channel coding. Some widely used soft computingtool like Genetic Algorithms (GAs) may be explored for this optimization work. An extension of the proposed work may be to design VLSI chip using ASIC or FPGA, as standard JPEG compression, channel coding, lifting and nonlinear mapping used in this work can easily be mapped in hardware platform.

7. References

Allatar, A. M.; Lin E. T. & Celik, M. U. (2003). Watermarking Low Bit-rate Advanced Simple Profile MPEG-4 Bitstreams, *IEEE Trans. on Circuits and Systems for Video Tech.*, Vol.13,787-800.

Bose, R. (2002) *Information theoy coding and crypography*, Tata McGraw-Hill.

Boyer, J. P.; Duhamel, P. J. & Blanc-T, Asymptotically optimal scalar quantizers for QIM watermark detection. *Proc. IEEE ICME*, pp 1373-1376.

Chen, B. & Wornell, G. W. (2001). Quantization index modulation: a class of provably good methods for digital watermarking and information embedding. IEEE Trans. on Information Theory, Vol. 47, 1423- 1443.

Choi, Y. & Aizawa, K. (200). Digital watermarking using inter-block correlation: extension to JPEG coded domain, *Proc. IEEE Int. Conf. Information Technology: Coding andComputing*, pp. 133-138.

Elbasi, E. (2007). Robust MPEG Video watermarking in wavelet domain. Trakya Univ. Jour. Sci, Vol. 8, 87-93.

Fridrich, J; Goljan, M., Chen, Q., & Pathak, V. (2004). Lossless data embedding with file size preservation, Proc. EI, Security, Steganography, Watermarking Multimedia Contents VI, SPIE, Vol.5306, pp. 354-365.

Gonzalez, R. C. & Woods, R. E. Digital image processing, Pearson Education, New Delhi, India.

Hartung, F. & Kutter, M. (1999). Multimedia Watermarking Techniques, Proc. IEEE, Vol. 87, 1079--1107.

Huang, H-Y.; Fan, C-H. & Hsu, W.-H.(2007). An effective watermark embedding algorithm for high JPEG compression, Proc. of IAPR Conference on Machine Vision Applications, pp. 256-259.

Karakos, D. & Papamarcou, A. (2003). A relationship between quantization and watermarking rates in the presence of additive Gaussian attacks, IEEE Trans. on Information Theory, Vol. 49,1970-1982.

Langelaar, G. C.; Setyawan, I. & Lagendijk, R. L. (2000). Watermarking digital image and video data, IEEE Signal Process. Mag., Vol. 17, 20-46.

Luo, W.; Heileman, G. L. & C. E. Pizano.(2002). Fast and robust watermarking of JPEG files, Proc. IEEE 5th Southwest Symp. Image Analysis and Interpretation, pp. 158-162.

Maity, S. P.; Delpa, C., Braci, S., Boyer, R. (2009a). Hidden QIM watermarking on compressed data using channel coding and lifting, Proc. of third Int. Conf. on Pattern Recognition and Machine Intelligence, Vol. 5909, pp. 414-419.

Maity, S. P.; Kundu, M. K. & Maity, S. (2009b). Dual purpose FWT domain spread spectrum image watermarking in real-time, Special issues: circuits & systems for realtime security & copyright protection of multimedia, Journal of Computers & Electrical Engg., Elsevier, Vol.35, 415-433.

Maity, S. P.; Phadikar, A. & Kundu, M. K. Image error concealment based on QIM data hiding in dual-tree complex wavelets, International Journal of wavelets, Multiresolution and Information Processing (Article in press).

Maor, A. & Merhave, N. (2004). On joint information embedding and lossy compression, Proc. of IEEE Int. Symp. On Info. Th., pp. 194.

Maor, A. & Merhave, N.(2005). On joint information embedding and lossy compression in the presence of a stationary memoryless attack channel, EEE Trans. on Info. Th., Vol. 51, 3166-3175.

Mobasseri, B. J. & Berger, R. J. (2005). A foundation for watermarking in compressed domain, IEEE Signal Processing Letter, Vol.12, 399-402.

Nakajima, K. & Tanaka, K. (2005). Rewritable data embedding on MPEG coded data domain, IEEE Proc. of ICME, pp. 682- 685.

F. A. P. Petitcolas. (2000). Watermarking schemes evaluation, IEEE Signal Proc. Mag., Vol.17, 58-64.

Taniguchi, M. (2005). Scaling detection method for watermarked MPEG content, Proc. IEEE Int. Conf. Image Proc., Vol. 1, pp. 225-228.

Voloshynovskiy, S. & Pun, T. (2002). Capacity security analysis of data hiding technologies, Proc. IEEE International Conference on Multimedia and Expo, pp. 477--480.

Wang, Z.; Bovik, A. C., Sheikh, H. R., Simoncelli, E.P. (2004). Image quality assessment: from error measurement to structural similarity, IEEE Transactions on Image Processing, Vol. 3, 1--14.

Wong, P. H. W. & Au, O. C. (2000). Data hiding and watermarking in JPEG compressed domain by DC coefficient modification, Proc. SPIE Security and Watermarking of Multimedia Contents, Vol. 3971, pp. 237-244.

Wong, P. H. W. & Au, O. C. (2001). Data hiding technique in JPEG compressed domain, Proc. of SPIE Security and Watermarking of Multimedia Contents, Vol. 4314, pp. 309--320.

Wu, G. & Yang, H. (2005). Joint watermarking and compression using scalar quantization for maximizing robustness in the presence of additive Gaussian attacks, IEEE rans. on Signal Processing, Vol. 53, 834-844.

5

Spread Spectrum Watermarking: Principles and Applications in Fading Channel

Santi P. Maity[1], Seba Maity[1], Jaya Sil[1] and Claude Delpha[2]
[1]*Bengal Engineering and Science University, Shibpur*
[2]*Laboratoire des Signaux et Systemes, Universite Paris, SUPELEC, CNRS*
[1]*India*
[2]*France*

1. Introduction

Spread spectrum (SS) modulation based watermarking methods are widely used and popular, satisfying two important characteristics, namely (i) it may help in achieving high document-to-watermark ratio (DWR) leading to low distortion due to watermark insertion and (ii) it can also help to achieve robustness against forced removal of hidden data (Cox et al. 1997; Maity et al, 2007a). In SS watermarking, the bits composing the desired message are modulated using spreading code patterns and are added to the host (original) signal. The message may consist of a random number with zero mean and unit variance like an independent and identically distributed (i.i.d) Gaussian sequence, a string of binary data (binary signaling) or a group of symbols where each symbol consists of combination of binary data (M-ary signaling) (Malver & Florencio, 2003; Maity & Kundu, 2011). The associated problems in SS watermark system are the effect of host signal interference (HSI), poor payload due to spectrum spreading and poor detection performance for the widely used correlator in presence of non-stationary fading attack i.e. gain attack (Kundur & Hatzinakos, 2001).

The objective of this chapter is to propose SS watermark design for two applications, namely (i) an algorithm with low computation cost and complexity with ease of hardware realization enabling faithful assessment of wireless channel condition under fading attack, and (ii) multicarrier SS watermarking for estimation of fading parameters using genetic algorithm (GA), the second one may be applicable for error concealment or collusion resilient system design. At the end, the readers would understand how to incorporate various other wireless communication concepts in designing watermarking system for various other applications like error concealment, tamper detection, security in data transmission, equalizer design in digital communication etc.

The rest of the chapter is organized as follows: Section 2 makes a brief literature review on related works, limitations followed by motivation and the scope of the present work. Section 3 presents two proposed watermarking methods, first one for quality of services (QoS) assessment in wireless channel, while the second one is designed for estimation of fading attack in multicarrier watermarking system. Section 4 presents performance evaluation with discussion. Finally conclusions are drawn in Section 5 along with scope of the future works.

2. Review of related works, limitations, motivations and scope of the work

In this section, we present a brief literature review on SS watermarking with an objective to discuss their merits, limitations and finally scope of the proposed work.

2.1 Related works and limitations

The widely accepted form of single bit SS watermarking was proposed by Cox et al. (Cox et al. 1997), where an i.i.d Gaussian sequence is embedded to the perceptually most significant Discrete cosine transform (DCT) coefficients. The decoder requires the knowledge of original un-watermarked image in order to eliminate the effect of HSI during extraction of the watermark. Several solutions reported in other works are put together in review work (Maity et al, 2009d) that discusses reduction or nullifying the effect of HSI. The approaches include various signal processing methods, like preprocessing the host prior to embed the watermark (Langelaar, 2000), use of pre-whitening schemes prior to correlation detection for minimizing the variance of HSI (Kumar & Sreenivas, 2007), statistical whitening techniques based on stochastic modeling (Kim, 2000), exploiting the white spectral nature of linear prediction residual (Seok & Hong, 2010) or the Savitzky-Golay residual (Cvejic & Seppanen, 2002), the symmetric phase only match filtering (Haitsma et al., 2000) and cepstral filtering (Kirovski & Malvar, 2003) etc. To increase payload in SS watermarking, the concept of M-ary modulation and code division multiple access (CDMA) are used (Maity & Kundu, 2007a). It has been shown that performance improvement in former makes it impractical in real-time due to the exponential increase in computation cost with large M-values, while CDMA based algorithms are interference limited (Maity & Kundu, 2004; Maity & Kundu, 2011). A modified M-ary watermark decoding algorithm using a tree-structure was proposed that reduces the number of correlators to $2 \log_2 M$ (Xin & Pawlak, 2008). However, this algorithm results in higher rate of decoding errors than the direct correlation algorithm especially for blind watermark extraction.

In communication, SS modulation exploits large process gain (PG) to protect desired signal from the jammer (Simon et al., 2002). This anti-jamming property is used in SS watermarking to provide high degree of robustness against forced removal of hidden information. In watermarking, PG implies distribution of each bit of watermark information on (large) number of independent host samples and is governed by the length of the spreading code pattern. Increase in process gain in watermarking offers two-fold advantages, namely reduction in per sample embedding distortion for a given watermark power i.e. allowable embedding distortion. Secondly, it also increases resistance against forced removal of embedded watermark. However, it does not ensure improved watermark detection in presence of fading-like attack. This is due to the fact that large PG reduces per sample watermark power i.e. watermark-to-noise ratio (WNR) value in fading operation which in turn degrades bit error rate (BER) performance (Sklar, 1988; Maity & Maity, 2009c) for the decoded watermark. In the work (Maity & Maity, 2009c), a new model for SS watermark embedding and decoding is proposed where each watermark bit is spread over N-mutually orthogonal signal points. Minimum mean square error combining (MMSEC) strategy is then used for robustness against fading-like attack.

2.2 Motivation and scope of the present work

Nowadays fading-like operation becomes appealing as a typical attack in watermarking. To the best of our knowledge, its importance was first highlighted in (Kundur & Hatzinakos,

2001) where the authors hypothesize that many common multimedia signal distortions, including cropping, filtering, and perceptual coding, are not accurately modeled as narrow band interference. During recent times, watermarking finds typical application in error concealment for image and video transmission through radio mobile fading channel (Maity et al. 2010). Moreover, for image signals, fading or gain-like attack operation may occur during the scanning process where light is not distributed uniformly over the paper. In an intelligent collusion system, colluders may apply non-equal i.e. variable gain weight factors which is analogous to fading-like operation (Cha & Kuo, 2009).

To this aim, this chapter proposes two SS watermarking schemes. Firstly, an algorithm of a fragile SS watermarking technique is proposed for digital image that can be extended to video signal application by embedding watermark information in different frames. As watermarking is applied here for some non-conventional application (unlike copyright protection, authentication etc.), reference watermark pattern embedded in the multimedia signal is already available to the end user. The watermarked signal is transmitted through radio mobile channel (Maity et al, 2007b). Like a tracing signal, the watermark tracks the transmitted data, since both are suffered from the same channel degradation. The alteration in hidden watermark information is used and is compared with reference one to estimate wireless channel condition dynamically which in turn access the QoS and controls transmission bit rate.

In second algorithm, a multicarrier SS watermarking scheme is developed using couple of communication tool sets, such as each watermark bit is spread over N-mutually orthogonal set of host samples (multicarrier concept), CDMA concept for payload improvement, Minimum mean square error combining (MMSEC) for exploiting frequency diversity gain. The decision variable for each watermark bit decoding is obtained from the weighted average of N-decision statistics that leads to better stability against fading-like attack operation. Watermark detection performance can be improved at relatively low cost using single user detection of CDMA (however, detection performance can be improved lot using multiuser detection but at relatively high computation cost) provided that the knowledge of fading attack gains are incorporated. To this aim, estimation for such attack gains is done using GA (Maity et al, 2009e).

3. Proposed spread spectrum watermarking method

This section describes two SS watermarking scheme. We denote them as Algorithm 1 and Algorithm 2. We present the algorithms one after another.

3.1 Algorithm 1:SS watermarking for QoS assessment in wireless channel

Campisi et al (Campisi et al, 2003) developed DCT domain fragile digital watermarking scheme for blind quality assessment of multimedia services. However, this work does not discuss about the required computation cost and complexity to validate the practical implementation of the algorithm for such (near) real time application. Furthermore, Campisi work employs global embedding principle for an entire frame and thus fails to identify the relative degradation at different portion within the frame. We develop a SS watermarking scheme using fast Walsh transform (FWT) for a digital image.

FWT is chosen for embedding space as its binary integer value kernel offers binary modulation effect in data hiding that leads to better robustness against noise addition

(Maity et al, 2009b). Not only this advantage, FWT offers low computation cost as floating point addition-multiplication is not required during convolution with digital images for forward and inverse transform. The computation cost is further reduced as we implement block based SS watermarking unlike the whole image (video frame) decomposition used in other work (Campisi et al, 2003). Moreover, the kernel of Walsh transform being symmetric, only one hardware block is sufficient to implement both forward and inverse transform. It can also be shown mathematically that change in image information due to watermarking is less for FWT compared to other embedding spaces like discrete cosine transform (DCT) and discrete wavelet transform (DWT). Moreover, the orthogonal row-columns of FWT offer good degree of independencies among the coefficients. Watermarking on these coefficients may be looked like frequency diversity in multiple independent paths and thus leads to robustness against fading operation.

We use a gray scale image as cover image and a binary image as watermark. The cover image of size (M_c x N_c) is partitioned into (8 x 8) non-overlapping blocks. Fast Walsh transform is applied in each block to decompose image signal. The widely used code pattern for SS modulation technique is pseudo noise (PN) sequence and is generated using LFSR (Linear feedback shift register). The size of the PN sequence is identical to the size of the Walsh coefficient matrix. Thus a set of PN matrices denoted by (P_i) of number ($M_m.N_m$) are generated where N=(M_w x M_w) denotes the size of watermark. Watermark information is embedded according to the following rule.

$$X^e = X \pm \sum_{i=1}^{N} \alpha . P_i$$

where X is Walsh coefficient of the cover image, X^e is the Walsh coefficient after watermark embedding, α is the modulation index, P_i is the PN matrix and '+' indicates watermark bit b embedding as 1, while '-' indicates b=0. Two dimensional discrete inverse Walsh transform of the modified coefficients would then generate watermarked image.

The watermarked image is decomposed using Walsh transform. Correlation value between Walsh coefficients and each code pattern of the set (P_i) is calculated. We have a total of ($M_m.N_m$) (equal to the number of watermark bits) correlation values (Γ_i) where i= 1, 2,.. M_m. N_m. From these correlation values, we calculate mean correlation value (T), used as the threshold or decision variable for binary watermark decoding.

The decision rule for the decoded watermark bit is as follows:

(i) for $\Gamma_i \geq T$, the extracted bit is '0'
(ii) for $\Gamma_i < T$, the extracted bit is '1'

3.1.1 VLSI architecture

A brief outline of the very large scale integration (VLSI) architecture for the proposed algorithm is reported here. Design is made using XILINX SPARTAN series FPGA. Interested readers may consult (Maity et al, 2009b) for details of this hardware design. Hardware design of watermark embedding process consists of four subblocks or modules namely (1) Walsh transformation module, (2) code generation module, (3) data embedding module and (4) inverse Walsh transformation module shown in Fig. 1. The VLSI architecture of watermark embedding unit is shown in Fig. 1.

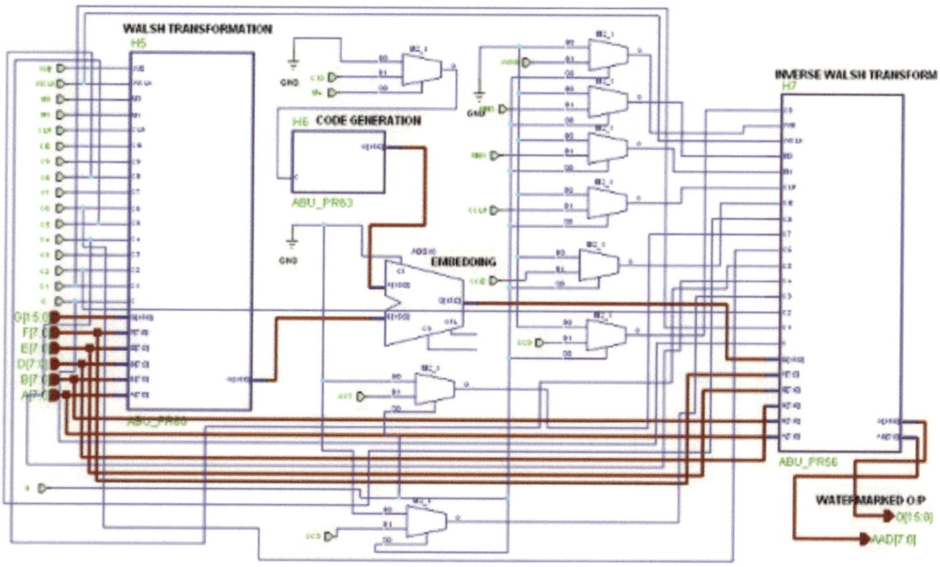

Fig. 1. VLSI architecture of embedding unit

Data is fed to the input pin G [15:0] of Walsh transformation block with the clock C1. The MUX with control input M4 allows the resultant spreading code to be added with Walsh coefficients at desired time. The output from the adder is fed to the G [15:0] input pin of inverse Walsh transformation block. Watermarked output is obtained at the output pin of this block. The other MUXs allow the various signals to flow into the inverse transformation block at the desired time.

The VSLI architecture of watermark decoding unit is shown in Fig. 2. The major sub blocks are: (1) Walsh transform module (2) Correlation calculation module (3) Mean correlation and threshold calculation module.

Watermarked data is fed to the input pin G[15:0] of the Walsh transform block. The output of this block is passed through the correlation calculation block. The function of the correlation calculation block is to calculate the correlation between the spreading functions and Walsh coefficients block. Then the correlation values are passed through a mean correlation and threshold calculation block. At the output of the block, the message bits are detected.

3.2 Multicarrier SS watermark with variable embedding rate

Multicarrier communication (MC), like orthogonal frequency division multiplexing (OFDM) becomes appealing to tackle inter symbol interference (ISI) problem for high data rate transmission in fading radio mobile channel. The integration of OFDM with CDMA, in the form of MC-CDMA, is also developed in high payload watermarking for collusion resilient fingerprinting (Cha & Kuo, 2009) and error concealment in time-varying channel (Maity et al. 2010). To this aim, estimation for such attack gains is done using GA. Independent fading attack on each mutually orthogonal host samples are assumed so that the embedded watermark bits on any host sample experience the same gain (analogous to fading gain for subcarriers in multicarrier system).

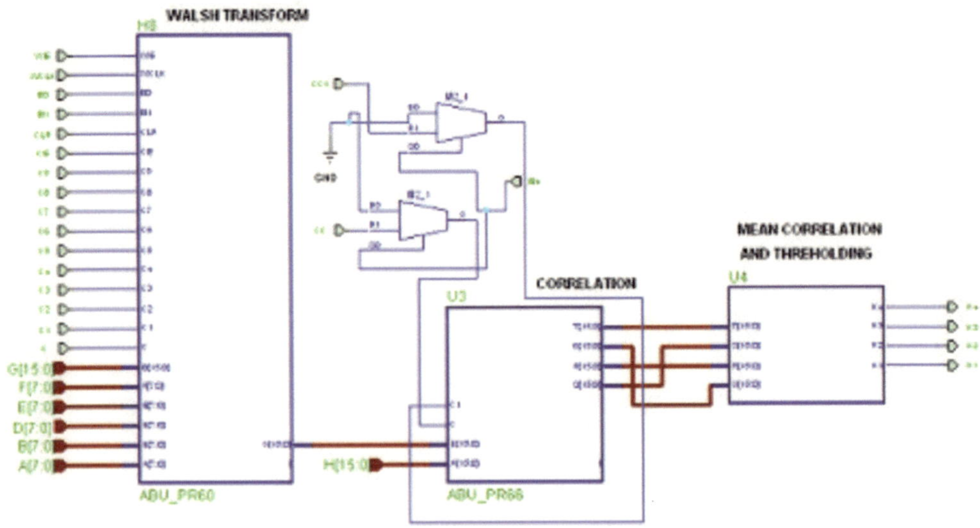

Fig. 2. VLSI architecture of watermark decoding unit

Let us assume that the host signal **X** is decomposed onto N-mutually orthogonal signal points, where each signal point corresponds to a vector or signal in N-dimensional signal space. So, the cover **X** can mathematically be represented as $X=\{X_1, X_2, X_3,........X_N\}$ where X_i is the signal coefficient corresponding to complete orthogonal basis function set. Let us also assume that the watermark (**W**) is a binary valued signal i.e. $\mathbf{W}=\{b_1, b_2, b_3,......., b_N\}$, where $b_i \in \{1,-1\}$ and i=1, 2, ...m. In SS watermarking, each watermark bit is spread over N-signal points where each host signal point is added with an element of the respective bit's code pattern. We use binary valued unit energy PN codes as spreading function. The watermarked signal, **X'**, may also be considered as a N-dimensional vector $\{X'_1, X'_2, X'_3,........X'_N\}$. Since $\{X'_1, X'_2, X'_3,........X'_N\}$ essentially correspond to mutually orthogonal points, the watermarked signal can be written as

$$X' = X'_1 + X'_2 + ... + X'_N = \sum_{k=1}^{K}\sum_{n=1}^{N} X_n \pm \gamma.P_n^k \quad (1)$$

where $n,k \in z$ and γ is the embedding strength. The symbol P_n^k corresponds to the n-th binary element of k-th code pattern. The symbol ± indicates antipodal embedding, i.e. if `+' is used for embedding `0', `-' for `1'.

To accommodate variable embedding rates with high overall payload, we modify the watermark embedding method by allocating all host signals points for some of the watermark bits. These watermark bits are those for which HSI and the cross correlation values among the code patterns are high. At the same time, odd and even mutually orthogonal host signal points are shared alternately for the other watermark bits which do not suffer much from HSI and cross-correlation values. The watermarked signal can now be written as

$$X' = \sum_{k=1}^{K_1} \sum_{n=1}^{N} (X_n \pm \gamma . P_n^k) + \sum_{k=1}^{K_2} \sum_{\forall n=odd}^{N} (X_n \pm \gamma . P_n^k) + \sum_{k=1}^{K_3} \sum_{\forall n=even}^{N} (X_n \pm \gamma . P_n^k) \quad (2)$$

where the total embedded watermark bits $K=k_1+k_2+k_3$. The first term of (2) corresponds to watermarking on all host points, while the second and the third terms represent watermarking on alternate odd and even sample points, respectively. Fig. 3 shows the block diagram of the proposed variable rate SS watermarking scheme.

Let us assume that an attacker modifies the n-th watermarked signal point by an amount α_n which takes values randomly from a complex valued i.i.d Gaussian distribution, of which Rayleigh fading is one case. Furthermore, we assume that the watermarked signal is also corrupted by additive white Gaussian noise (AWGN) when transmitted through the communication channel. The distorted and the noise corrupted watermarked signal at the input to the decoder can be written as

$$X'' = \sum_{k=1}^{K_1} \sum_{n=1}^{N} \alpha_n . X_n \pm \gamma . P_n^k + \sum_{k=1}^{K_2} \sum_{n=\forall n=odd}^{N} \alpha_n . X_n \pm \gamma . P_n^k + \sum_{k=1}^{K_3} \sum_{\forall n=even}^{N} \alpha_n . X_n \pm \gamma . P_n^k + \eta \quad (3)$$

Where, η is the contribution due to AWGN.

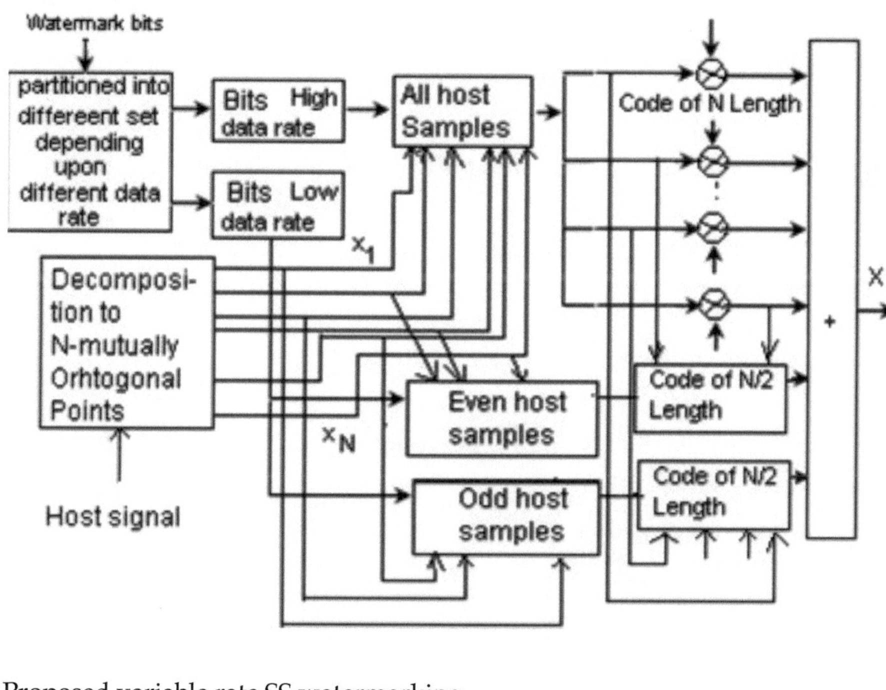

Fig. 3. Proposed variable rate SS watermarking

The received watermarked signal is first projected onto N-orthogonal signal points and is then correlated using j-th spreading code resulting in $r^j=\{r_1^j, r_2^j\},......r_N^j\}$. It is assumed that j-th watermark bit is embedded in all N-orthogonal signal points. The decision variable for the j-th bit at n-th signal point is denoted by r_n^j and can be written as follows:

$$r_n^j = < X''_n ,\ P_n^j \ > = < P_n^j ,\ \sum_{k=1}^{K_1}\sum_{n=1}^{N} \alpha_n.X_n \pm \gamma.P_n^k + \sum_{k=1}^{K_2}\ \sum_{n=\forall n=odd}^{N} \alpha_n.X_n \pm \gamma.P_n^k + \\ \sum_{k=1}^{K_3}\ \sum_{\forall n=even}^{N} \alpha_n.X_n \pm \gamma.P_n^k + \eta_n \ > = \ \alpha_n.\gamma + \sum_{k=1,k\neq j} \alpha_n.\gamma.\rho_{kj} + \eta_j \tag{4}$$

where η_j is a Gaussian random variable with mean 0 and variance $N_0/2$. The symbol ρ_{kj} indicates cross-correlation due to the j-th and k-th code patterns. The expression of (4) is obtained assuming the inner product of P_{nj} and X_n is zero i.e. HSI is assumed to be zero. The concept developed in (Malver & Florencio, 2003) can also be applied to reduce the effect of the signal as source of interference for the case of non-rejection of HSI. The first term of (4) results from the auto-correlation value of j-th code pattern with zero lag, the second term is the sum of cross-correlation values among the different combinations of code patterns (except j-th code) and the third term is the AWGN noise component spread by j-th code pattern. The second term is called multiple bit interference (MBI) effect.

3.2.1 Proposed GA based attack estimation

The goal of this SS watermarking method is to embed data on each signal point based on its data hiding capacity and subsequently reliable decoding even after fading-like attack. Since our SS watermarking method is designed for variable data rate, each host/watermarked signal point has different data hiding capacity as well as detection performance against fading attack. The goal of this work is to estimate this fading attack on each signal point using GA. The fitness function `F' depends on both data hiding capacity `C' and detection error probability p_e that corresponds to BER for watermark decoding. We first define `F' and GA based minimization is presented later.

Formation of fitness function: We assume that actual fading attack at n-th signal point is α_n and its estimated value is denoted by $\hat{\alpha}_n$. The error in estimated value is represented by e_n. We may use for probability density function (pdf) of the square of the estimation error as central Chi-square distribution and can be written as follows:

$$f(|e_n^2|) = \frac{1}{\sigma_n^2} e^{\frac{-|e_n|^2}{\sigma_n^2}} \tag{5}$$

where $\sigma_n{}^2$ is the variance of estimation error. We assume watermark embedding strength γ is made `1' for simplification of analysis. Moreover, for binary watermark embedding the choice of different values of γ to design adaptive watermark system is also not much effective. So, in terms of estimated attack values and its corresponding error terms, the expression of (4) can be written as follows:

$$r_n^j = \hat{\alpha}_n + e_n + \sum_{k=1,k\neq j}^{K} \hat{\alpha}_n \rho_{kj} + \sum_{k=1,k\neq j}^{K} e_n \rho_{kj} + \eta_j = \hat{\alpha}_n + e_n + \sigma_I^2 + \sigma_{Ie}^2 + \sigma_N^2 \tag{6}$$

The first, second, third, fourth and fifth term of (6) can be designated as signal term corresponding to the embedded bit, estimated error in signal term, variance of interfere i.e. interference power due to all embedded bits at n-th signal point, interference power due to all embedded bits for estimation error at n-th signal point, and noise power at n-th signal point, respectively. For large payload, the third and the fourth term is a random variable with normal distribution (according to central limit theorem).

We define a term SINR (signal-to-interference noise ratio) corresponding to j-th watermark bit at n-th signal point as follows:

$$(\mathrm{SINR})_n^j = \frac{(|\hat{\alpha}_n| + |e_n|)^2}{\alpha_I^2 + \alpha_{Ie}^2 + \alpha_N^2} \tag{7}$$

We assume SINR for all host signal points are independent, so total SIR corresponding to the j-th watermark bit is

$$(\mathrm{SINR})^j = \sum_{n=1}^{N} (\mathrm{SINR})_n^j \tag{8}$$

The data hiding capacity corresponding to j-th watermark bit can be written as

$$C^j = \log(1 + \mathrm{SINR}^j) \text{ bits/sample} \tag{9}$$

Total data hiding capacity corresponding to j-th watermark bit for the host signal can be written as $C = \sum_{\forall j} C^j$.

We now define fitness function `F' as function of data hiding capacity and detection probability $p_e$ i.e. $F=f(C, p_e)$. One form of realization of `F' may be developed from the weighted average of C and p_e. It is preferable to minimize `F' when target is to maximize C and minimize p_e. It is logical to express C as $C_{norm} = \frac{C_{\hat{\alpha},e}}{C_{\alpha=1}}$, that indicates normalization of the capacity. The symbol $C_{\alpha=1}$ corresponds to non-fading situation and obviously data hiding capacity with reliable decoding will be high. It is obvious that the value of $C_{norm} = \frac{C_{\hat{\alpha},e}}{C_{\alpha=1}}$ is less than 1 but our target is to achieve this value close to 1. The p_e is calculated as follows:

$$P_e = \frac{1}{K} \sum_{k=1}^{K} (b_k - \hat{b}_k) \tag{10}$$

where, K is total watermark bits, b_k and $\hat{b}_k$ are the embedded and the detected k-th watermark bit, respectively.

The objective function `F' can be defined as

$$F = \alpha_1(1 - C_{norm}) + \alpha_2 \rho_e = \alpha_1\left(1 - \frac{C_{\hat{\alpha},e}}{C_{\alpha=1}}\right) + \alpha_2 \rho_2 \tag{11}$$

where α_1 and α_2 are the weighting factors of data hiding capacity and detection reliability, respectively. Each weighting factor represents how important each index is during the searching process of GA. For example, if both indices are equally important, each one should be 0.5 so that the relationship $\alpha_1 + \alpha_2 = 1$ must hold.

Optimization of fitness function using GA: The steps for implementing optimized attack estimation are presented below:

Step 1. Initialization of twenty sets of random values for $\{\hat{\alpha}_1, \hat{\alpha}_2, ... \hat{\alpha}_n, e_1, e_2, ... e_n\}$ are done. The values of α are taken from Rayleigh distribution while the values of e's are taken from (5). Then the value of C and p_e are calculated for each set.

Step 2. Using the procedure outlined in previous subsection, the value of fitness function `F' is calculated for each of $\{\hat{\alpha}_1, \hat{\alpha}_2, ... \hat{\alpha}_n, e_1, e_2, ... e_n\}$ using (11).

Step 3. An upper bound of F value (F_U) is determined based on the calculated `F' values. The value of $F_U$ acts as a threshold and is adjustable. This is required so that the needful number of sets for $\{\hat{\alpha}_1, \hat{\alpha}_2, ...... \hat{\alpha}_n, e_1, e_2, ...... e_n\}$ values for which `F' values lie below the F_U are duplicated and the remaining sets having `F' values higher than F_U are ignored from the population. This process is done from the concept of selection of GA based algorithm.

Step 4. A binary string is generated through decimal-to-binary conversion for each selected set of $\{\hat{\alpha}_1, \hat{\alpha}_2, ... \hat{\alpha}_n, e_1, e_2, ... e_n\}$ value and thus a set of strings are calculated for all selected combinations. Now, crossover and mutation operations are done with above probabilities.

Step 5. Operation as described in step 4, when applied to the selected sets, generates a new set of $\{\hat{\alpha}_1, \hat{\alpha}_2, ... \hat{\alpha}_n, e_1, e_2, ... e_n\}$ value. This set is considered as population for next iteration/generation of the proposed GA based optimization problem.

Step 6. Repeat step 1 to step 5 for the desired number of iterations or till a predefined acceptable values for C and p_e are achieved.

4. Performance evaluation and discussion

In this section we present the performance of the proposed SS watermarking scheme one after another.

4.1 Performance analysis of algorithm 1

We report (1) the experimental results that highlight the effectiveness of the proposed scheme to access QoS and (2) results of hardware design in term of number of CLBs (Configurable Logic Blocks).

1. *Result for QoS assessment*

We consider (256 x 256), 8 bits/pixel grayscale image as host image and a binary image as sample watermark. We use PSNR (Peak signal-to- noise ratio) as objective measures to quantify visual quality of the watermarked image i.e. the offered services. PSNR values are 40.23 dB and 36.45 dB when watermark information is embedded in digital image using FWT and DCT, respectively.

The algorithm takes approximately 1 second for embedding and 2 seconds for extraction while algorithm in (Campisi et al, 2003) takes 3.5 seconds for embedding and 6.5 seconds for decoding, both implemented in MATLAB 6 platform running on a Pentium III 400MHz PC system. In Universal mobile telecommunication services (UMTS), multimedia signals are compressed first and thus a coded bit stream is obtained. This coded bit stream is then transmitted through noisy channel. Mobile station (MS), the end user of mobile communication system, extracts the tracing watermark from the supplied services and compare with the original watermark pattern. Since the original multimedia signal is not available to the MS, the relative quality of the tracing watermark is the indication about the quality of the offered services. The presented QoS assessment scheme has been tested for JPEG and JPEG-2000 coder followed by additive white Gaussian noise offered by the transmission channel. This corresponds to the relative quality of the tracing watermark that in turn indicates PSNR value, i.e. quality of the offered services. Fig. 4 represents relative quality of the tracing watermark when extracted from the various noisy compressed images i.e. quality of the offered services. In practical UMTS environment a fraudulent user, to obtain any benefit, declares that the received quality is lower than the provided one. An ad hoc solution may be adopted against false declaration on QoS through(i) an improvement of service quality of base station by lowering the emitted bit rate in few seconds as it implies that the channel is not well suited for the current bit rate for the given BER or (ii) interrupt the communication process for a few seconds. The solution as in (ii) is due to the fact that if there occurs frequent declarations of poor or null quality from a MS, the admission call manager may refuse the access to further calls of the same user, al least until the MS has moved to a region with less noise or interference (Campisi et al, 2003).

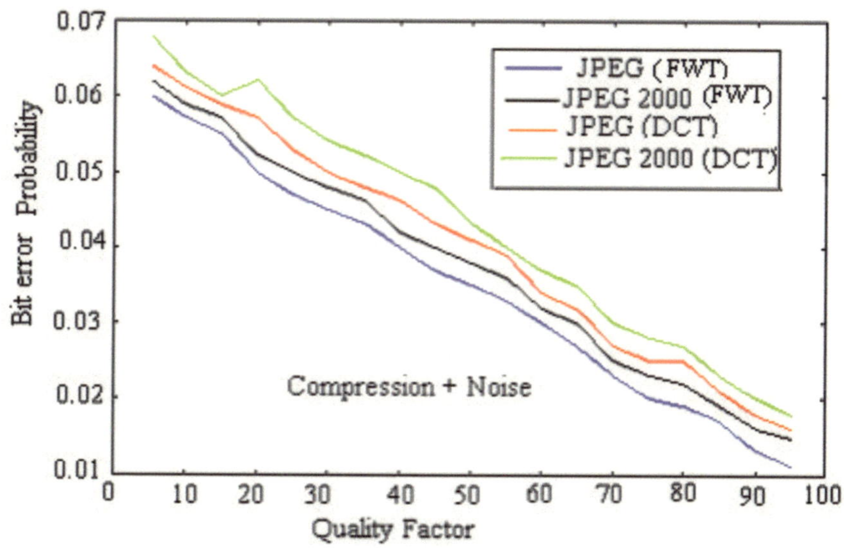

Fig. 4. Quality of tracing watermark for QoS

In mobile radio channel signal is degraded due to multipath effect. Fig. 5 shows that both the original and watermarked images are affected by the channel in similar fashion after Rayleigh and Rician fading and as expected QoS is better for the latter (due to the presence of stationary dominant signal along with multipath components) compared to the former (only multipath components are present). Multipath channels being independent, embedded watermark would experience different amount of channel distortion while watermarked signals traverse through them. The relative quality values (P_e) of the tracing watermarks indicate the condition of the different channels. BER can be used for calculation of weight factors in diversity techniques as the same are determined in maximal ratio combiner (space or antenna diversity) or RAKE receiver (SS time diversity) based on the value of SNR (Signal-to-noise ratio) (Prasad, 1996). Quality improvement for the offered services is achieved by 3.5 dB under multipath effect, while the value of sigma (standard deviation of noise) for different paths are varied by 4.

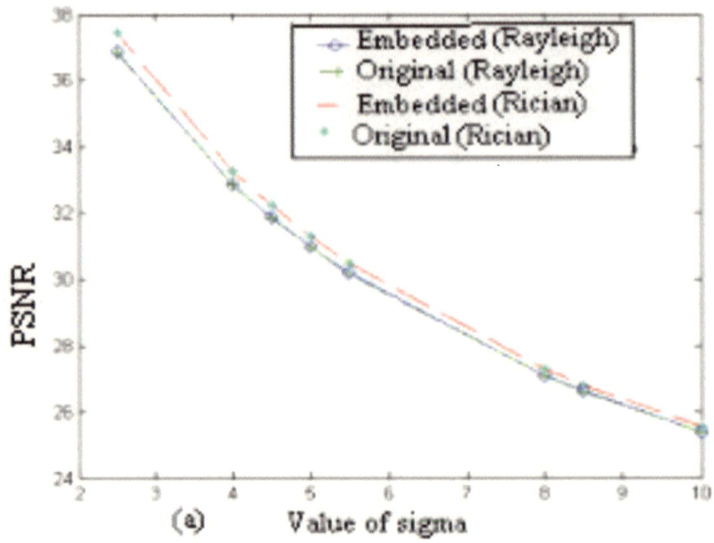

Fig. 5. Quality of various offered services in MS

2. *Result of Hardware design*

The VLSI design is implemented for a gray scale image of size (8 x 8) and a 4-bit binary watermark with element number values '1' and '0'. The choice of (8 x 8) block size is to make the scheme compatible with DCT based JPEG compression operation. The chip used is XCS40 which contains 784 CLB, out of which 730 CLBs are consumed, 430 for embedding unit and 300 unit for decoding unit. The maximum clock frequency is 80 MHz and clock cycle 344 cycles/ (8 x 8).

4.2 Performance analysis of algorithm 2

This section represents performance analysis of the proposed attack estimation method in terms of SINR performance with the number of watermark bits, BER performance with the number of watermark bits, optimization performance for non-variable and variable embedding rate with number of generations. The host image is a 8 bits/pixel gray scale image of size (512x 512). We embed watermark image shown in Fig. 6(b) and PSNR value of the watermarked image [shown in Fig.6(c)] is found 43.24 dB. Fig. 6(d) shows the watermarked image after fading attack and Fig. 6(e) shows the extracted watermark image. Fig. 6(f) shows the watermarked image after removing decoded watermark using the estimated attack parameters.

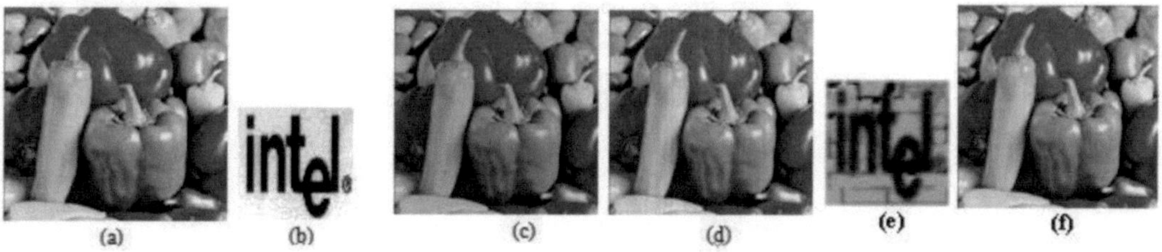

Fig. 6. (a) Host image, (b) watermark image, (c) watermarked image, (d) watermarked image after fading attack, (e) extracted watermark using estimated attack parameters, (f) watermarked image after removal of watermark bit

Fig. 7 shows the graphical representation of actual SINR (with the actual knowledge of fading attack) and the estimated SINR value (obtained using the estimated attack parameters) for number of generations 100. Difference in SIR decreases with the increase of number of embedding bits, which is due to the fact that interference power i.e. σ^2_I is much larger (due to the strong correlation among the code patterns) compared to $\sigma^2_I e$ under high payload condition and the estimated attack parameters converge to the actual values. This has been further supported by BER (bit error rate) performance with the same number of generations/iterations for change in watermark bits as shown in Fig. 8.

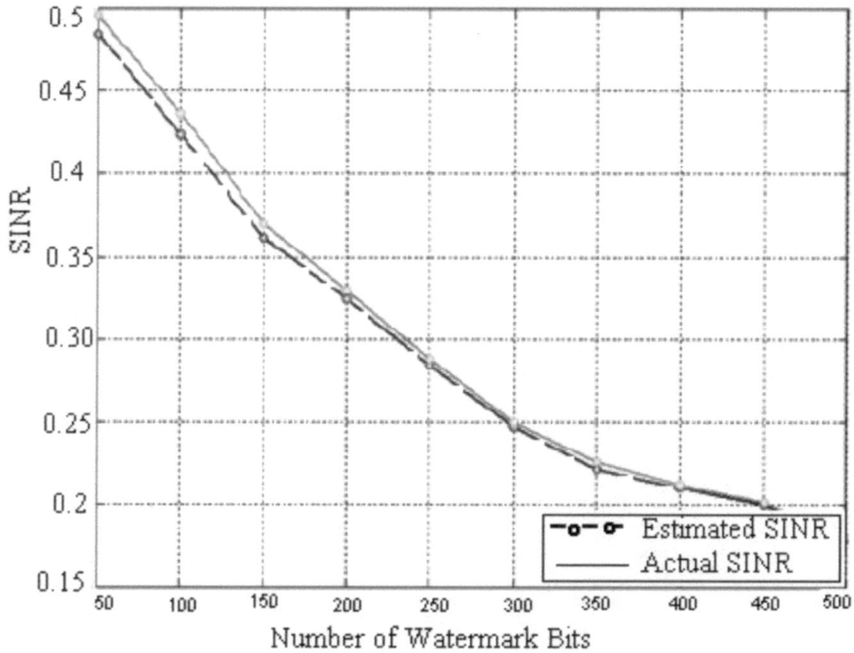

Fig. 7. Comparison of SINR values for the estimated and actual attack parameters with the variation of number of watermark bits

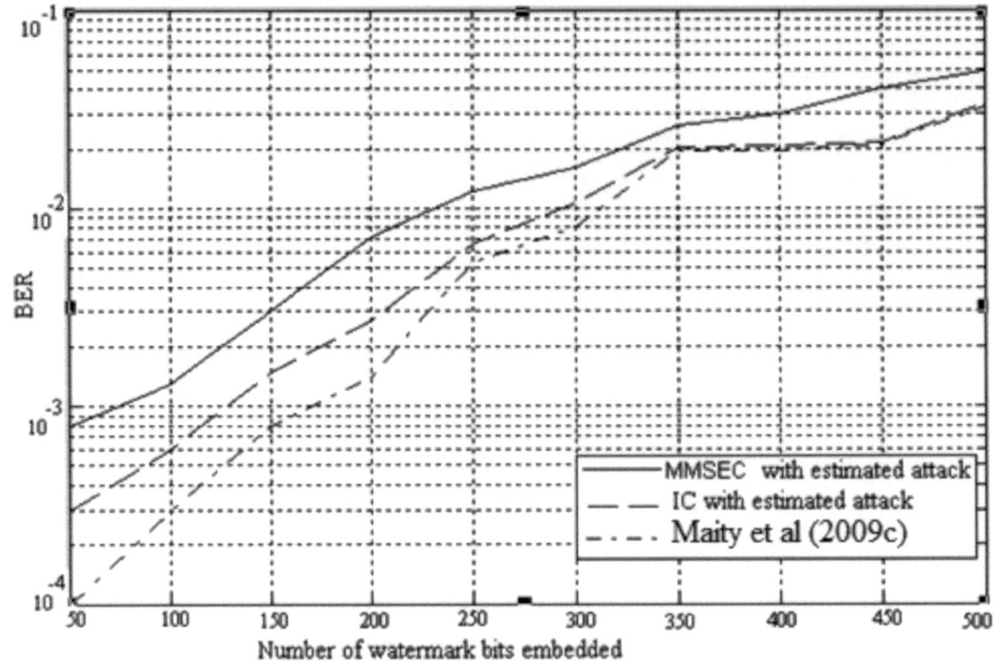

Fig. 8. BER performance with the variation of number of watermark bits

We also test the generation effect for the estimated attack parameters followed by watermark decoding reliability. Fig. 9(a) shows the watermark image embedded on host image shown in Fig. 6(a). Figs. 9(b)-(d) show the extracted watermark images from the watermarked image shown in Fig. 9(c) using estimated attack parameters after generation/iteration number 50, 75 and 100, respectively. The visual quality of the extracted message/watermark is represented by mutual information I(W;W') where random variables W and W' represent the watermark image and its decoded version obtained from the watermarked images with fading-like attack. Fig. 9(b), 9(c) and 9(d) reveal the fact that the visual recognition of the retrieved watermark images increase more and more close to the original watermark image. The I(W;W') values for the extracted messages are 0.0894, 0.1012 and 0.1252, respectively. The improvement in decoding is borne out by the property of GA which produces better solutions for the estimated attack parameters leading to the improvement in watermark decoding reliability. This is due to the number of generations/iterations are increased. The estimation of fading attack would help for error concealment during transmission of watermarked signal through radio mobile channel.

We also compare the performance of the proposed methods with other watermarking methods reported in (Cox et al. 1997), (Kundur & Hatzinakos, 2001) and (Malver & Florencio, 2003). For compatibility with the proposed technique, embedding is performed for multiple bit watermarking in (Cox et al. 1997) and (Malver & Florencio, 2003) also. A 512-bit randomly generated equiprobable binary watermark was embedded in all cases using the watermarking principles as described in (Cox et al. 1997), (Kundur & Hatzinakos, 2001) and (Malver & Florencio, 2003). All the watermarked images are then undergo similar fading attack. The fading attack parameters then estimated using the GA based proposed method described in this work. The estimated fading parameters are then used to improve watermark decoding reliability. Fig. 10(a) shows the improvement in visual quality after removing the effect of fading attack for different number of generations, while Fig. 10(b) shows the watermark decoding reliability using the estimated fading parameters after JPEG compression operation at different quality factors.

(a) (b) (c) (d)

Fig. 9. Watermark images, (b), (c) and (d) decoded watermarks using estimated fading attack parameters at generation number of 50, 75 and 100, respectively

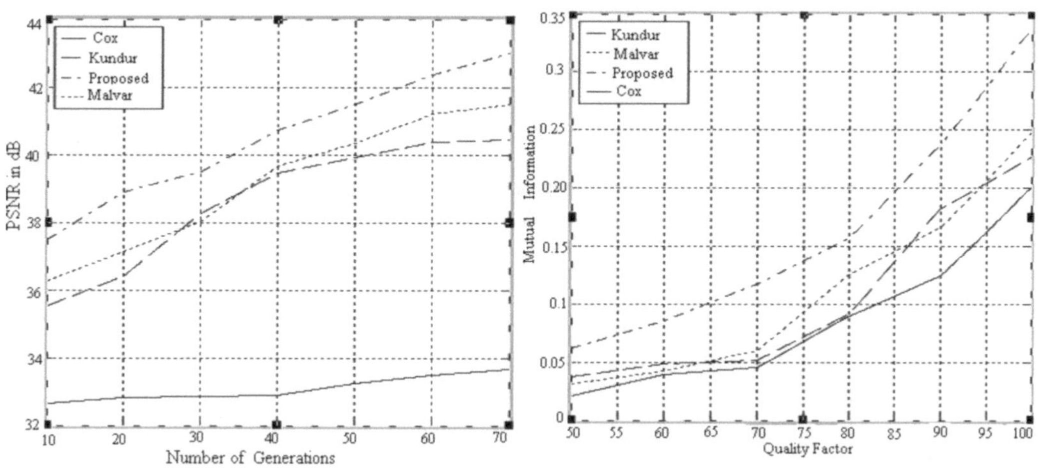

Fig. 10. (a) Improvement in visual quality using estimated fading parameter, (b) Watermark decoding reliability after JPEG compression using estimated fading parameter

We see the effect of number of iterations on estimation of attack parameters for both variable and non-variable embedding rate SS watermarking system for watermark payload of 500 bits. The graphical results in Fig. 11 show that variable embedding system provides much better BER and capacity performance compared to non-variable system. The average `F' value is stable for the former, while the same for non-variable system is improved with the increase of number of iterations. In other words, attack estimation converges quickly for the proposed variable embedding rate system compared to (Maity et al 2009a).

We also study the performance of the proposed algorithm for gray scale watermark embedding. One typical application, as specified earlier, may be in error concealment in digital image transmission over fading channel. To make our algorithm 2 compatible to error concealment application we consider host image itself as watermark. Lifting based n-level 2D-DWT is performed on the original image to decompose it into its high-pass and low-pass subbands. The number of levels in wavelet decomposition is implementation dependent; however, four levels are demonstrated in the experimentation. The approximation subband i.e. low-low (LL) subband is selected as an important feature. The extracted feature is then converted into bit string (8-bit/coe_cients) and is used as a watermark to be embedded to the host image according to the algorithm proposed here. This introduces sufficient redundancy in the watermarked image to be transmitted over fading channel.

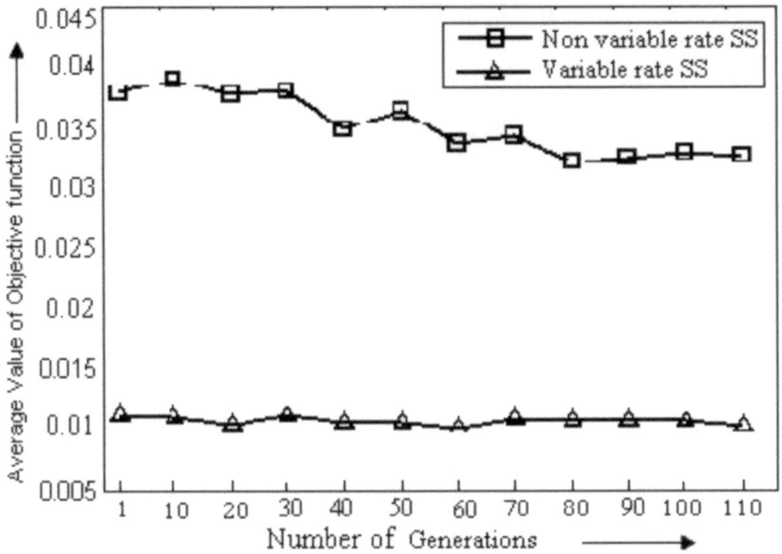

Fig. 11. Effect of number of iterations on estimation of attack parameters

Fig. 12 shows a set of test (host) images, while Fig. 13 shows the LL subband used as watermark. Fig. 14 shows the respective watermarked images with MSSIM and PSNR values after embedding watermark shown in Fig. 13. The extracted watermark images (without applying any attack operation over watermarked images) are shown in Fig. 15.

Fig. 12. Host images (a) Lena, (b) Fishing Boat, (c) Pepper, (d) Cameraman, (e) Baboon, (f) Opera, (g) Pueblo bonito, (H) F16

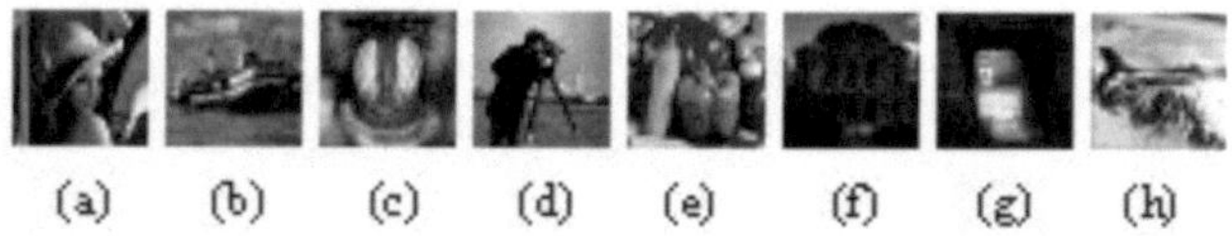

Fig. 13. Watermark digests for (a) Lena, (b) Fishing Boat, (c) Pepper, (d) Cameraman, (e) Baboon, (f) Opera, (g) Pueblo bonito, (H) F16

Fig. 14. Watermarked images (a) Lena, (b) Fishing Boat, (c) Pepper, (d) Cameraman, (e) Baboon, (f) Opera, (g) Pueblo bonito, (H) F16

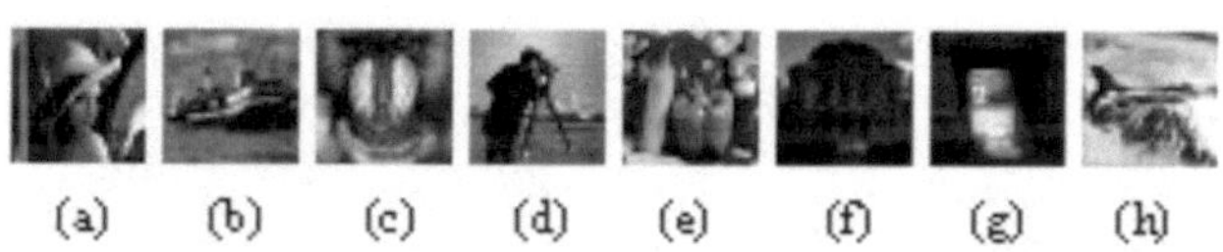

Fig. 15. Extracted watermark images (a) Lena, (b) Fishing Boat, (c) Pepper, (d) Cameraman, (e) Baboon, (f) Opera, (g) Pueblo bonito, (H) F16

In order to show the robustness of the proposed method over fading-like gain operation and subsequent application to error concealment, we simulate our test for different random gain operation from Rayleigh distribution. One way of implementation is accomplished by transmitting watermarked image over Rayleigh fading channel using MC-CDMA at different SNR. The small value of SNR represents that the channel is under deep fade, while large value of SNR indicates the reverse one. Fig. 16 (a) and (b) show the watermarked images transmitted through Rayleigh fading channel at SNR=3dB and SNR=5 dB, respectively. The corresponding extracted watermark images are shown in Fig. 16(c) and (d), respectively. The respective better quality images after applying error concealment operation using the extracted watermark images are shown in Fig. 16 (e) and (f), respectively. Degraded and error concealed images are shown with associated PSNR and MSSIM values.

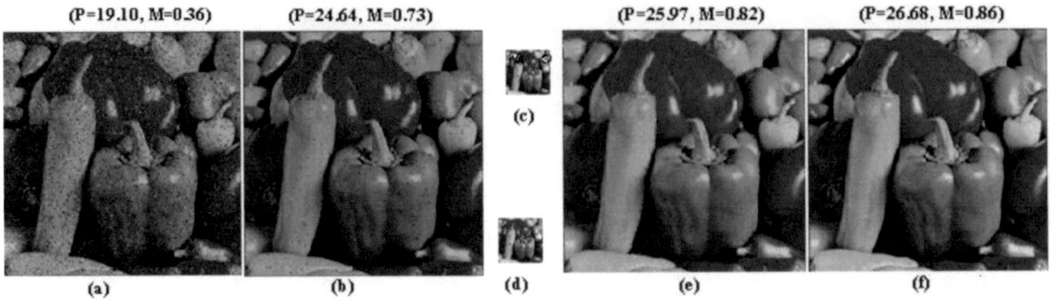

Fig. 16. Watermarked images after transmitting through Rayleigh fading channel at (a) SNR=3dB; (b) SNR=5dB; (c) extracted watermark from (a); (d) extracted watermark from (b); (e) Error concealed image using extracted watermark (c); (f) Error concealed image using extracted watermark (d).

5. Conclusions and scope of future works

This chapter proposes two SS watermarking scheme application to fading channels. First, a low cost SS watermarking scheme along with hardware design is proposed and tested for blind assessment of QoS for digital images in radio mobile channel. The novelty of the scheme lies in the choice of FWT for image decomposition that offers low loss in structural information for the offered multimedia services, high resiliency to compression operations and ease of hardware realization. The estimation of the tracing watermark at MS will provide detailed information about the quality of services due to watermark embedding, status of the link, information relating to billing purpose etc. Furthermore, the quality of the tracing watermarks may be exploited in diversity techniques for cancelation of the fading effect arising out of multipath propagation.

A new model of multi carrier spread spectrum watermarking with variable embedding rate is proposed in second algorithm. GA is used to estimate the fading-like attack and is incorporated for BER calculation using MMSEC decoder. Simulation results show that detection performance similar to multiple group combined multistage interference cancelation is possible to achieve with low computation cost. Estimated attack parameters offers better detection and capacity performance for variable rate system compared to non-variable rate system. Simulation is also done for gray scale watermark images and robustness performance is studied for quality improvement through error concealment in Rayleigh fading channel.

Future work may be extended for the first algorithm to design a dedicated hardware chip for larger image sizes. On the other hand, an adaptive watermark embedding power control system can be designed for the proposed variable rate SS watermarking system.

6. References

Campisi, P.; Carli, M., Giunta, G. & Neri, T. (2003). Blind quality assessment for multimedia communications using tracing watermarking, *IEEE Trans. on Signal Processing,* Vol. 51, 996-1002.

Cha, B.-Ho & Kuo, C. C. Jay. (20009). Robust MC-CDMA based fingerprinting against time-varying collusion attacks, *IEEE Trans. On Information Forensics and Security*, Vol. 4, 302-317.

Cox. I. J; Killian, J., Leighton, F. T. & Shamoon, T. (1997). Secure spread spectrum watermarking for multimedia, *IEEE Trans. Image Process*, Vol.6, 1673-1687.

Cvejic, N. & Seppanen, T. (2002). Audio prewhitening based on polynomial filtering for optimal watermark detection, *Proc. of European Signal Process. Conf*erence.

Haitsma, J. A.; van der Veen, M., Kalker, T. & Bruekers, F. (2000). Audio watermarking for monitoring and copy protection, *Proc. of the ACM multimedia workshop*, pp. 119-122.

Kim, H. (2010). Stochastic model based audio watermarking and whitening filter for improved detection, Proc. IEEE Int. Conf. on Acoustics, Spech and Signal Proc., pp. 1971-1974.

Kirovski, D. & Malvar, H. S. (2003). Spread spectrum watermarking of audio signals, *IEEE Trans. Signal Process.*, Vol. 51, 1020-103.

Kumar, K. S. & Sreenivas, T. (2007). Increased watermark-to-host correlation of uniform random phase watermarks in audio signals. *Signal Processing*, 87, 61-67.

Kundur, D. & Hatzinakos, D. (2001). Diversity and attacks characterization for improved robust watermarking, IEEE Trans. on Signal Proc., Vol. 29, 2383-2396.

Langelaar, G. C.; Setyawan, I. & Lagendijk, R. L. (2000). Watermarking digital image and video data, IEEE Signal Process. Mag., Vol. 17, 20-46.

Maity, S. P. & Kundu, M. K. (2004). A blind CDMA image watermarking scheme in wavelet domain, *Proc. IEEE Int. Conf. on Image Proc. (ICIP-2004)*, pp. 2633–2636.

Maity, S. P.; Kundu, M. K. & Das, T. S. (2007a). Robust SS watermarking with improved capacity, *Pattern Recognition Lett.*, Vol. 28, 350-356.

Maity, S. P.; Kundu, M. K. & Maity, S. (2007b). An efficient digital watermarking scheme for dynamic estimation of wireless channel condition. Proc. Of Int. Conf. on computing: theory and applications. Indian Statistical Institute, Kolkata, India, pp. 671–675.

Maity, S. P.; Maity, S. & Sil, J. (2009a). Spread spectrum watermark embedder optimization using Genetic Algorithms, Proc. of 7th Int. Conf. on Adv; in Pattern Recognition, ISI Kolkata, 4-6 February, pp. 29-32.

Maity, S. P.; Kundu, M. K. & Maity, S. (2009b). Dual purpose FWT domain spread spectrum image watermarking in real-time, *Special issues: circuits & systems for realtime security & copyright protection of multimedia, Computers & Electrical Engg.*, Vol. 35, 415-433.

Maity, S. P. & Maity, S. (2009c). Multistage spread spectrum watermark detection technique using fuzzy logic, *IEEE Signal Proc. Letters*, Vol.16, 245-248.

Maity, S. P.; Phadikar, A. & Delpha, C. (2009d). Spread spectrum watermarking: from zero-rate embedding to high payload system , Proc. Of Int. Conf. on Multimedia Information Networking and Security, 525-529.

Maity, S. P.; Maity, S. & Sil, J. (2009e). Estimation of Fading Attack on High Payload Spread Spectrum Watermarking with Variable Embedding Rate using Genetic Algorithms, *Proc. of Third Int. Conf. on Imaging for Crime Detection and Prevention (ICDP-09)*.

Maity, S. P.; Maity, S. & Sil, J.(2010). Multicarrier spread spectrum watermarking for secure error concealment in fading channel, *Springer Telecommunication System*, Vol. 49, 219-229, 2012.

Maity, S. P. & Kundu, M. K. (2011). Performance improvement in spread spectrum image using wavelets. *International Journal of wavelets, Multiresolution and Information Processing*, Vol. 9, 1-33.

Malvar, H. S. & Florencio, A. F. (2003). Improved spread spectrum: a new modulation technique for robust watermarking, *IEEE Tran. On Signal Proc.*, Vol. 51, 898-905.

Prasad, R. (1996). CDMA for wireless personal communication , Artech House, Boston.

Seok, J.W. & Hong, J. W. (2001). Audio watermarking for copyright of digital audio data, *IEEE Electronic Lett.*, Vol. 37, 60-61.

Simon, M. K.; Omura, J. K., Sholtz, R. A. & Levitt, B. K. (2002). Spread Spectrum communication Hnadbook, New York:McGraw-Hill.

Sklar, B. (1988). Digital communication , PH, Englewood Cliffs, NJ.

Xin, Y. & Pawlak, M. (2008). M-ary phase modulation for digital watermarking. Int. Journal of Appl. Math. Comput. Science, Vol. 18, 93-104.

6

Optimization of Multibit Watermarking

Joceli Mayer
Research Laboratory on Digital Signal Processing, Federal University of Santa Catarina Brazil

1. Introduction

This Chapter presents a Multibit Improved Spread Spectrum modulation (MISS) by properly adjusting the energy of the pseudo random sequences modulated by Code Division (CDM). We extend the one-bit spread spectrum watermarking approach proposed by Henrique S. Malvar and Dinei A. F. Florencio (2003) to multibit watermarking by using an optimization procedure to achieve the best performance possible in robustness and transparency while mitigating the cross correlations among sequences and the host interference. The proposed multibit approach also tradeoffs the resulting watermarking distortion with the host interference rejection. This Chapter extends the approach published in Mayer (2011). We describe the improved modulation method and present results to illustrate the performance.

1.1 Spread spectrum modulation

Spread spectrum modulation is a mature and popular approach for hiding information in a host [I. J. Cox, J. Kilian, F. T. Leighton, T. Shamoon (1997)]. The basic idea is to spread one message bit over many samples of the host data. The spreading can be achieved by modulating the host data with a sequence obtained from a pseudo-random generator, for instance.

In general and independently of the media type, the embedding in the sample domain of one antipodal bit b can be achieved by additive embedding [I. J. Cox, J. Kilian, F. T. Leighton, T. Shamoon (1997)]

$$\boldsymbol{c} = \boldsymbol{c}_0 + \bullet b\boldsymbol{p} \tag{1}$$

where $\boldsymbol{c}_0$ is the vector representation of the M samples of the host data, $\boldsymbol{p}$ is the vector representation of the spread sequence of size M, $\bullet$ is a scaling parameter, b is an antipodal bit $\in \{-1, +1\}$, $\boldsymbol{w} = \bullet b\boldsymbol{p}$ is the embedded watermark and $\boldsymbol{c}$ is the vector representation of the resulting watermarked data of size M. The embedding can be applied to any document type (voice, audio, image, video, text, etc) and in any feature space (samples, linearly transformed domain using wavelet (WT), discrete cosine (DCT) or Fourier transform (FT), or another space). By spreading the information over the chosen domain, all spread spectrum modulation techniques [I. J. Cox, M. L. Miller, J. A. Bloom (2002)] can provide robustness to non-malicious attacks such as compression, filtering, histogram equalization and A/D and D/A conversions, as well as to tampering attacks [I. J. Cox, J. Kilian, F. T. Leighton, T. Shamoon (1997); I.J. Cox, M.L. Miller, A.L. Mckellips (1999); Santi P. Maity and Malay K. Kundu (2004); Z. Jane Wang, Min Wu, Hong Vicky Zhao, Wade Trappe, K. J. Ray Liu (2005)]. Spread spectrum watermarking can be made robust to geometric operations such as rotation, cropping and scaling by employing a pre-processing tailored to the specific attack [I. J. Cox, J. Kilian, F. T. Leighton, T. Shamoon (1997); Yanmei Fang, Jiwu Huang, Shaoquan Wu (2004)]. There has been a great deal of effort towards the generation and shaping of sequences $\boldsymbol{p}$, that can improve the performance of the watermarking system [Mauro Barni and Franco Bartolini (2004)]. Reduction of the perceptual impact can be achieved by exploiting the human perceptual masking in either the frequency or the sample domain [E.J. (1999); Joceli Mayer and José C. M. Bermudez (2005); Joseph J.K.Ó. Ruanaidh and Gabriella Csurka (1999); Martin Kutter and Stefan Winkler (2002); Santi P. Maity and Malay K. Kundu (2004)]. The system performance can be measured by estimating the probability of detection considering channel distortions and/ or malicious attacks, by evaluating the distortion resulting from the insertion of the watermark signal into the host data, by determining the computational resource requirements (speed of detection, required memory), or by other practical constraint imposed by the application. Some recent results [Henrique S. Malvar and Dinei A. F. Florencio (2003); M. Barni, N. Memon, T. Kalker, P. Moulin, I.J. Cox, M.L. Miller, J.J. Eggers, F. Bartolini, F. Pérez-González (2003); Perez-gonzalez & Pun (2004)] indicate that informed embedding spread spectrum watermarking can provide a competitive performance when compared to techniques based on the dirty-paper approach [Moulin & Koetter (2005)], especially in practical situations when scaling attacks are considered and the noise and the host signals cannot be properly modeled by Additive White Gaussian Noise (AWGN) sequences.

Some simple and popular schemes focus on combining classical 1-bit spread spectrum modulation with an informed embedding strategy. An "erase and write" strategy has been initially proposed in I. J. Cox, M. L. Miller, J. A. Bloom (2002) and named "Peaking DS" (PEAK) in Delhumeau et al. (2003). It consists of pre-canceling the host interference before embedding:

$$\boldsymbol{w} = \bullet \boldsymbol{p} - \frac{< \boldsymbol{p}, \boldsymbol{c}_0 >}{< \boldsymbol{p}, \boldsymbol{p} >} \boldsymbol{p} \tag{2}$$

where $< \boldsymbol{p}, \boldsymbol{c}_0 >$ stands for the inner product of $\boldsymbol{p}$ and $\boldsymbol{c}_0$. Improved Spread Spectrum (ISS) is an extension to PEAK that maximizes the robustness to an AWGN attack of known power $\bullet^2$, at constant distortion [Henrique S. Malvar and Dinei A. F. Florencio (2003)]. A compromise is made between the power of the watermark portion devoted to host-interference cancellation and its information-carrying portion, the latter essential for robustness to attacks.

1.2 Multibit spread spectrum watermarking

Many applications require a higher payload watermarking [Mauro Barni and Franco Bartolini (2004)]. In these cases, one bit watermarking can be extended to convey more bits of information. By using a codebook of sequences, which should be known by both the encoder and the decoder, a multibit watermark can be designed to convey N bits of information. In most cases, only a secret key K is needed to recreate the sequences at decoder. This key is usually shared by the sender and receiver using a secure protocol and neither the host image or the sequences are required to be known by the receiver in the blind decoding watermarking. Three modulation approaches are possible: basic message coding, Time Division Multiplexing (TDM) and Code Division Multiplexing (CDM). Basic message coding [I. J. Cox, M. L. Miller, J. A. Bloom (2002)] requires a unique sequence $\boldsymbol{w}_i$ for each n-bit message m_i, resulting in a codebook with 2^N possible messages. Issues associated with this approach include computational complexity for generating and, in some cases, storing the codebook. Moreover, the detection process requires a search for a sequence in a space of 2^N vectors of dimension

M. Depending on the required payload (N bits), this multibit approach may require a huge computational complexity [Mauro Barni and Franco Bartolini (2004)]. The search complexity can be considerably reduced by structuring the sequences into a binary tree [Wade Trappe, Min Wu, Jane Wang, K. J. Ray Liu (2003)], which requires the storage of the sequences. On the other hand, using a binary tree may increase both the storage requirements and the probability of detecting the wrong message when the sequences are not perfectly orthogonal to each other. For instance, consider that a pseudo random generator (PN) based on a secret key K is used to generate the codebook. For security, only the intended decoder agent should detain the knowledge of the sequence $\boldsymbol{p}$ or of the key K that generated the sequence. Assume that the Lehmer generator [? is used with $L = 2^{31} - 1$, where L is the period of the generator. To embed messages into images with $S^2 = 512^2 = 2^{18}$ pixels, the generator can provide, without overlapping sequences, a maximum of $L/\ S^2 = 2^{31}/\ 2^{18} = 2^{13}$ sequences and messages. This means that only 13 bits can be embedded in the host data. By allowing overlapping, the generator can provide $2^{31} - 1$ different sequences, resulting in messages of at most 30 bits.

Alternatives based on the spread spectrum approach aimed at reducing the complexity of multibit watermarking include the use of message multiplexing such as TDM and CDM [Mauro Barni and Franco Bartolini (2004)]. The computational complexity required for detection is linear in N ($O(N)$ for embedding N bits), whereas the basic message coding and orthogonal modulation require an exponential ($O(2^N)$) number of detections [Z. Jane Wang, Min Wu, Hong Vicky Zhao, Wade Trappe, K. J. Ray Liu (2005)]. In TDM, the host signal is divided into N subsets of size $M/\ N$. Then 1-bit spread spectrum watermark embedding is performed on each subset. A combination of these multiplexing techniques can provide a desired tradeoff for a given application. For instance, a mixed embedding based on TDM and basic message coding is employed in [Min Wu and Bede Liu (2003)] to mitigate the computational complexity associated with the basic message coding approach. Random sample shuffling is often necessary for TDM to deal with the uneven capacity of each signal segment (non-stationary signals) [Min Wu and Bede Liu (2003)]. CDM multiplexing is discussed next.

1.3 CDM spread spectrum watermarking

In general, a watermarking technique employing CDM embeds N bits into the host data (or in a feature space) $\boldsymbol{c}_0$, resulting in the watermarked signal

$$\boldsymbol{c} = \boldsymbol{c}_0 + \boldsymbol{w} = \boldsymbol{c}_0 + \bullet \sum_{j=1}^{N} b_j \boldsymbol{p}_j \tag{3}$$

The host data vector $\boldsymbol{c}_0$ (samples, coefficients of a transformed domain or host features) and the watermarked signal $\boldsymbol{c}$ can represent speech, image or video signals where their samples are organized as a vector of dimension M. In this case, the watermark is $\boldsymbol{w}$. The multi-bit message vector $\boldsymbol{b}$ is composed by N antipodal bits $b_j, j = 1, \ldots, N$. The scaling factor • controls the energy of the resulting multibit watermark $\boldsymbol{w}$. Each M-dimensional vector $\boldsymbol{p}_j, j = 1, \ldots, N$, contains a spread sequence (the j-th spread sequence) with M samples, usually obtained using a pseudo random generator. Vectors $\boldsymbol{p}_j$ can be shaped applying a masking vector $\boldsymbol{x}$, resulting in an adjusted vector $\boldsymbol{p}_j * \boldsymbol{x}$, where $*$ represents element by element vector multiplication. This perceptual masking can be designed to achieve a more transparent embedding according to a perceptual-based criterion.

Techniques with different performances and tuned to specific applications can be derived using different combinations of spreading sequences, masking operators, weighting factor evaluation techniques and embedding domains [Henrique S. Malvar and Dinei A. F. Florencio (2003); Perez-gonzalez & Pun (2004); Santi P. Maity and Malay K. Kundu (2004); Yanmei Fang, Jiwu Huang, Shaoquan Wu (2004)]. When the sequences p_j are designed such that they do not overlap with each other, the CDM becomes a TDM multiplexing. This approach was used in Martin Kutter (1999) to deal with ISI. Thus, TDM can be seen as a special case of CDM [I. J. Cox, M. L. Miller, J. A. Bloom (2002)].

CDM has been widely employed for watermark embedding in both the sample and transformed domains [Joseph J.K.Ó. Ruanaidh and Gabriella Csurka (1999); Santi P. Maity and Malay K. Kundu (2004); Yongqing Xin and Miroslaw Pawlak (2004)]. On the other hand, the perceptual impact of the CDM embedding on the fidelity increases with the number N of bits embedded when the spreading sequences overlap with each other, generating intersymbol interference (ISI) [Martin Kutter (1999)]. This impact can be mitigated by using M-ary modulation [Martin Kutter (1999)], which, on the other hand, increases the detection complexity and precludes the error performance to degrade graciously [Mauro Barni and Franco Bartolini (2004)]. The cross-correlation effects can be mitigated by designing spreading sequences using pseudo random generators followed by the Gram-Schmidt orthogonalization, by using orthogonal sequences created from a Walsh-Hadamard basis [J. Mayer, A. V. Silverio, J. C. M. Bermudez (2002); Santi P. Maity and Malay K. Kundu (2004)] or through other orthogonalization techniques. Performance improvement can be also achieved by employing Wiener pre-filtering to mitigate host correlation [Hernández & Pérez-González (1999)]. Many approaches in the literature propose to embed the watermark into reduced length regions of the data. These include many space-domain block-based embedding schemes [Borges & Mayer (2006); Paulo V. K. Borges, Joceli Mayer (2005)] and frequency-domain schemes that segment the watermark representation using, for instance, the DCT with 8x8 blocks or wavelet decompositions. Unfortunately, however, the pseudo random generators used in practice generate highly cross-correlated short sequences. The degrading effect of cross-correlated sequences on the detector performance becomes especially important in applications that require small bit error rates (BER). The improvements proposed in this Chapter for CDM address the low BER case for highly cross-correlated sequences.

2. Improved CDM

The traditional CDM watermarking approach in (3) scales the watermark energy by a factor $\bullet^2$. This approach is inefficient because it relies on a single factor • to adjust the energy of all sequences. Given a fixed gain factor • designed to minimize some cost function, many patterns p_j can be introduced with more (or less) energy than the minimum necessary to satisfy the robustness or the fidelity constraints. Moreover, the patterns need to be designed considering the interferences caused by the host image, by the cross-correlation among sequences and by the perceptual shaping mask x. Otherwise, the designed patterns will provide sub-optimal embedding, resulting in losses in transparency and robustness. An analysis of alternative pattern generating methods can be found in J. Mayer, A. V. Silverio, J. C. M. Bermudez (2002). Perceptual masking might affect the orthogonality of the spreading sequences and compromise the detector performance [Joceli Mayer and José C. M. Bermudez (2005)]. In some schemes perceptual masking is not employed or even implemented in an alternative way. The proposed approach also addresses this interference by considering the masking effects on the ISI. We address the watermark embedding issue by allowing a different gain factor $\bullet_j$ for each pattern [Joceli Mayer, Rafael Araujo da Silva (2004)]. Thus, we propose to embed N bits into the host data by using

$$\boldsymbol{c} = \boldsymbol{c}_0 + \sum_{j=1}^{N} \bullet_j b_j \boldsymbol{p}_j * \boldsymbol{x} \tag{4}$$

In the following we assume that the spreading sequence vectors $\boldsymbol{p}_j$ are zero-average. We also assume that the additive transmission channel noise $\boldsymbol{\eta}$ is zero-mean, statistically independent and identically distributed (i.i.d.), with an even probability density function (pdf), but not necessarily Gaussian. We also define a decision variable d_i, relative to bit b_i, which is computed at the detector using linear correlation of the spreading sequence with the received watermarked signal:

$$d_i = \langle \boldsymbol{p}_i, \boldsymbol{c} + \boldsymbol{\eta} \rangle$$

$$d_i = \langle \boldsymbol{p}_i, \boldsymbol{c}_0 \rangle + \left\langle \boldsymbol{p}_i, \sum_{j=1}^{N} \bullet_j b_j \boldsymbol{p}_j * \boldsymbol{x} \right\rangle + \langle \boldsymbol{p}_i, \boldsymbol{\eta} \rangle$$

$$d_i = R_i^{\boldsymbol{c}_0} + R_i^{\bullet} + \left\langle \boldsymbol{p}_i, \sum_{j=1}^{N} \bullet_j b_j \boldsymbol{p}_j * \boldsymbol{x} \right\rangle$$

$$= R_i^{\boldsymbol{c}_0} + R_i^{\bullet} + \sum_{j=1}^{N} \bullet_j R_{ij} \tag{5}$$

where $R_i^{\boldsymbol{c}_0} = \langle \boldsymbol{p}_i, \boldsymbol{c}_0 \rangle$, $R_i^{\bullet} = \langle \boldsymbol{p}_i, \boldsymbol{\eta} \rangle$ and $R_{ij} = b_j \left\langle \boldsymbol{p}_i, \boldsymbol{p}_j * \boldsymbol{x} \right\rangle$ are, respectively, the correlation of $\boldsymbol{p}_i$ with the host image, the correlation of $\boldsymbol{p}_i$ with the noise and the cross-correlation between $\boldsymbol{p}_i$ and the pattern $\boldsymbol{p}_j$ multiplied, element by element, by the mask $\boldsymbol{x}$. Notice that we employ linear correlation for detection, as is usually the case in most practical watermarking systems. However, the linear correlation is optimal only when the involved signals are Gaussian distributed. A discussion about the optimality of the linear detector is given in Mauro Barni and Franco Bartolini (2004).

For the noiseless case, $R_i^{\bullet} = 0$ and we can guarantee a specified detection level $d_i = \bullet b_i$, for $i = 1, \cdots, N$, by solving (5) for the gain factor vector $\boldsymbol{\alpha} = [\bullet_1, \cdots, \bullet_N]^T$:

$$\begin{bmatrix} R_{11} & R_{12} & \cdots & R_{1N} \\ R_{21} & R_{22} & & \vdots \\ \vdots & & \ddots & \\ R_{N1} & \cdots & & R_{NN} \end{bmatrix} \cdot \begin{bmatrix} \bullet_1 \\ \bullet_2 \\ \vdots \\ \bullet_N \end{bmatrix} = \begin{bmatrix} \bullet \cdot b_1 - R_1^{\boldsymbol{c}_0} \\ \bullet \cdot b_2 - R_2^{\boldsymbol{c}_0} \\ \vdots \\ \bullet \cdot b_N - R_N^{\boldsymbol{c}_0} \end{bmatrix} \tag{6}$$

This approach simultaneously takes into account the interferences from the host image, patterns and shaping mask in order to enforce that $d_i = \bullet b_i$ for all bits. Notice that $R_{ij} << R_{ii}$ (disregarding the mask $\boldsymbol{x}$) for practical pseudo-random generators, assuring that the matrix in Eq. (6) is almost diagonal and has rank N so that there exists a solution for $\boldsymbol{\alpha}$. Considering an additive noise with known power, the parameter $\bullet$ can be determined to compensate for the effect of the $R_i^{\bullet}$ correlations, as discussed in Joceli Mayer and José C. M. Bermudez (2005).

3. Extending PEAK and ISS schemes

The proposed approach extends the single-bit PEAK Delhumeau et al. (2003) strategy to multibit and also tradeoffs the host interference rejection with the resulting watermark energy. The PEAK strategy is a special case of ISS using $\bullet = 1$. As reported by Henrique S. Malvar and Dinei A. F. Florencio (2003), $\bullet = 1$ usually provides a good but not optimal performance for the single-bit case. In this section, we investigate the extension of ISS to multibit by introducing the • factor. In our development, the factor • represents the amount of host interference being cancelled, where $\bullet = 1$ indicates complete cancelation.

The proposed approach extends (6) proposed in Joceli Mayer and José C. M. Bermudez (2005) by introducing the parameter •, similarly as the one-bit ISS scheme, to tradeoff host rejection with watermark energy. For the noiseless case, $R_i^{\bullet} = 0$, the resulting detection level $d_i = \bullet b_i + (1 - \bullet)R_i^{co}$ is affected by the residual of host correlation, for $i = 1, \ , N$. This clearly indicates that the constant robustness property [Joceli Mayer and José C. M. Bermudez (2005)] cannot be achieved when $\bullet \neq 1$. For a given pair • and •, this detection level can be enforced by solving the following system for α:

$$\begin{bmatrix} R_{11} & R_{12} & R_{1N} \\ R_{21} & R_{22} & \\ & & \\ R_{N1} & & R_{NN} \end{bmatrix} \cdot \begin{bmatrix} \bullet_1 \\ \bullet_2 \\ \\ \bullet_N \end{bmatrix} = \begin{bmatrix} \bullet b_1 + (1 - \bullet)R_1^{co} \\ \bullet b_2 + (1 - \bullet)R_2^{co} \\ \\ \bullet b_N + (1 - \bullet)R_N^{co} \end{bmatrix} \tag{7}$$

The resulting detection level, considering an additive channel noise, is given by:

$$d_i = \bullet b_i + (1 - \bullet)R_i^{co} + R_i^{\bullet} \tag{8}$$

and the error probability can be different for each bit:

$$PE_i = Pr(R_i^{\bullet} > \bullet - (1 - \bullet)R_i^{co}, b_i = -1) + Pr(R_i^{\bullet} < -\bullet - (1 - \bullet)R_i^{co}, b_i = 1) \tag{9}$$

Thus, our average bit error probability is given by:

$$P_{eM} = \frac{1}{N} \sum_{i=1}^{N} PE_i \tag{10}$$

After solving (7), the resulting introduced distortion will be:

$$s_W^2 = \left(\sum_{i=1}^{N} \bullet_i \bullet \boldsymbol{p}_i \right)^T \left(\sum_{i=1}^{N} \bullet_i \bullet \boldsymbol{p}_i \right) \tag{11}$$

We employ an optimization approach to find the proper • and • parameters, as follows. For a given desired maximum average probability, PM, we compute the $J * K$ points from $P_{eM}(\bullet_j, \bullet_k)$ and $s_W^2(\bullet_j, \bullet_k)$ for each pair $(\bullet_j, \bullet_k)$. The search range is defined by $\bullet_j = \bullet_{min} + j * (\bullet_{max} - \bullet_{min}) / J$, $j = 0, \cdots, J - 1$ and $\bullet_k = \bullet_{min} + k * (\bullet_{max} - \bullet_{min}) / K$, $k = 0, \cdots, K - 1$, where J and K are the chosen number of points and $< \bullet_{min}, \bullet_{max}, \bullet_{min}, \bullet_{max} >$ are positive values chosen tipically as $< 0, 5, 0, 1 >$. For each pair $(\bullet_j, \bullet_k)$ it is required to compute the resulting $P_{eM}(\bullet_j, \bullet_k)$, and if it is less than PM, the value $s_W^2(\bullet_j, \bullet_k)$ is also required by first solving (7). The pair that results in the smallest $s_W^2(\bullet_j, \bullet_k)$, restricted to $P_{eM}(\bullet_j, \bullet_k) < PM$, will be chosen. It is possible that no pair satisfies the restriction, in this case PM needs to be increased. The approach requires, in the worst case, $J * K$ computations of P_{eM}, (7) and of resulting s_W^2. These cost functions, $s_W^2(\bullet_j, \bullet_k)$, $P_{eM}(\bullet_j, \bullet_k)$ are illustrated at Fig. 1.

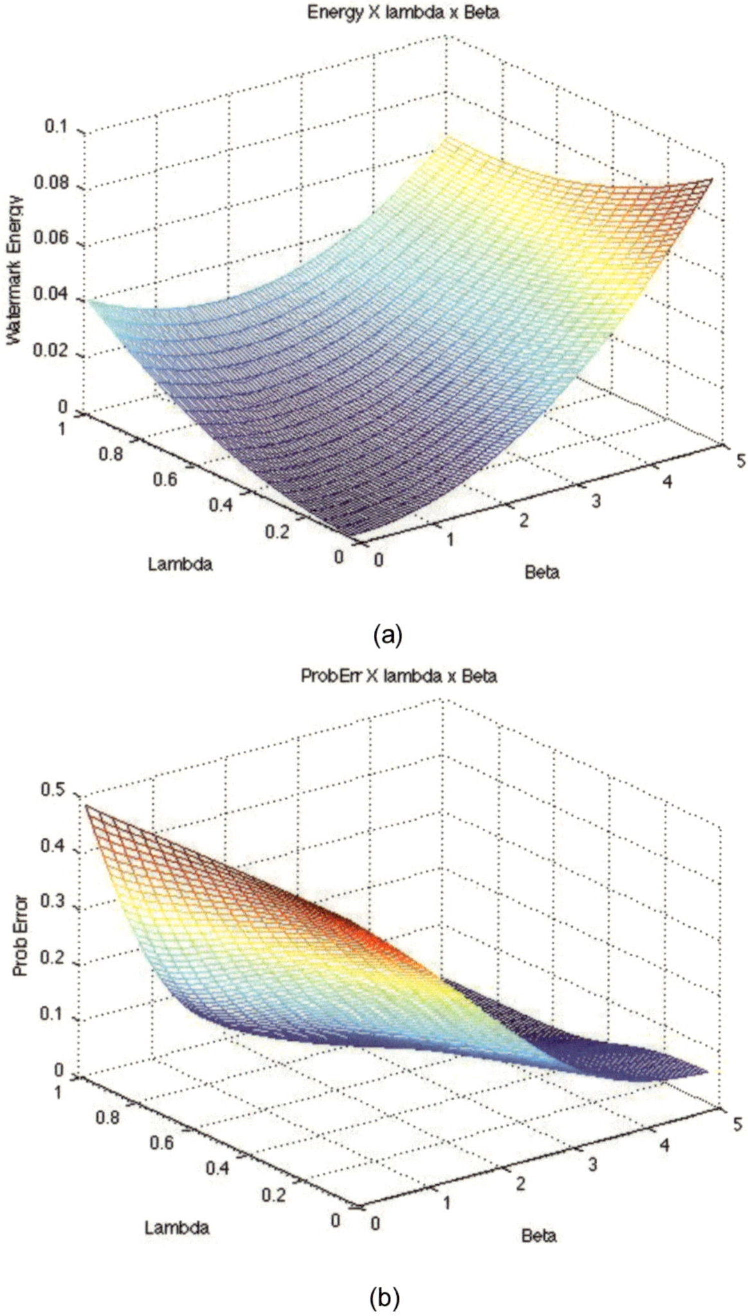

Fig. 1. (a) Watermark energy versus parameters • and • . (b) Probability of error versus parameters • and • . Optimized performance: very transparent ($s_W^2 = 0.0587$) and the Monte Carlo simulation validate the specified probability of error (Pe $\leq$ 1E-6) resulting in the measured of $P_{eM} = 7.93E - 7$.

(a)

(b)

Fig. 2. (a) Original Image, (b) Watermarked Image (very low perceptual impact, $s_W^2 = 0.0587$, embedded with 10 bits using the MISS).

(a)

(b)

Fig. 3. (a) Difference between the original and the watermarked Image (scaled by 10 and added 128), (b) Watermarked Image attacked with AWGN noise ∼N(0,10). Very robust to AWGN, $P_{error} \leq 1E-6$.

4. Experiments

The figures 2 and 3 show the performance using the proposed optimization, presenting high transparency and very low probability of error for the AWGN attack. Perceptual masking is not implemented in this example designed to observe the benefits of mitigating host interference and cross correlation among patterns. By contrasting to the traditional multibit CDM, in (3), on a Monte Carlo experiment with 1000 trials, AWGN noise $\sim$ N(0,10), and adjusting the schemes for the same watermark energy in all tests, the resulting average error probability (P_{eM}) and its deviation for CDM was $P_{eM-CDM} = 0.0425 \pm 0.0478$ while for the proposed Multibit Improved Spread Spectrum, we found $P_{eM-MISS} = 0.019 \pm 0.00047$. The MISS approach provides considerably smaller probability of error in both average and deviation when compared to the traditional CDM.

Note that the MISS is based on Spread Spectrum (SS) modulation and presents similar robustness to compression and filtering attacks as other related SS techniques [Delhumeau et al. (2003); Henrique S. Malvar and Dinei A. F. Florencio (2003)]. Particularly, the proposed approach is designed to extend the ISS technique to multibit embedding. Thus, it is expected from the MISS approach the same performance achieved by ISS approach for 1-bit embedding. MISS provides a superior multibit embedding than the PEAK approach [Delhumeau et al. (2003)] as it finds the best values for • and • at the multibit embedding.

5. Conclusions

We presented an extension of the ISS and PEAK algorithms to multibit spread spectrum. The proposed scheme estimates the probability of error for AWGN and the expected distortion for each combination of parameters • and •. The scheme outperforms previous proposed multibit CDM spread spectrum modulation [Joceli Mayer and José C. M. Bermudez (2005)] as it finds the least energy necessary for the watermark given a target probability of error. The proposed modulation approach, coined as MISS, is applicable to image, audio, speech and video media. Further improvement can be achieved by extending the proposed optimization by using one parameter $\bullet_i$ per message bit.

6. References

Borges, P. V. K. & Mayer, J. (2006). Analysis of position based watermarking, *Pattern Analysis & Applications, Springer London* 9(1): 70–82.

Delhumeau, J., Furon, T., Hurley, N. & Silvestre, G. (2003). Improved polynomial detectors for side-informed watermarking, *Proc. SPIE* .

E.J., W. R. P. C. D. (1999). Perceptual watermarks for digital images and video, *Proceedings of the IEEE* 87(7): 1108–1126.

Henrique S. Malvar and Dinei A. F. Florencio (2003). Improved spread spectrum: A new modulation technique for robust watermarking, *IEEE Trans. on Signal Processing* 51(4): 898–905.

Hernández, J. & Pérez-González, F. (1999). Statistical analysis of watermarking schemes for copyright protection of images, *IEEE Proc., Special Issue on Identification and Protection of Multimedia Information* 87(7): 1142–1166.

I. J. Cox, J. Kilian, F. T. Leighton, T. Shamoon (1997). Secure spread spectrum watermarking for multimedia, *IEEE Transactions on Image Processing* 6(12): 1673–1687.

I. J. Cox, M. L. Miller, J. A. Bloom (2002). *Digital Watermarking*, Morgan Kaufmann.

I.J. Cox, M.L. Miller, A.L. Mckellips (1999). Watermarking as communications with side information, *Proceedings of the IEEE* 87(7): 1127–1141.

J. Mayer, A. V. Silverio, J. C. M. Bermudez (2002). On the design of pattern sequences for spread spectrum image watermarking, *Int. Telecommunications Symposium, ITS* .

Joceli Mayer and José C. M. Bermudez (2005). Multi-bit informed embedding watermarking with constant robustness, *IEEE Intl. Conf. on Image Processing, ICIP* 1: 804–821.

Joceli Mayer, Rafael Araujo da Silva (2004). Efficient informed embedding of multi-bit watermark, *IEEE International Conference on Acoustics, Speech, and Signal Processing, ICASSP*, Vol. 1, pp. 389–392.

Joseph J.K.Ó. Ruanaidh and Gabriella Csurka (1999). A bayesian approach to spread spectrum watermark detection and secure copyright protection for digital image libraries, *IEEE Comp. Society Conf. on Comp. Vision and Pattern Recognition*, pp. 207–212.

M. Barni, N. Memon, T. Kalker, P. Moulin, I.J. Cox, M.L. Miller, J.J. Eggers, F. Bartolini, F. Pérez-González (2003). Signal processing forum: What is the future for watermarking ? (part 2), *IEEE Signal Processing Magazine* 20(6): 53–57.

Martin Kutter (1999). Performance improvement of spread spectrum based image watermarking schemes through m-ary modulation, *Lecture Notes in Computer Science, Springer Verlag* 1768: 238–250.

Martin Kutter and Stefan Winkler (2002). A vision-based masking model for spread-spectrum image watermarking, *IEEE Trans. on Image Processing* 11(1): 16–25.

Mauro Barni and Franco Bartolini (2004). *Watermarking Systems Engineering - Enabling Digital Assets Security and Other Applications*, Marcel Dekker.

Mayer, J. (2011). Improved spread spectrum multibit watermarking, *IEEE Intl. Workshop on Information Forensics and Security - WIFS'11* .

Min Wu and Bede Liu (2003). Data hiding in image and video: Part i-fundamental issues and solutions, *IEEE Trans. on Image Processing* 12(6): 685–695.

Moulin, P. & Koetter, R. (2005). Data-hiding codes, *Proceedings IEEE* 93(12): 2083–2127.

Paulo V. K. Borges, Joceli Mayer (2005). Informed positional embedding for multi-bit watermarking, *IEEE Intl. Conf. on Acoustics, Speech, and Signal Processing, ICASSP*, Vol. 2, pp. 809–812.

Perez-gonzalez, O. K. S. V. F. D. F. & Pun, T. (2004). Spread spectrum watermarking for real images: is everything so hopeless?, *Proceedings of 12th European Signal Processing Conference, EUSIPCO*.

Santi P. Maity and Malay K. Kundu (2004). A blind CDMA image watermarking scheme in wavelet domain, *Intl. Conf. on Image Processing, ICIP*, pp. 2633–2636.

Wade Trappe, Min Wu, Jane Wang, K. J. Ray Liu (2003). Anti-collusion fingerprinting for multimedia, *IEEE Trans. on Signal Processing* 51(4): 1069–1087.

Yanmei Fang, Jiwu Huang, Shaoquan Wu (2004). CDMA-based watermarking resisting to cropping, *Proc. of the 2004 Intl. Symposium on Circuits and Systems, ISCAS*, Vol. 2, pp. 25–28.

Yongqing Xin and Miroslaw Pawlak (2004). Multibit data hiding based on cdma, *Canadian Conf. on Electrical and Computer Engineering*, Vol. 2, pp. 935–938.

Z. Jane Wang, Min Wu, Hong Vicky Zhao, Wade Trappe, K. J. Ray Liu (2005). Anti-collusion forensics of multimedia fingerprinting using orthogonal modulation, *IEEE Trans. on Image Processing* 14(6): 804–821.

7

A Novel Digital Image Watermarking Scheme for Data Security Using Bit Replacement and Majority Algorithm Technique

Koushik Pal[1], G. Ghosh[1] and M. Bhattacharya[2]
[1]Institute of Radio Physics and Electronics, University of Calcutta, Kolkata
[2]Indian Institute of Information Technology and Management, Gwalior
India

1. Introduction

Recent history has witnessed the rapid development in information technologies that has given an extended and easy access to digital information. Along with several developments it leads to the problem of illegal copying and redistribution of digital media. As a result the integrity and confidentiality of the digital information has come under immense threat. The concept of an emerging technology, digital watermarking came in order to solve the problems related to the intellectual property of media. (P.W.Wong, 1998). Digital Watermarking is a technique which allows an individual to add hidden copyright notices or other verification messages or even classified information to digital media. (Rafael C Gonzalez and Richard E. Woods, 2002), (Cox I. J., Miller M., Bloom J., 2002).

Watermarks can either be visible or invisible. Here in this chapter we utilize the invisible technique. This is used in public information settings such as digital images libraries, museums, and art galleries and also in defense communication where data security is of prime importance. Watermark embedding utilizes two kinds of methods; one is in the spatial domain and the other in the transform domain. In the spatial domain the watermark is directly embedded into the image pixels whereas in the frequency domain the image is decomposed into blocks and then mapped into the transform domain (M. Kutter, F. A. P. Petitcolas, 1999).

This is basically a process of hiding information in an image known as cover image. Copyright protection is achieved by robust watermarking while image authentication is usually achieved by fragile watermarking techniques. In the fragile watermarking scheme if any alteration of the message is found then it is broken and it can be easily detected as tampered by the provider of the watermark. In general, fragile schemes modify the least-significant-bits LSB planes of the original image in an irreversible way. Often a secret key is also used to encrypt the information (P.W. Wong, 1998). Invertible watermarking is a new process which enables the exact recovery of the original image upon extraction of the embedded information (M.L. Miller, I.J. Cox, J.M.G. Linnartz and T. Kalker, 1999). This work implements both authentication and confidentiality in a reversible manner without affecting the image in any way. Security of images imposes three mandatory characteristics: confidentiality, reliability and availability (J. Fridrich,2002).

Confidentiality means that only the entitled persons have access to the images.

Reliability has two aspects, **integrity**: the image has not been modified by a non-authorized person; **authentication proofs** that the image belongs indeed to the correct person and is issued from the authorized source.

Lastly availability is the ability of an image to be used by the entitled persons in the normal conditions of access and exercise.

This chapter presents a new digital watermarking method through bit replacement technology, which stores multiple copies of the same data that is to be hidden in a scrambled form in the cover image. In this chapter an indigenous approach is described for recovering the data from the damaged copies of the data under attack by applying a majority algorithm to find the closest twin of the embedded information. A new type of non-oblivious detection method is also proposed. The improvement in performance is supported through experimental results which show much enhancement in the visual and statistical invisibility of hidden data.

1.1 LSB watermarking and its limitation

The most straight-forward method of watermark embedding would be to embed the watermark into the least-significant-bits (LSB) of the cover object (Ling Na Hu Ling Ge Jiang, 2002). Given the extraordinarily high channel capacity of using the entire cover for transmission in this method, a smaller object may be embedded multiple times (D. Osborne, D. Abbott, M. Sorell, and D. Rogers, 2004). Even if most of these are lost due to attacks, a single surviving watermark would be considered as a success. LSB substitution however despite of its simplicity brings a host of drawbacks. Although it may survive from all these transformations such as cropping, any addition of noise or lossy compression, a better attack would be to simply set the LSB bits of each pixel to defeat the watermark with negligible impact on the cover object. Furthermore, once the algorithm is discovered, the embedded watermark could be easily modified by an intermediate party. An improvement on basic LSB substitution would be to use a pseudo-random number generator to determine the pixels to be used for embedding based on a given "seed" or key (P.W. Wong, 1998). The algorithm however would still be vulnerable to replace the LSB's with a constant. Even in locations that were not used for the watermarking bits, the impact of the substitution on the cover image would be negligible.

LSB modification proves to be a simple and fairly powerful tool for steganography (Johnson, N. F., Duric, Z., and Jajodia, S., 2001), however it lacks the basic robustness that watermarking applications require.

1.2 Attack and distortion

In practice, a watermarked image may be altered either on purpose or accidentally. The watermarking system should be robust enough to detect and extract the watermark. Different types of alteration which is known as attack can be done to degrade the image quality by adding distortions.

The distortions are limited to those factors which do not produce excessive degradations; otherwise the transformed object would be unusable. These distortions also introduce degradation on the performance of the watermark extraction Algorithm. Methods or a combination of methods considered unintentional are used intentionally as an attack on a watermarked document in order to render the watermark undetectable. Compression is a common attack as data transferred via network is often compressed using JPEG (most commonly). High quality images are often converted to JPEG to reduce their size. Another method is deletion or shuffling of blocks. In images rows or columns of pixels may be deleted or shuffled without a noticeable degradation in image quality. These may render an existing watermark undetectable. Salt and pepper noise is another type of attack that replaces the intensity levels some of the pixels of an image resulting loss of information from those pixels. Some of the best known attacks are mentioned here; they may be intentional or unintentional, depending on the application. In this paper we have taken two very popular attacks known as Salt and pepper noise and image compression.

In present chapter the section 2 contains proposed watermarking method for data authentication. Section 3 describes image quality matrices, section 4 presents the experimental results, section 5 explains flow diagram and section 6 discusses the conclusion of the work.

2. Proposed watermarking technique for data authentication

Our proposed methodology for data hiding does not follow the conventional LSB technique because of its inherent limitations. We have developed a new digital watermarking scheme that uses several bits of the cover image starting from lower order to higher order to hide the information logo. Here we generally hide several sets of the same data forming the information logo into the cover image. So if some of the information is lost due to attack, we can still collect the remaining information from the cover image and can reconstruct the hidden information very closer to the original one.

The detailed step wise algorithm along with the pseudo code written in MATLAB for both the embedding scheme and the recovery scheme is given here. The flow diagram of both the embedding and recovery process is also given in section 5 for better understanding.

2.1 Embedding the digital watermark

Step 1. *Two images are taken as input:*

First of all, the cover image is taken as input. Then the message or information logo is taken as input. The cover image is taken to be a gray scale image. The logo or information is a binary image basically a sequence of 0's and 1's.

Step 2. *The size of the images is extracted:*

Next to make the program compatible to run for any size of the cover image and information logo keeping in mind the data carrying capacity of the cover image the dimensions of the respective images are extracted and stored in to two variables..

Step 3. *Normalize and reshape the logo:*

After normalizing the information logo it is being reshaped in one dimension.

Step 4. *Transforming the cover image into wavelet domain using DWT:*

The cover image is transformed to wavelet domain using discrete wavelet transform. Here we use 'haar' transform to do the DWT. Here the 1st level DWT was used to obtain more capacity for hiding the information. The cover image is decomposed into 4 subdomains as HH, HL, LH and LL according to different frequencies of the cover image.

Step 5. *Calculate the length of transformed cover image and 1 D logo*
Step 6. *Calculate the size of each sub domain decomposed cover image and reshape them in to 1D*
Step 7. *Determine the maximum coefficient value of each of the 4 sub domain*
Step 8. *Finding the position to hide the information logo into the transformed logo:*

The position for hiding the binary logo in each sub domain must be in between zero and the maximum coefficient value of that sub domain.

Step 9. *Hiding a number of sets of same information logo in HL and LH domain:*

More than one set of same information is being hidden in HL and LH band or domain for easier and good quality recovery. The hiding process in each of these domains follows a specific formula. The formula is that the black dots in each sets of 1D information logo is hidden in a position of information logo position from where a constant value is subtracted.

Step 10. *Reshaping the decomposed image back to its normal dimension*
Step 11. *Write the watermarked image to a file and display it.*

2.2 Recovery of the embedded watermark

We have assumed that the cover image that is hiding the watermark is available at the receiving end. So again in the process of recovery we first take the original image that has been used to hide the information. Along with that we also send the receiver of the message, 3 keys which essentially act as private keys. These keys are required to decrypt and to the extract the encrypted, embedded messages.

Step 1. *take input the watermarked and original image*
Step 2. *Find 1st level decomposition of both the two inputs using DWT*
Step 3. *Find the size of each sub domain of both the two decomposed input image*
Step 4. *reshape each of the decomposition of both watermarked and original cover image into 1 D*
Step 5. *take two input keys equal to the dimension of logo to find the size of 4 decompositions of logo*
Step 6. *Determining maximum coefficient values of original cover image*
Step 7. *Finding positions that were used to hide logo for each decomposition*
Step 8. *Extracting positional sets for different sets of logo from each decomposition*
Step 9. *Recovery of different sets of logo from each of the sub bands using majority algorithm and construction of final logo from the different recovered sets*
Step 10. *after reshaping display each of the recovered sets of logo and the final constructed logo*

3. Image quality metrics

To measure the amount of visual quality degradation between original and watermarked images different types of image quality metrics are used. In present work we have used *peak signal-to-noise ratio* (PSNR) and structural similarity index measure (SSIM).

3.1 Peak Signal-to-Noise Ratio (PSNR)

It is the ratio between the maximum possible power of a signal and the power of corrupting noise that affects the fidelity of its representation. PSNR is usually expressed in terms of dB for wide range signals The PSNR is most commonly used as a measure of quality of reconstruction of lossy compression. The cover image in this case is the original data, and the information logo is the error introduced by watermarking. When comparing deformed image with the original one an *approximation* to human perception of reconstruction quality is made, therefore in some cases one reconstruction may appear to be closer to the original than another, even though it has a lower PSNR. So a higher PSNR would normally indicate that the reconstruction is of higher quality.

It is most easily defined via the mean square error **(MSE)** which is for two $m \times n$ monochrome images I and K where one of the images is considered a noisy approximation of the other and is defined as:

$$MSE = \frac{1}{m\,n}\sum_{i=0}^{m-1}\sum_{j=0}^{n-1}[I(i,j) - K(i,j)]^2$$

The PSNR is defined as:

$$\begin{aligned} PSNR &= 10 \cdot \log_{10}\left(\frac{MAX_I^2}{MSE}\right) \\ &= 20 \cdot \log_{10}\left(\frac{MAX_I}{\sqrt{MSE}}\right) \end{aligned}$$

Here, MAX_I is the maximum possible pixel value of the image. When the pixels are represented using 8 bits per sample, this is 255.

3.2 Structural Similarity Index Measure (SSIM)

It is a method for measuring the similarity between two images. The SSIM index is a full reference metric, in other words, the measuring of image quality based on an initial distortion-free image as reference. SSIM is designed to improve on traditional methods like PSNR and MSE which have proved to be inconsistent with human eye perception. The resultant SSIM index is a decimal value between -1 and 1, and value 1 is only reachable in the case of two identical sets of data. The SSIM metric is calculated on various windows of an image. The measure between two windows x and y of common size $N \times N$ is:

$$SSIM(x,y) = \frac{(2\mu_x\mu_y + c_1)(2\sigma_{xy} + c_2)}{(\mu_x^2 + \mu_y^2 + c_1)(\sigma_x^2 + \sigma_y^2 + c_2)}$$

Where μ_x the average of x;

μ_y the average of y;

σ_x^2 the variance of x;

σ_y^2 the variance of y;

σ_{xy} the covariance of x and y;

$c_1 = (k_1 L)^2$, $c_2 = (k_2 L)^2$ two variables to stabilize the division with weak denominator;

L the dynamic range of the pixel-values (typically this is $2^{\#bits\ per\ pixel} - 1$);

k_1=0.01 and k_2=0.03 by default.

4. Results and discussions

In this section several experimental results are given to show the outcomes of the proposed watermarking technique.

In section 4.1. three sets of cover image along with three information logo are taken as input and watermarked image as result of embedding technique. The computed value of quality matrices are also given to find the image quality.

In section 4.2. watermarked images and recovered information logos are given.

In section 4.3. outcomes of same recovery technique has shown but under two attacks known as salt and pepper noise and image compression. For salt and pepper noise the percentage is varied up to 40% and compression up to 5%. The required noisy watermarked images and recovered logo from those images are presented.

In this section eight different sets of recovered logo and the final constructed logo using majority algorithm are also given for two different examples.

4.1 Embedding of watermark into cover image

From table 1 we can see that the results obtained from the quality metric are very satisfactory and hence we can conclude from the obtained data that the watermarked image is not very much different from the original cover image that is being used. Also we can observe that the difference between the watermarked image and the original is appearing all most same to human visual system to detect.

Higher PSNR value indicates good quality of picture. After embedding the information logo in the cover image like *Lina, Tower, Fruits* etc. we have found a quite higher PSNR value.

Similarly SSIM is another measuring metric used for finding the similarity between the two images. Here we found that after embedding the information logo the similarity between cover image and watermarked image is almost close to 1 as 0.98 which describes a good *structural similarity* between these two images

4.2 Recovery of watermark from watermarked image without any attack

From table 2 we can see that the hidden watermark image i.e. the logo or information is successfully recovered from the watermarked image. Primarily we have considered the communication is ideal and hence no external interference has been included. In practice in the real world scenario we have to consider the noise and which are being incorporated in present experiment into the sent watermarked image. There are chances of unauthorized users in reality where the watermarked image can also be easily altered by unauthorized access from unwanted users.

4.3 Recovery of watermark from watermarked image under attacks

In watermarking terminology, an attack is any processing that may impair detection of the watermark or communication of the information conveyed by the watermark. The processed watermarked data is then called attacked data.

Cover image (dimension 256X256)	**Message image (dimension 16X16)**	**Watermarked image (dimension 256X256)**	**PSNR in dB**	**SSIM**
			42.343	0.988 9
Lena	S logo	Watermarked Lena		
			41.806	0.978 1
Tower	K logo	Watermarked Tower		
		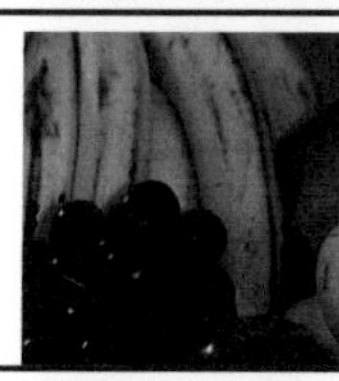	41.506	0.9853
Fruit	Max Payne logo	Watermarked Fruit		
			42.893	0.9798
Hat	M Logo	Watermarked Hat		
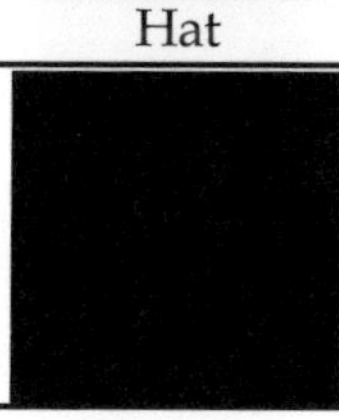			42.1347	0.9621
Baboon	C Logo	Watermarked Baboon		

Table 1. Cover image, message image and watermarked image with PSNR and SSIM value

There are two kinds of watermark attacks: non-intentional attacks, such as compression of a legally obtained, watermarked image or video file, and intentional attacks, such as an attempt by a multimedia pirate to destroy the embedded information and prevent tracing of illegal copies of watermarked digital video. In present chapter we have considered two types of attack as *(i) salt and pepper noise and (ii) image compression.*

Watermarked Image (dimension 256X256)	Recovered message image (dimension 16X16)

Lena	S logo

Tower	K logo
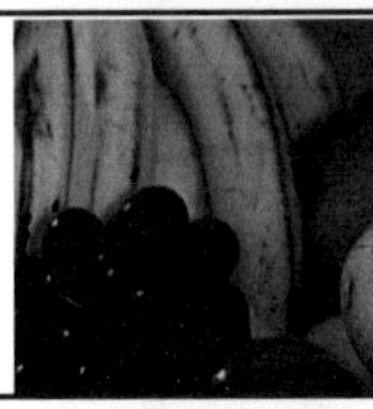	
Fruit	Max Payne logo

Hat	M Logo
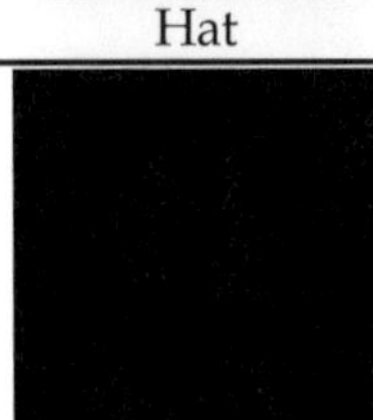	
Baboon	C Logo

Table 2. Watermarked image and recovered logo from it without any attack.

4.3.1 Majority algorithm technique

After recovering 8 different sets from attacked watermarked image we have to find the best sets of pixel which is much closer to the original hidden or embedded information logo. The rest portions' black dots are replaced by white dots. For this every sets of recovered logo is checked with each other to find the similarity. From the following results it can easily understandable the strength of this algorithm. The recovered 8 sets are practically not recognizable but the final derived logo is quite recognizable and the quality matrices also reflect the strength of this new algorithm.

Two sets of result are given here to understand the algorithm. K logo and S logo both have been constructed from 8 different recovered sets after 40% salt and pepper noise attack.

Recovered K logo from 1st set	Recovered K logo from 2nd set	Recovered K logo from 3rd set	Recovered K logo from 4th set	
				**Derived K logo from these 8 set using Majority Algorithm**
Recovered K logo from 5th set	Recovered K logo from 6th set	Recovered K logo from 7th set	Recovered K logo from 8th set	

Table 3. Constructed K logo from recovered 8 sets using Majority Algorithm Technique

		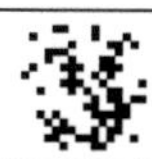		
Recovered S logo from 1st set	Recovered S logo from 2nd set	Recovered S logo from 3rd set	Recovered S logo from 4th set	
				**Derived S logo from these 8 set using Majority Algorithm**
Recovered S logo from 5th set	Recovered S logo from 6th set	Recovered S logo from 7th set	Recovered S logo from 8th set	

Table 4. Constructed S logo from recovered 8 sets using Majority Algorithm Technique

4.3.2 Salt and pepper noise

Salt and pepper noise is a form of noise typically seen on images. It represents itself as randomly occurring white and black pixels. An effective noise reduction method for this type of noise involves the usage of a median filter, morphological filter or a contra harmonic mean filter. Salt and pepper noise creeps into images in situations where quick transients, such as faulty switching, take place.

In this section we have demonstrated proposed technique after using the salt and pepper noise to corrupt the images up to 40 %. This algorithm can recover embedded information from the tempered watermarked image after this attack using majority algorithm.

Watermarked image (dimension 256X256)	Attacked image (Salt and Pepper noise)	Reconstructed message image or logo from 8 different recovered sets (dimension 16X16)
		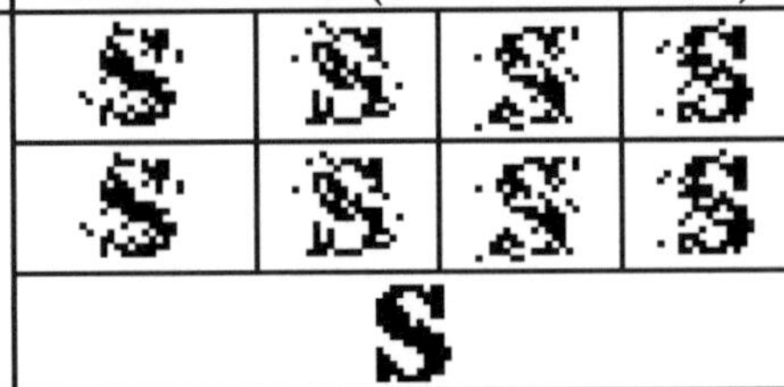
Lena	10%	S logo
		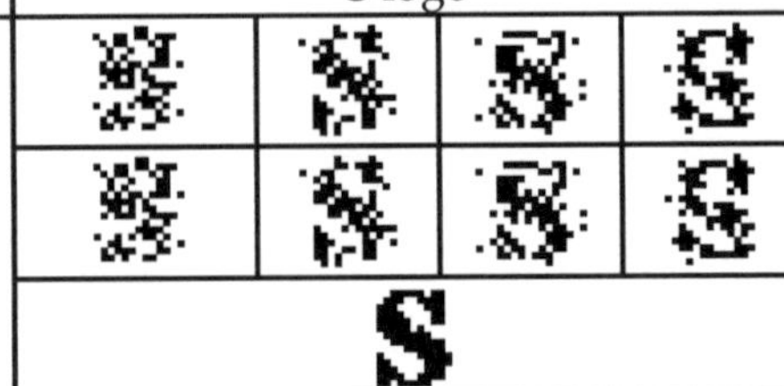
Lena	20 %	S logo
		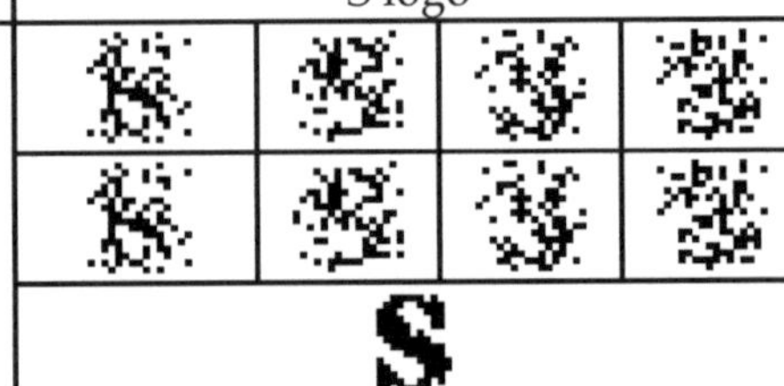
Lena	30 %	S logo
		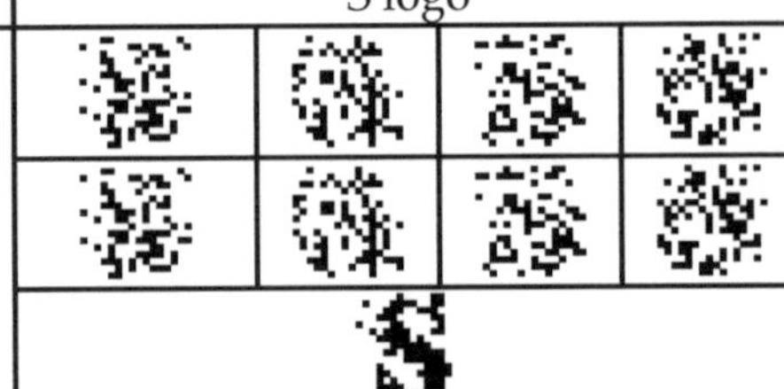
Lena	40 %	S logo

Table 5. Watermarked image, attacked image and recovered logo using majority algorithm technique

From the above set of results it is clear that the proposed algorithm can withstand even 40% salt and pepper attack with ease and the information logo that is derived from the watermarked image closely resembles the information logo that was embedded into the image.

Hence we can say that the proposed algorithm efficiently handles salt and pepper noise.

Similarly in the next table the strength of the proposed algorithm is demonstrated against the salt and pepper attack with some different sets of data.

Watermarked image (dimension 256X256)	**Attacked image (Salt and Pepper noise)**	**Reconstructed message image or logo from 8 different recovered sets (dimension 16X16)**
	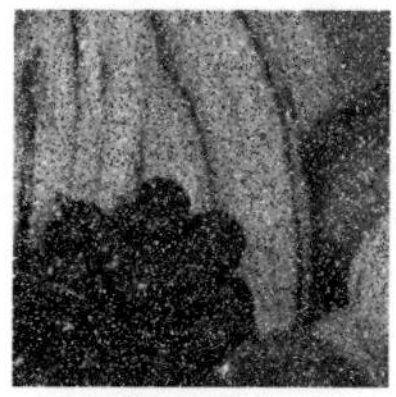	 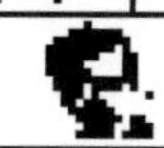
Fruit	30 %	Max Payne
		 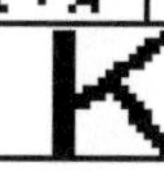
Tower	30 %	K logo
		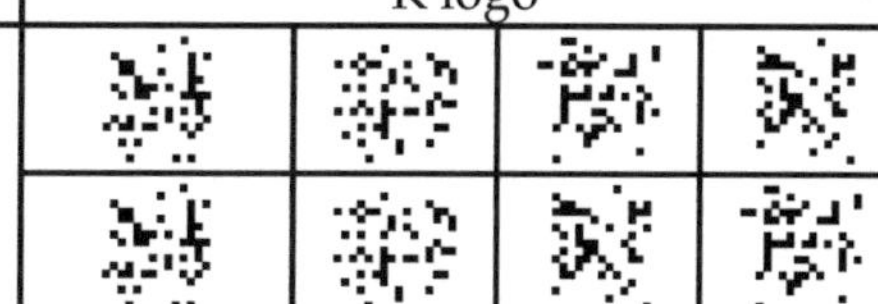 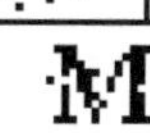
Hat	40 %	M Logo
	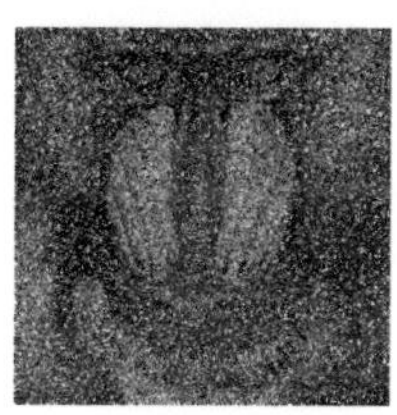	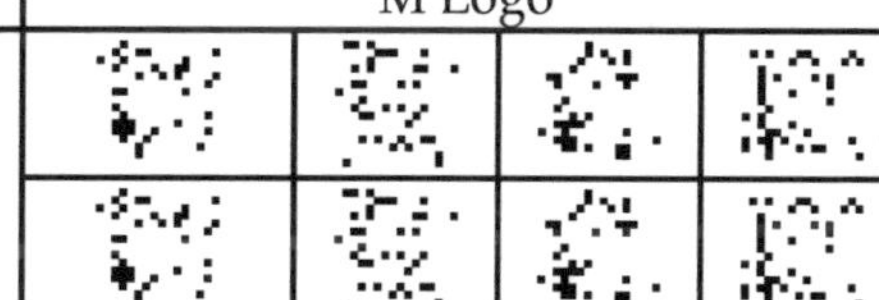 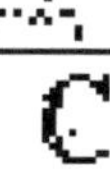
Baboon	40 %	C Logo

Table 6. Four different sets of Watermarked image, salt and pepper noise attacked image and recovered logo using majority algorithm technique

4.3.3 Image compression

The objective of image compression is to reduce irrelevance and redundancy of the image data in order to be able to store or transmit data in an efficient form. Image compression may be lossy or lossless. Lossless compression is preferred for medical imaging.

The proposed algorithm also demonstrates its strength against the compression attack as well.

Watermarked image (dimension 256X256)	Attacked image	Reconstructed message image or logo from 8 different recovered sets (dimension 16X16)

Tower	2 % Compression	K logo
	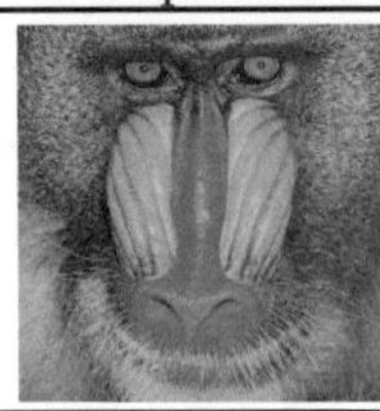	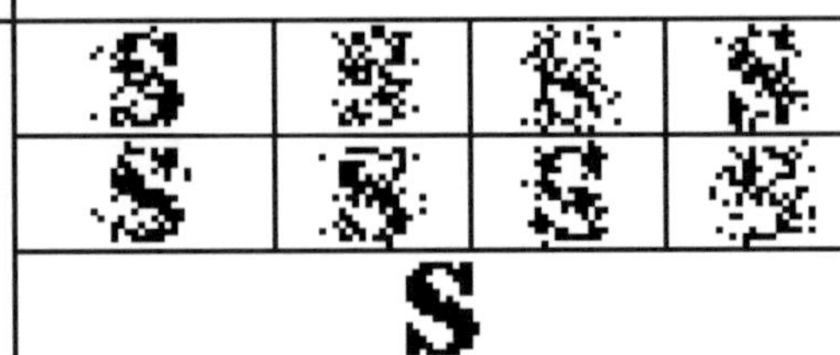
Baboon	5 % Compression	S logo

Table 7. Watermarked image, attacked image and recovered logo using majority algorithm

SSIM is used for finding the similarity between the two images. The similarity between original logo and the recovered logo from the watermarked image is measured using SSIM. Following results describe that the proposed algorithm is quite efficient for Salt and pepper Noise up to 40 % and JPEG Compression up to 5% as the SSIM is close to 1.

Used Logo (dimension 16X16)	Types of Attack	Amount of distortion	SSIM
S Logo	Salt and pepper Noise	20%	0.9554
		30%	0.9032
		40%	0.7954
S Logo	Compression	1%	0.9687
		2%	0.8654
		5%	0.7496

4.3.4 Applying the proposed technique on medical images

Medical images are very special as they are very informative. They need more care when we use them. Every medical image contains much more information which may be needed in future. So we have to keep the information of these images intact. The proposed algorithm can also be used on medical images like X ray, MRI, CT Scan for data hiding and authentication.

Here we use some medical images as cover image, some trade mark logo as information, and salt and pepper noise and image compression as attack. Here we can see the proposed algorithm can recover embedded information logo from both types of attacked image up to

40% for salt and pepper noise and up to 3% for compression attack. Even after attack the hidden information logo can be efficiently recovered and is easily recognizable. The good SSIM values of the following table ensure the close similarity between the original and recovered logo.

Watermarked image (dimension 256X256)	**Attacked image**	**Reconstructed message image or logo from 8 different recovered sets (dimension 16X16)**
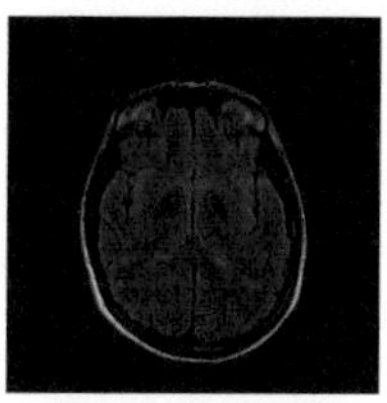		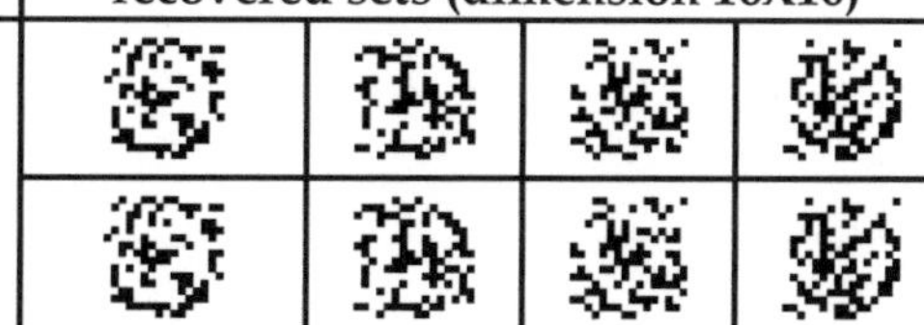  **SSIM** 0.7863
MRI of Brain (Top View)	40% Salt and Pepper	R logo
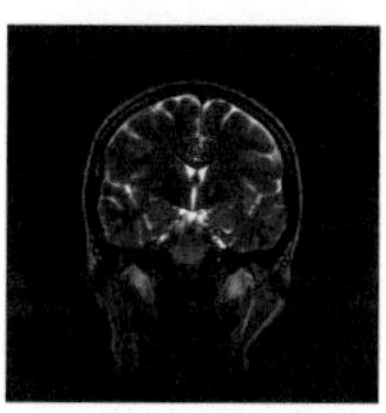	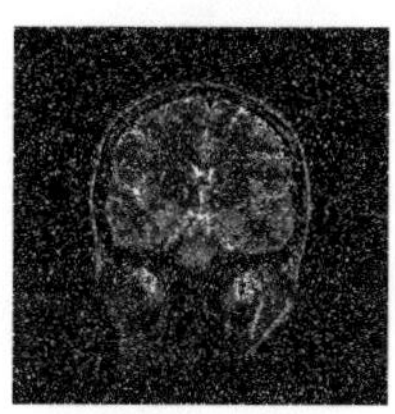	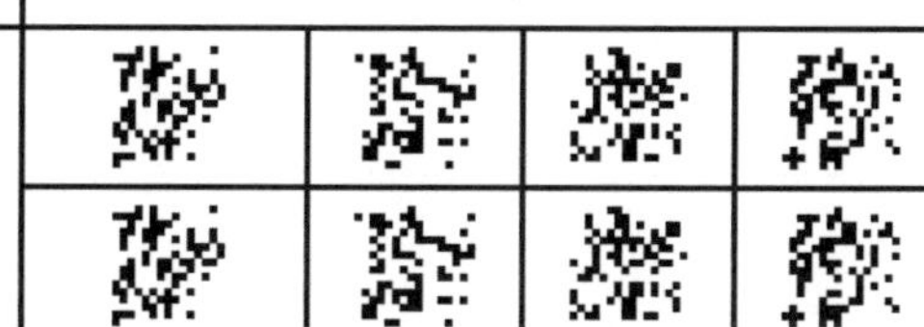  **SSIM** 0.7801
MRI of Brain (Rear View)	40% Salt and Pepper	JS logo
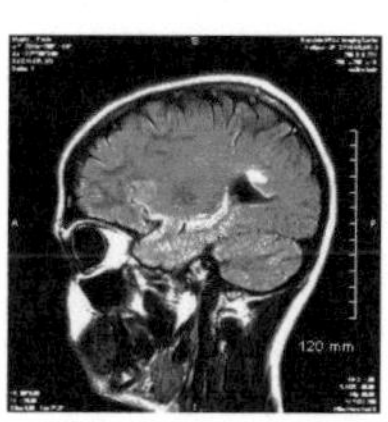	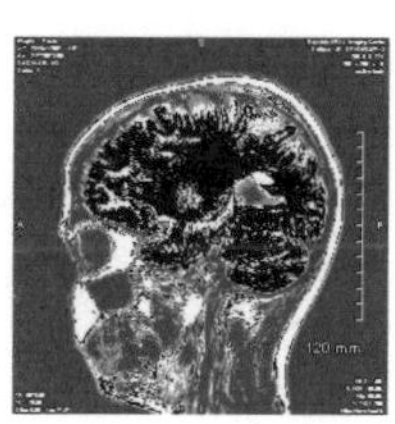	  **SSIM** 0.8291
Brain CT Scan (Side View)	3% compression	Man logo

Table 8. Recovery of information logo from different attacked watermarked medical images

5. Design flow of the proposed scheme

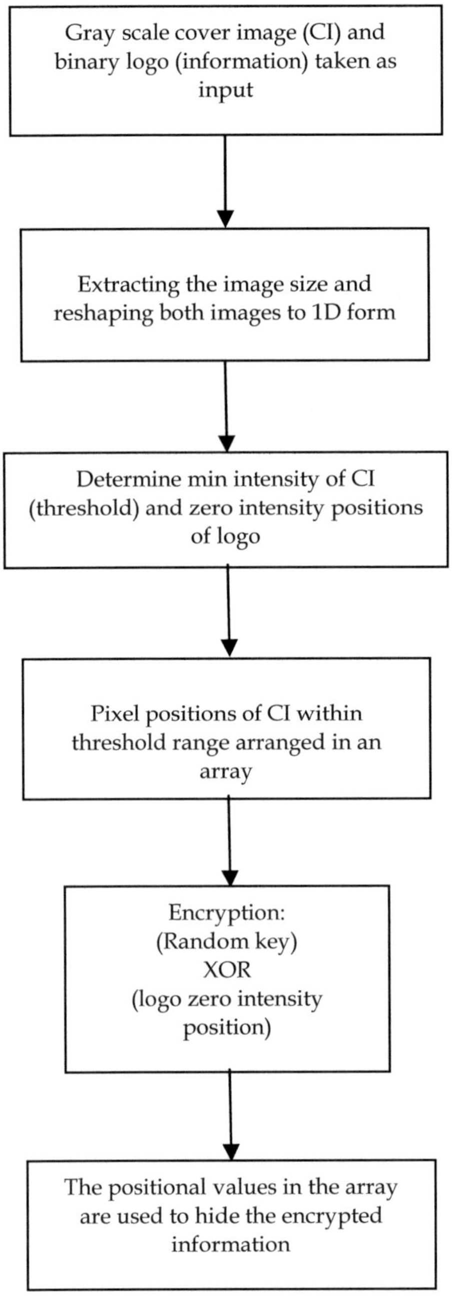

Fig. 1. Embedding or hiding technique

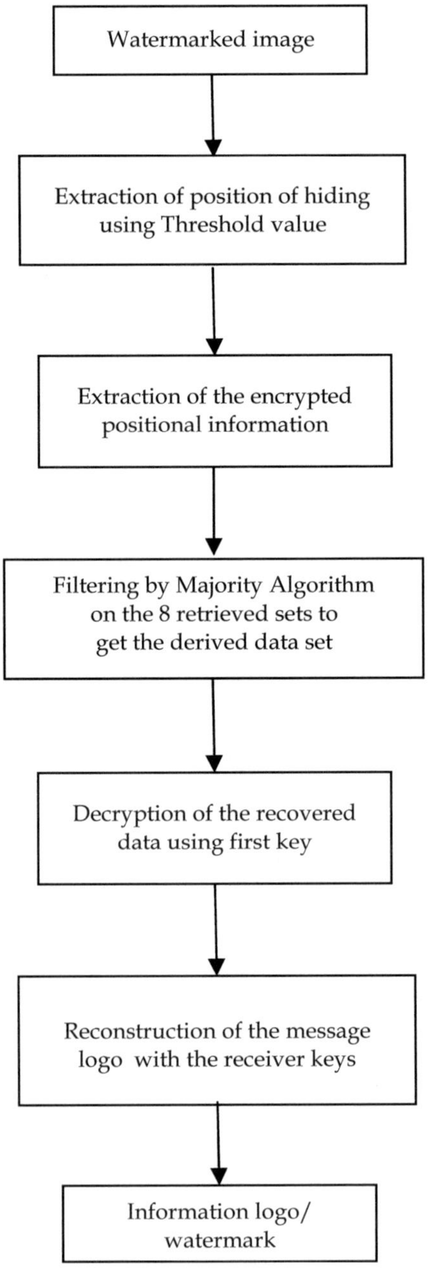

Fig. 2. Decoding or Recover Technique

6. Conclusion

Digital Watermarking has emerged as an important area of research. It mainly deals with the addition of hidden messages or copyright notices into digital media. There are many algorithms available for watermarking and it can be done for different media. They can also be attacked in different ways. Digital Watermarking has many applications in the digital world today. The digital watermarking can be thought as digital communication scheme where an auxiliary message is embedded in digital multimedia signals and is available wherever the later signals move. Therefore the detection reliability is significantly enhanced by embedding rather than by transmitting the same watermark through different sub channels (bands). Thus, this diversity technique can give very good results in detecting the watermark, considering the fact that many watermark attacks are more prone to fading.

The proposed algorithm aims at obtaining a solution to the several problems of digital communication and also for data hiding. It has been seen that the proposed algorithm is robust against compression and 'salt and pepper' noise attack and also utilizes a private key which is required for the recovery of the hidden information and hence lending security to the algorithm. The results obtained show satisfying statistics of the performance of the proposed algorithm. The obtained PSNR and SSIM value supports the quality of the encryption method. It is also seen that the embedded information is successfully recovered from the watermarked image by using majority algorithm technique. The majority algorithm technique is very much efficient and a newer approach which is very unique and easy to understand.

Hence we can conclude by stating the fact that the proposed algorithm provides a method for secure communication and data hiding.

7. Acknowledgement

It is my pleasure to express my heartiest thank to all the faculty members of Institute of Radio physics and Electronics, University of Calcutta, Kolkata for their heartiest cooperation.

I am also thankful to all the faculty members of Electronics and communication Engineering Department of Guru Nanak Institute of Technology, sodepore, Kolkata for their ungrudging support.

I am also very grateful to my family members for their continuous encouragement.

8. References

Cox I. J., Miller M., Bloom J., 2002, "Digital Watermarking," Morgan Kaufmann Publishers.

D. Osborne, D. Abbott, M. Sorell, and D. Rogers. Multiple embedding using robust watermarks for wireless medical images. In IEEE Symposium on Electronics and Telecommunications, page section 13(34), Timisoara, Romania, Oct. 2004.

E.T. Lin and E.J. Delp, "A Review of Fragile Image Watermarks," in Proceedings of the Multimedia and Security Workshop at ACM Multimedia'99, ACM, Ed., Orlando, Florida, USA, Oct. 1999, pp. 35-39.

F. Hartung and M. Kutter, "Multimedia watermarking techniques, "Proceedings of the IEEE, vol. 87, no. 7,pp. 1079–1107, July 1999.

J. Fridrich et al, Lossless Data Embedding for All Image Formats, Proc. SPIE Photonics West, Security and Watermarking of Multimedia Contents, pp. 572–583, 2002.

Johnson, N. F., Duric, Z., and Jajodia, S., 2001, "Information Hiding: Steganography and Watermarking - Attacks and Countermeasures," Kluwer Academic Press.

Ling Na Hu Ling Ge Jiang, Blind Detection of LSB Watermarking at Low Embedding Rate in Grayscale Images. M. Celik, G. Sharma, E. Saber and A. Tekalp. Hierarchical watermarking for secure image authentication with localization. IEEE Trans. Image Process, 11(6):585–595, June2002.

M. Kutter and F. A. P. Petitcolas. A fair benchmark for image watermarking systems. In Proc. SPIE Security and Watermarking of Multimedia Contents, volume 3657, pages 226–239, San Jose, CA, USA, Jan. 1999.

M.L. Miller, I.J. Cox, J.M.G. Linnartz and T. Kalker, "A Review of Watermarking Principles and Practices," in Digital Signal Processing for Multimedia Syatems, K.K. parhi and T. Nishitani Eds. New York: Marcel Dekker Inc., 1999, pp. 461-485.

P.W. Wong, "A public key watermark for image verification and authentication", in Proceedings of the IEEE International Conference on Image Processing, Chicago, IL, October 1998, pp. 455-459.

P. Wong, "A watermark for image integrity and ownership verification, " Final Program and Proceedings of the IS&T PICS 99, pp. 374-379, Savanna, Georgia, April 1999.Conference on Image Processing, 1, 455-459.

Rafael C Gonzalez and Richard E. Woods, Digital Image Processing, Prentice Hall, 2002, ISBN-81-7808-629-8

Shi Y. Q., 2005, "Reversible Data Hiding," IWDW 2004, Korea, Lecture Notes in Computer Science 3304, pp. 1-12.

8

Hardcopy Watermarking for Document Authentication

Robinson Pizzio
Universidade do Sul de Santa Catarina - Unisul
Brazil

1. Introduction

Watermarking techniques have been extensively studied and applied to digital text and image documents for applications such as author and/or content authentication. However, most of these techniques are not designed or intended to be robust to the PS channel and associated distortions. General office/business documents and the associated flow of office information usually, for many different reasons, need to suffer a digital-to-analog conversion through printing and scanning processes, which brings to authentication methods the necessity of robustness to this process.

Many approaches in the literature deals with the document hardcopy authentication problem. Brassil et al. propose in Brassil et al. (1999) authentication methods based on shift coding (line, word, etc.). Those methods, in order to be robust to the PS channel, require uniformly spaced centroids, which are not easily achieved in practice. Wu et al. develop in Wu & Liu (2004) an authentication method where some pixels of the characters are flipped from black to white or vice versa, which requires a high quality printing and scanning process. More recently, the text luminance modulation (TLM) approach was investigated in Borges & Mayer (2006b); Víllan et al. (2006). In order to embed information, this approach modulates the luminance of the characters by changing the character color intensity or gray level. This approach provides a very low perceptual impact, high capacity, and robustness to the PS channel. Most of the works are intended for invisible watermark embedding. On the other hand, binary one-dimension (1D) or multi-level two-dimension (2D) barcodes are quite visible and yet can also be applied for document authentication Quintela & Pérez-González (2003); Víllan et al. (2005). Visible watermarking provides a way to certify legal copies and also a way to quick recognize that the document has been authenticated. This approach of using a logo/seal has been used for centuries for document authentication of authorship and information contents. These are very interesting properties to be considered in authentication applications. Still, visible watermarking has not received significant attention from researchers for applications like hardcopy document authentication. For image copyright protection, visible watermarking has been studied in Braudaway et al. (1996), M.S. Kankanhalli (1999), and Y. Hu (2003), for example, but none of the methods is able to survive the PS process. Also, they do not carry any information besides the visual logo inserted in the image.

In this work we present a document authentication technique which inserts visible logos to the document. In contrast to traditional invisible watermarking techniques, visible logos can provide instant recognition of the copyrights of the document. Although visible, the inserted logos are unobtrusive, which means that they are sufficiently transparent in order to allow a clear interpretation of the information conveyed by the text. We illustrate that the proposed technique is able to use a very transparent logo and yet provide a robust detection. In our method, in addition to the recognition of the visible logo, we also authenticate the document by coding information bits (a code generated from the sensitive parts of the document like names, dates, or values, for instance) associated with the position of the inserted logos. This coding approach, coined position based watermarking (PBW), was originally exploited by Borges and Mayer in Borges & Mayer (2003), but it was not designed specifically to be robust to the PS channel. Also, the PBW was originally designed and analyzed only to the insertion of invisible Gaussian marks in digital images. In order to be robust to the PS process, and able to be applied for document authentication, this paper proposes to improve the PBW technique. Moreover, our method can be used along with barcodes, TLM and other techniques. A combination of these methods with the proposed one can provide superior robustness and high payload when compared to an isolated technique. Moreover, these techniques can be designed to have a very small interference among them.

Besides, we analyze the applicability of the developed method for the case where the authenticated document is printed on recycled paper. For this case, we characterize the noise imposed by the recycled paper, estimate the autocorrelation function of this noise, and a new detector is derived. Also, some new analyses are presented.

To achieve the development of the new binary document authentication method proposed here, this paper brings the following contributions: (i) the definition of a simple but effective analytical model to the PS channel; (ii) the derivation of optimal detectors and optimal detection threshold for cases of white or recycled paper documents; (iii) identification and characterization of the segmentation noise; (iv) characterization of the pattern noise for a recycled paper; and (v) the determination of the position error identification during logo detection. The remain of this paper is organized as follows. In Section 2 some of the main distortions found in the PS channel are discussed and a simple but effective channel model is proposed. Details on the logos insertion and detection processes, the development of an optimal detection threshold for the proposed method, an error probability analysis, the lower bound capacity of the method, and the analysis of the position error are all presented in Section 3. The analysis of the applicability of the method for recycled paper documents is presented in Section 4. Also in this section we characterize the recycled paper noise and a new detector is derived. The new detector depends on the autocorrelation matrix of the recycled paper noise and this matrix is deduced in Section 5. Some experiments to illustrate the discussions and performance of the method are in Section 6. Section 7 concludes this paper and present some future works.

2. Printing-scanning channel

2.1 PS channel distortions

When a grayscale document is printed, digital halftoning (gray to binary conversion) takes place in order to print with bilevel devices. Moreover, the spreading of the toner or ink on the hardcopy introduces another distortion similar to a blurring effect Norris & Smith (2004).

In the scanner, another blurring distortion is generated by the optics and motion of the inline CCD. Geometric distortions, including rotation, cropping and scaling take place in the scanning process. A misplacement of the paper over the flatbed scanner may rotate the document. Cropping appears both during manual placement and scanning region selection. Scaling is originated by employing different system resolutions.

Furthermore, both devices have non-linear gains. An offset gain is generated by the printing process due to the toner or ink black color offset. Another non-linear gain is generated by scanner non-linear filters and color adjustments.

2.2 PS channel model

Taking into account the distortions imposed by the PS channel, we investigate a simple model for those distortions in order to design and evaluate our method. In this way, we point out below some considerations and the final model proposed for tests.

As halftoning is device dependent, we propose to convert the grayscale logo to a bilevel representation employing our own halftoning technique. This approach prevents the halftoning noise generated by the printer's algorithm and allows us to choose a simplified analytical model for the PS channel when compared to the some existing models Borges & Mayer (2006b); Quintela & Pérez-González (2003). Moreover, we disregard the non-linear gain due to toner and consider the printing blurring effect as a low-pass filtering. Blurring due to the scanner is also modeled as a low-pass filtering.

Regarding geometric distortions, we assume that significant rotation can only occur if someone badly operates the scanner by mistake. For authentication applications, the user is interested in help the authentication process and does not attempt to remove or deteriorate the watermark by rotation. Thus, we are not concerned with rotation as a distortion to be modeled and assume that proper placement is done by the user. Regarding cropping, we are eliminating the margins of the document and preserving only its internal content. Moreover, internal cropping is not considered in our model because the user is assumed to avoid it in order to keep the document authentication. Scaling is a problem intrinsic to the scanning process but it can be reversed by many different methods already available in the literature Zitová & Flusser (2003). In our experiments we assume a controllable environment where all the resolutions employed on the system are known and rescaling can be achieved by a bicubic interpolation when necessary. We also disregard non-linear gains, since we are detecting the logos by a correlation based template matching (CBTM) method, which is quite robust to small non-linear disturbances.

Considering the assumptions above, our PS channel model is written as:

$$\mathbf{Yr} = (\mathbf{Dw} * \mathbf{H}) + \eta_e \tag{1}$$

where $\mathbf{Yr}$ is the watermarked document processed by the PS channel; $\mathbf{Dw}$ is the digital watermarked document; '*' represents the 2D convolution; the noise term η_e represents the electronic noise of the devices and is assumed to be an uncorrelated Gaussian noise, $\eta_e \approx \mathcal{N}(0, \bullet_e^2)$. Moreover, we assume that $\mathbf{H}_p$ and $\mathbf{H}_s$ model the blurring effect of the printing and scanning, respectively. Considering that the low-pass effect due to scanning prevails over that of printing, we can write $\mathbf{H}_s * \mathbf{H}_p \approx \mathbf{H}_s = \mathbf{H}$. We can model it as a Butterworth low-pass filter described by

$$H(u,v) = \frac{1}{1 + [D(u,v)/D_0]^{2n}}$$

where n is the filter order, D_0 is the cutoff frequency, and $D(u,v)$ is the Euclidean distance from point u, v to the origin (center) of the frequency spectrum. The parameters of the filter are estimated by comparing the frequency responses of an original digital document image and its PS version after several experiments. During the tests we found out that the order n and cutoff frequency D_0 are device dependent. Indeed, we could determine typical values for laser and for inkjet printers. The best approximation of the frequency response for the PS process in the case of laser printers are $n = 3$ and $D_0 = 0.4$, and $n = 1$ and $D_0 = 0.12$ for inkjet printer.

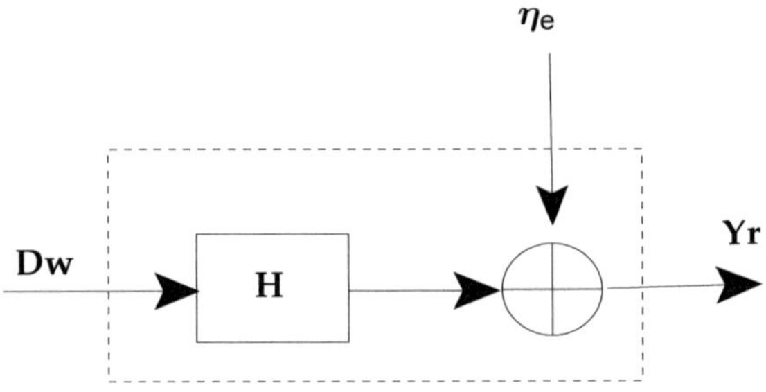

Fig. 1. PS channel model.

3. Proposed method

3.1 The insertion

Let us consider a binary text document **D** of size $M' \times N'$ and a grayscale logo **L** of size $M \times N$, both with pixel amplitudes in the $[0,1]$ range. The insertion of the logos is an additive process which is not applied over the characters. The insertion position coding rule is derived from Borges & Mayer (2003).

Once the insertion position is defined according to the authentication bits, we compute $\mathbf{Y} = \mathbf{X} + (\mathbf{L}_{ht} - 1)$ to effectively insert the logo. **X** is a document region to be marked, $\mathbf{L}_{ht}$ represents the bilevel version of the original grayscale logo with adjusted energy, and **Y** is the watermarked document region. The subtraction by 1 is employed to guarantee the insertion of the logo only in the background of the document leaving the characters intact after negative saturation (quantization). The block diagram of the insertion process is shown in Fig. 2, where • controls the watermark strength. Considering that the logo is previously defined and does not convey any authentication bits and that the halftoning method employed is known, the $\mathbf{L}_{ht}$ logo is a deterministic signal in the process. The chosen detector relies on these assumptions.

3.2 The detection

A correlation based template matching, which is equivalent to the matched filter (MF) detector, is employed for the detection of the logos. It is well known that this is the optimum detector for deterministic signal (logo filtered by **H**) corrupted by additive white Gaussian noise Kay (1998). This is the assumed scenario depicted in Fig. 1. The mathematical definition of the

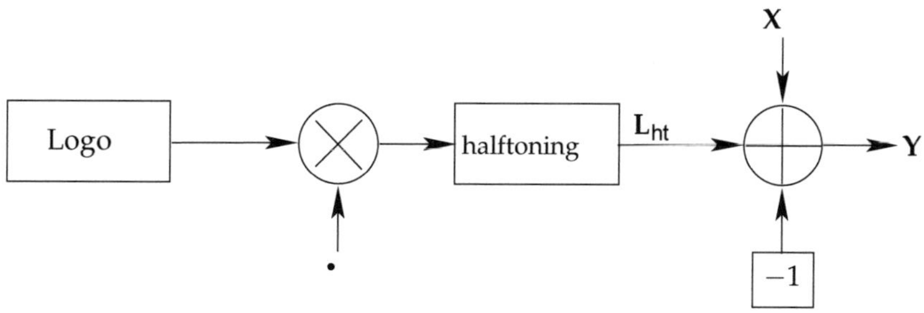

Fig. 2. Block diagram of the insertion process.

detector is given by

$$\bullet = \langle \mathbf{Yp}, \mathbf{L}_{ps} \rangle = \sum_{i=1}^{M} \sum_{j=1}^{N} Yp_{ij} L_{ps_{ij}}, \tag{2}$$

where **Yp** is a region of the watermarked document already processed by the PS channel, and $\mathbf{L}_{ps} = \mathbf{L}_{ht} * \mathbf{H}$ is the halftoned logo ($\mathbf{L}_{ht}$) pre-filtered by the low-pass filter (**H**) modeling our PS channel. Therefore, as $\mathbf{L}_{ht}$ and **H** are deterministic variables, $\mathbf{L}_{ps}$ will also be deterministic. Fig. 3 depicts the detection process. The CBTM operation needs to be performed to each pixel of the whole document and it is very time consuming. Taking advantage of the convolution theorem of the Fourier Transform, we speed up the detection by performing it on the frequency domain Gonzalez (1992). The received document is composed of the

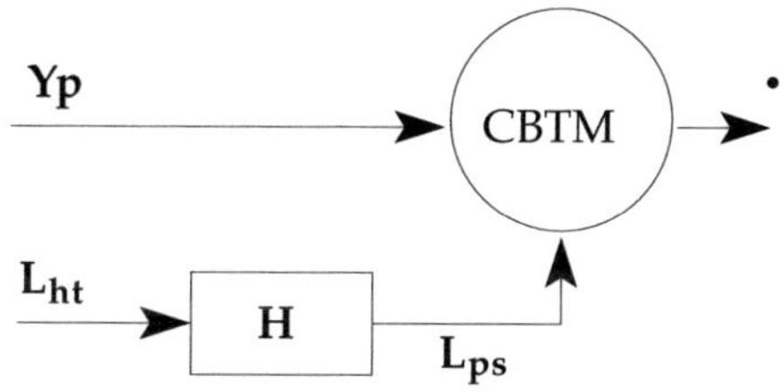

Fig. 3. Block diagram of the detection process.

logos, the characters and noise. As the logo positions carry the authentication information, characters are considered as perturbing noise. Thus we segment the characters from the received document before performing the detection. The segmentation relies on a global threshold obtained by Otsu's method Otsu (1979). Due to the PS blurring effect, the borders of the characters are degraded, preventing from a perfect segmentation. We named this degradation as *segmentation noise*. For binary documents watermarked with low energy and more transparent logos, our experiments illustrate that this segmentation noise follows a uniform distribution with values varying from 0.560 to 0.996 (1 is the white background of the document). In Fig. 4 we show a histogram that characterize this noise. In this Figure the vertical axis represents the logarithm of the pixel occurrence and the horizontal axis represents the pixel value. Results illustrate that the segmentation of the characters brings a significant improvement on the detection error probability.

3.3 Optimal detection threshold

Having defined the detection metric (2) we need now to determine the detection threshold in order to indicate the presence of one or more logos in the document. In general,

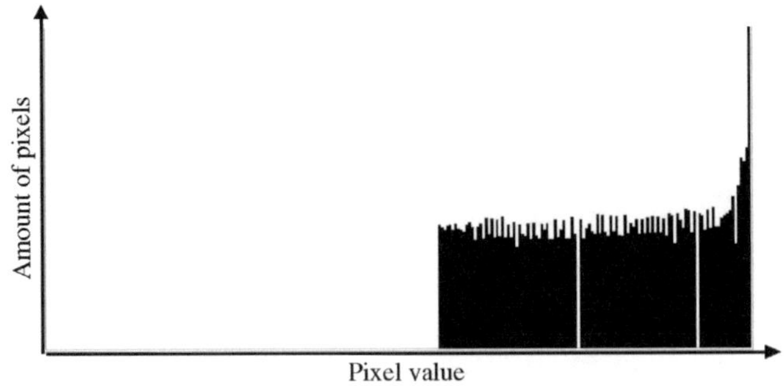

Fig. 4. Histogram of the segmentation noise.

the watermarking literature employs the Neyman-Pearson criterion Kay (1998) for the determination of the detection threshold. Considering the nature of our application we propose an optimal detection threshold based on the minimum error criterion as follows.

The total detection error probability (TDEP) Pe as a function of the threshold is defined as

$$Pe(\bullet) = P_0 P_{fa}(\bullet) + P_1 P_{fn}(\bullet) \quad (3)$$

where $P_{fa}(\bullet)$ and $P_{fn}(\bullet)$ are, respectively, the probabilities of false alarm and false negative detection for a given threshold $\bullet$; P_0 and P_1 represent the a priori probabilities of the unmarked and marked regions, respectively.

By noting that our detection metric $\bullet$ (eq. (2)) is a sum of statistically independent terms and considering the Central Limit Theorem (CLT), we can assume that the probability density function (pdf) of P_{fa} and P_{fn} can be approximated by a normal pdf. This assumption is verified in practice. Hence, the TDEP can be written as

$$\begin{aligned} Pe(\bullet) = & \frac{P_0}{\sqrt{2\bullet}\,\bullet_{\bullet_0}} \int_{\bullet}^{\infty} \exp\left[-\frac{(\bullet - \bullet_{\bullet_0})^2}{2\bullet^2_{\bullet_0}}\right] d\bullet + \\ & + \frac{P_1}{\sqrt{2\bullet}\,\bullet_{\bullet_1}} \int_{-\infty}^{\bullet} \exp\left[-\frac{(\bullet - \bullet_{\bullet_1})^2}{2\bullet^2_{\bullet_1}}\right] d\bullet \end{aligned} \quad (4)$$

where $\bullet_{\bullet_0}$ and $\bullet_{\bullet_1}$ are the mean values; $\bullet_{\bullet_0}$ and $\bullet_{\bullet_1}$ are the standard deviations about the means of the unmarked and marked regions respectively. To find the threshold $\bullet$ that minimizes the TDEP given the constrain $P_0 + P_1 = 1$, we differentiate $Pe(\bullet)$ with respect to $\bullet$ and equate the result to zero. Thus, we get a quadratic equation in the form

$$A\bullet^2 + B\bullet + C = 0 \quad (5)$$

where

$$\begin{aligned} A &= \bullet^2_{\bullet_0} - \bullet^2_{\bullet_1} \\ B &= 2(\bullet^2_{\bullet_1}\bullet_{\bullet_0} - \bullet^2_{\bullet_0}\bullet_{\bullet_1}) \\ C &= \bullet^2_{\bullet_0}\bullet^2_{\bullet_1} - \bullet^2_{\bullet_1}\bullet^2_{\bullet_0} + 2\bullet^2_{\bullet_0}\bullet^2_{\bullet_1} \log \frac{P_0 \bullet_1}{P_1 \bullet_0}. \end{aligned}$$

From equation (7), $\bullet^2_1 = \bullet^2_0$, and consequently $A = 0$. Therefore, equation (5) is reduced to a first order equation, and the optimal detection threshold is given by

$$B\bullet + C = 0. \tag{6}$$

3.4 Error probability

Let us define two regions: $\mathcal{H}_0$ the hypothesis of non-marked regions and $\mathcal{H}_1$ the hypothesis of the marked regions, so that

$$\begin{cases} \mathcal{H}_0 : \bullet_0 = \left\langle \mathbf{W}, \eta_s + \eta_e \right\rangle \cong \left\langle \mathbf{W}, \eta_s \right\rangle \\ \mathcal{H}_1 : \bullet_1 = \left\langle \mathbf{W}, \mathbf{W} + \eta_e + \eta_s \right\rangle \cong \left\langle \mathbf{W}, \mathbf{W} + \eta_s \right\rangle \end{cases}$$

where $\mathbf{W} = (\mathbf{L} * \mathbf{H})$ is a deterministic variable that represents the logo processed by the filter of the PS channel, η_s is an i.i.d. uniformly distributed variable that represents the segmentation noise, and η_e is an i.i.d. zero mean Gaussian distributed variable that represents the electronic noise. Also, considering that the segmentation noise η_s prevails over the electronic noise η_e, we assume $\eta_s + \eta_e \cong \eta_s$.

To determine the error probability, the mean and variance of the hypotheses $\mathcal{H}_0$ and $\mathcal{H}_1$ are derived. The mean of $\mathcal{H}_0$ hypothesis is

$$\bullet_{\bullet_0} = E\{\bullet_0\} = E\left\{ \sum_{i,j=1}^{M,N} W_{ij} \bullet_{s_{ij}} \right\} = \bullet_{\bullet_s} \sum_{i,j=1}^{M,N} W_{ij}.$$

Before the correlation process, the logo mean is removed so that $E\{\mathbf{L}\} = 0$. Besides, its assumed that the sum of the PS filter coefficients equals to one, such that the filtering process does not alter the mean. Therefore, $\sum_{i,j=1}^{M,N} W_{ij} = 0$, consequently, $\bullet_{\bullet_0} = 0$.

The variance of $\mathcal{H}_0$ hypothesis is given by

$$\bullet^2_{\bullet_0} = E\{\bullet^2_0\} - \bullet^2_{\bullet_0} = \left[\bullet^2_{\bullet_s} + \bullet^2_{\bullet_s} \right] \sum_{i,j=1}^{M,N} W^2_{ij}$$

where $\bullet_{\bullet_s}$ and $\bullet^2_{\bullet_s}$ are, respectively, the mean and variance of the segmentation noise and are given by

$$\bullet_{\bullet_s} = \frac{a+b}{2} \quad \bullet^2_{\bullet_s} = \frac{(b-a)^2}{12},$$

where a represents the beginning of the uniform distribution, and b represents the end of the distribution as depicted in Fig. 5.

The mean of $\mathcal{H}_1$ hypothesis is given by

$$\bullet_{\bullet_1} = E\{\bullet_1\} = \sum_{i,j=1}^{M,N} \left[W^2_{ij} + W_{ij} E\{\bullet_{s_{ij}}\} \right] = \sum_{i,j=1}^{M,N} W^2_{ij}$$

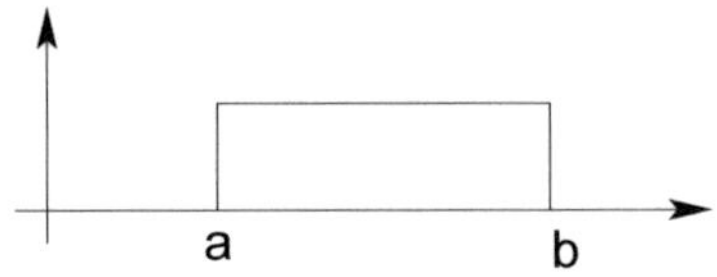

Fig. 5. Example of a uniform distribution.

and the variance is

$$\begin{aligned} \bullet^2_{\bullet_1} &= E\{\bullet^2_1\} - \bullet^2_{\bullet_1} \\ &= E\left\{\left[\sum_{i,j=1}^{M,N}(W_{ij}^2 + W_{ij}\bullet s_{ij})\right]^2\right\} - \bullet^2_{\bullet_1} = \bullet^2_{\bullet_0}. \end{aligned} \quad (7)$$

Now, recalling equation (4) we have

$$Pe = \frac{P_0}{2}\,\mathrm{erfc}\left(\frac{\bullet - \bullet_{\bullet_0}}{\sqrt{2\bullet^2_{\bullet_0}}}\right) + \frac{P_1}{2}\,\mathrm{erfc}\left(\frac{\bullet_{\bullet_1} - \bullet}{\sqrt{2\bullet^2_{\bullet_1}}}\right)$$

where erfc() is the complementary error function. Pe is the error probability of one detection. The total error probability must take into account all the $M'N'$ detections. If we miss one logo we could not decode the message. Thus, letting Q represents the amount of marked points and $K = M'N'$ the total amount of pixels of the document, the probability of missing the message (Pe_t) carried by the logos is

$$Pe_t = 1 - (1 - Pe)^{Q(K-Q)}. \quad (8)$$

3.5 Lower bound capacity

The capacity of our method is directly dependent on the document and logo size. Also, due to the statistical nature of the employed detectors, logo superposition is not allowed. Although we know that this restriction will compromise the capacity, error probability will not be affected, and we prefer this more conservative choice. Another important point to be considered is the necessity to define a region of insertion and not just a pixel of insertion for the logo. This fact will be properly discussed in section 3.6. For the capacity development we will consider an insertion region of size $J \times J$ pixels. Therefore, given a document with $M \times N$ pixels and a logo with $U \times V$ pixels, we can determine the available insertion area A_i by

$$A_i = \left(\frac{M}{J} - U + 1\right)\left(\frac{N}{J} - V + 1\right). \quad (9)$$

In order to ensure logo superposition avoidance we are considering the logo with the triple of his original size. This is the worse case but the safest in terms of error probability. Nevertheless, we know from experiments that it is possible to insert closer logos without over compromise the detection. Anyway, we decided to opt for a more conservative choice. So, the amount of available insertion positions in the document is given by

$$p = \left(\frac{M}{J} - U + 1\right)\left(\frac{N}{J} - V + 1\right) - (Q-1)(9UV-1) \quad (10)$$

where Q represents the amount of logos to be inserted. Note that equation (10) can produce not allowed results. If $p < Q$ we have more logos than available positions. This is not possible and one should change the size of the document or the size of the logo. The insertion is only possible if $p \geq Q$.

The combination of the p available positions with the Q amount of logos to be inserted gives us

$$\text{Comb}(p, Q) = \frac{p!}{(p - Q)!Q!}. \tag{11}$$

Now, the capacity C in bits can be obtained by

$$C = \log_2[\text{Comb}(p, Q)]. \tag{12}$$

The equation (12) gives us the lower bound capacity C of our method in bits. To illustrate this equation, in Fig. 6 we present the capacity plot for a 7000 × 5000 pixels document considering that the insertion region has 7 × 7 pixels. The graphics are presented for logo size of 64 × 64, and 128 × 128 pixels. In Fig. 7 we show similar plots but now considering that the insertion region has 3 × 3 pixels.

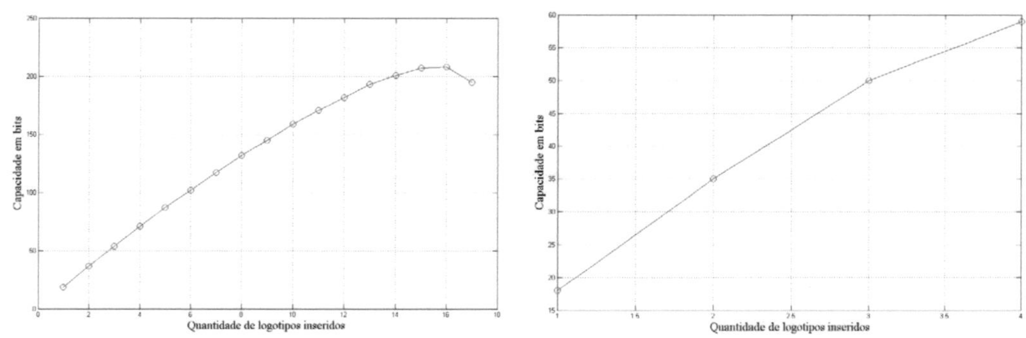

(a) 64 × 64 pixels logo. (b) 128 × 128 pixels logo.

Fig. 6. Capacity for a 7000 × 5000 pixels document with a 7 × 7 pixels insertion region.

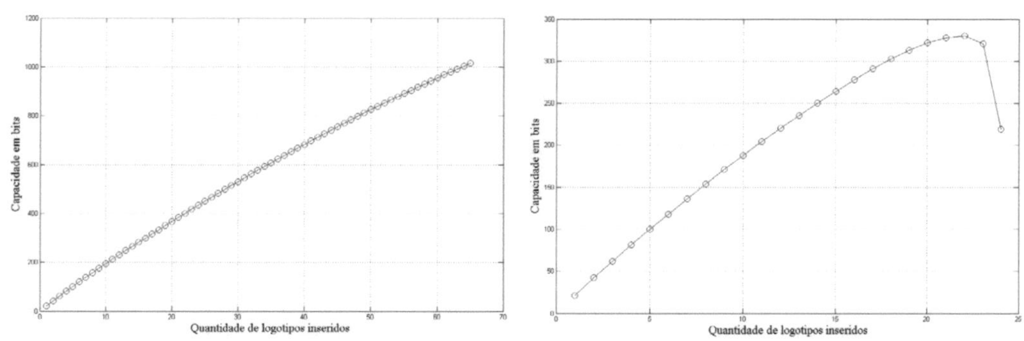

(a) 64 × 64 pixels logo. (b) 128 × 128 pixels logo.

Fig. 7. Capacity for a 7000 × 5000 pixels document with a 3 × 3 pixels insertion region.

3.6 Position error

The logo detection is performed by a correlation process. The message conveyed is coded in the logo insertion positions. Therefore, when we process a detection we are interested in identify the presence or not of a logo, and his position in the document. In order to estimate the logo position after detection, we determine the correlation peaks above the threshold. This peak is considered to be the insertion position. In Fig. 8 we show a graph that exemplify a detection. To estimate the insertion positions we determine the peaks above the threshold (horizontal dashed line).

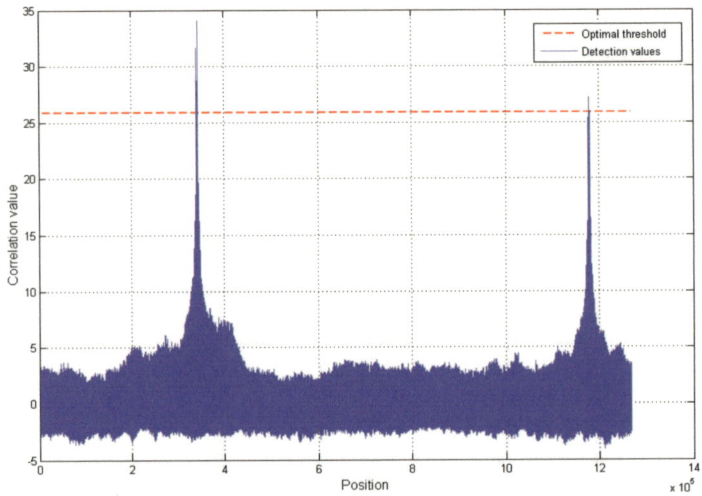

Fig. 8. Detection example.

In general, the logo is a correlated image and the whole authentication process is noisy. Due to the correlation of the logo and the noise of the entire process, there is a possibility that we make a mistake in the estimation of the logo position. We call this mistake as **position error**. In the sequel of this section we present the mathematical development that models the position error.

The logo detection is performed by a correlation process that can be generalized by

$$C[n] = \sum_{k} x[k]m[k-n] \tag{13}$$

where x represents the test logo and therefore, is a deterministic variable. m represents the logo presented in the document and this is given by

$$m[n] = x[n] + r[n]. \tag{14}$$

Taking into account the CLT, we assume that r is an i.i.d. noise with Gaussian distribution, $r \approx \mathcal{N}(0, \sigma_r^2)$. Also, we assume that this noise models all the distortions generated by the PS channel associated with the segmentation noise. So that we have

$$C[n] = \sum_{k} x[k]\{x[k-n] + r[k-n]\} = \sum_{k} x[k]x[k-n] + \sum_{k} x[k]r[k-n]. \tag{15}$$

Analyzing the mean of equation (15) we have

$$\bullet_{C[n]} = E\{C[n]\} = E\left\{\sum_k x[k]x[k-n] + \sum_k x[k]r[k-n]\right\}.$$

As x is a deterministic variable,

$$E\{C[n]\} = \sum_k x[k]x[k-n] + \sum_k x[k]E\{r[k-n]\} = \sum_k x[k]x[k-n] = C_x[n]. \tag{16}$$

The variance of equation (15) is given by

$$\bullet^2_{C[n]} = EC[n]^2 - E^2\{C[n]\} \tag{17}$$

$$= E\left\{\sum_k x[k]m[k-n]\sum_l x[l]m[l-n]\right\} - E^2\{C[n]\}$$

$$= C_x[n]^2 + \sum_k x[n]^2 E\{r[k-n]^2\} - E^2\{C[n]\} \tag{18}$$

From equation (16)

$$E\{C[n]\} = C_x[n], \tag{19}$$

therefore,

$$E^2\{C[n]\} = C_x[n]^2 \tag{20}$$

and equation (18) can be rewritten as,

$$\bullet^2_{C[n]} = C_x[n]^2 + \sum_k x[k]^2 E\{r[k-n]^2\} - C_x[n]^2 = \bullet^2_r \sum_k x[k]^2 = \bullet^2_r C_x[0]. \tag{21}$$

As can be seen in equation (21), the variance of the correlation process of the test logo with the document logo is dependent on the noise energy present in the document. For this reason, in some detections the correlation peak may not correspond to the exact insertion position of the logo but to a close adjacent position. This means that from the detection point of view the insertion point can not be a specific point but a small region of size $J \times J$ pixels. Which is called **insertion region**. In section 6.3 we present an experiment that illustrate how to define the size of the insertion region for a determined logo.

4. Applicability of the technique for recycled paper document

Considering that 90% of paper pulp is made of wood, recycling is a very important action that brings a good impact for the environment. Many companies have already decided to use just recycled paper for their whole bulk of office-like documents. For this reason we investigate the applicability of the Position Based Hardcopy Watermarking (PBHW) technique for the authentication of documents printed on recycled paper.

The very important point to be analyzed is the fact that a recycled paper is not white. It has a kind of noise imposed by the recycling process. We have analyzed this pattern of noise and concluded that it has an interesting characteristic. It can be easily modeled by a Gaussian distribution function with mean $\bullet_{pn} = 150$ and variance $\bullet^2_{pn} = 16.5$, $\eta_{pn} \approx \mathcal{N}(\bullet_{pn}, \bullet^2_{pn})$. In Fig. 9 it is depicted the histogram of a recycled paper page sample that illustrates the typical distribution of a recycled paper pattern noise.

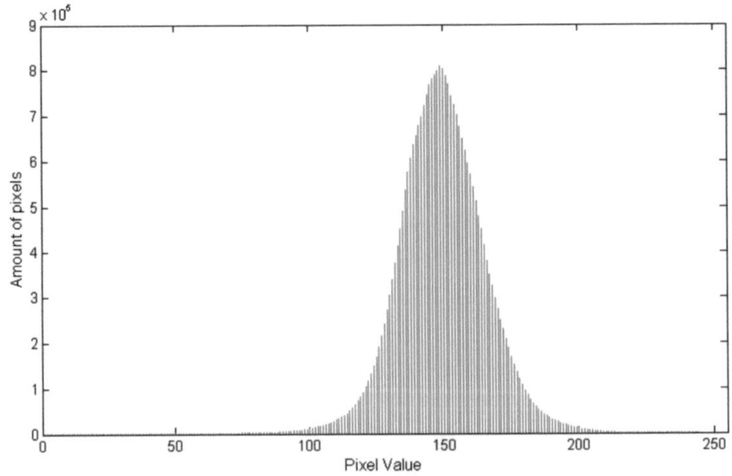

Fig. 9. Histogram of a recycled paper page sample.

The proposed PBHW technique makes use of a MF for logo detection. This detector is known to be optimum for deterministic signals corrupted by uncorrelated Gaussian noise Kay (1998). Taking into account the low-pass filtering characteristic of our PS channel, the Gaussian pattern noise η_{pn} of a recycled paper will become a correlated noise. Thus, the MF will be not optimum anymore. Therefore, we investigate a new detector.

4.1 Optimum detector for recycled paper document

Given a received signal **y**, the detection problem we are dealing with can be characterized by the detection of a deterministic signal **s** corrupted by correlated Gaussian noise η. Consequently, we have two statistical hypothesis to be verified:

$$\begin{cases} \mathcal{H}_0 : \text{No marked region. } \mathbf{y} = \eta \\ \mathcal{H}_1 : \text{Marked region. } \quad \mathbf{y} = \mathbf{s} + \eta \end{cases}$$

where $\mathbf{s} = \mathbf{w} * \mathbf{h}$, and $\eta = \eta_{pn} * \mathbf{h}$. Here **w** represents the logo, **h** represents the PS channel low-pass filter, and η_{pn} represents the recycle paper noise.

The likelihood ratio is given by

$$l(\mathbf{y}) = \frac{p(\mathbf{y}; \mathcal{H}_1)}{p(\mathbf{y}; \mathcal{H}_0)}.$$

Taking the log of both sides of the above equation, we have

$$\begin{aligned} \mathcal{L}(\mathbf{y}) &= \log l(\mathbf{y}) \\ &= \log \frac{p(\mathbf{y}; \mathcal{H}_1)}{p(\mathbf{y}; \mathcal{H}_0)}, \end{aligned}$$

where $p(\mathbf{y}; \mathcal{H}_i)$ represents the pdf of **y** when $\mathcal{H}_i$ is true.

Hence, as

$$p(\mathbf{y}; \mathcal{H}_0) = \frac{1}{(2\pi)^{N/2} |\mathbf{R}|^{1/2}} \exp\left[-\frac{1}{2}\mathbf{y}^T\mathbf{R}^{-1}\mathbf{y}\right]$$

$$p(\mathbf{y};\mathcal{H}_1) = \frac{1}{(2\bullet)^{N/2}|\mathbf{R}|^{1/2}} \exp\left[-\frac{1}{2}(\mathbf{y}-\bullet_y)^{\mathsf{T}}\mathbf{R}^{-1}(\mathbf{y}-\bullet_y)\right]$$

we have

$$\begin{aligned}
\mathcal{L}(\mathbf{y}) &= \log\frac{p(\mathbf{y};\mathcal{H}_1)}{p(\mathbf{y};\mathcal{H}_0)} \\
&= \log\frac{\frac{1}{(2\bullet)^{N/2}|\mathbf{R}|^{1/2}} \exp\left[-\frac{1}{2}(\mathbf{y}-\bullet_y)^{\mathsf{T}}\mathbf{R}^{-1}(\mathbf{y}-\bullet_y)\right]}{\frac{1}{(2\bullet)^{N/2}|\mathbf{R}|^{1/2}} \exp\left[-\frac{1}{2}\mathbf{y}^{\mathsf{T}}\mathbf{R}^{-1}\mathbf{y}\right]} \\
&= \frac{1}{2}\left[\mathbf{y}^{\mathsf{T}}\mathbf{R}^{-1}\mathbf{y}-(\mathbf{y}-\bullet_y)^{\mathsf{T}}\mathbf{R}^{-1}(\mathbf{y}-\bullet_y)\right] \\
&= \mathbf{y}^{\mathsf{T}}\mathbf{R}^{-1}\bullet_y-\frac{1}{2}\bullet_y{}^{\mathsf{T}}\mathbf{R}^{-1}\bullet_y.
\end{aligned}$$

In this way, the optimum detector for the presented situation is given by the logarithm of the likelihood ratio as

$$\mathcal{L}(\mathbf{y}) = \mathbf{y}^{\mathsf{T}}\mathbf{R}^{-1}\bullet_y-\frac{1}{2}\bullet_y{}^{\mathsf{T}}\mathbf{R}^{-1}\bullet_y. \tag{22}$$

From equation (22) we can say that the detector decides $\mathcal{H}_1$ if

$$\mathcal{L}(\mathbf{y}) = \mathbf{y}^{\mathsf{T}}\mathbf{R}^{-1}\mathbf{s}-\frac{1}{2}\mathbf{s}^{\mathsf{T}}\mathbf{R}^{-1}\mathbf{s} > \log\bullet.$$

As the fraction $\frac{1}{2}\mathbf{s}^{\mathsf{T}}\mathbf{R}^{-1}\mathbf{s}$ is independent of the observations, we say that

$$\mathbf{y}^{\mathsf{T}}\mathbf{R}^{-1}\mathbf{s} > \log\bullet + \frac{1}{2}\mathbf{s}^{\mathsf{T}}\mathbf{R}^{-1}\mathbf{s}.$$

Letting $\left(\log\bullet + \frac{1}{2}\mathbf{s}^{\mathsf{T}}\mathbf{R}^{-1}\mathbf{s}\right) = \bullet'$ we got

$$\mathbf{y}^{\mathsf{T}}\mathbf{R}^{-1}\mathbf{s} > \bullet'.$$

Now, the test statistic for the detector is given by

$$T_{pn}(\mathbf{y}) = \mathbf{y}^{\mathsf{T}}\mathbf{R}^{-1}\mathbf{s}. \tag{23}$$

Comparing equation (23) with the literature of detection theory, we note that the developed detector corresponds to the **generalized matched filter** (GMF) Kay (1998). Also, taking into account the CLT, we assume that the test statistic of equation (23) has a Gaussian distribution. Consequently, the optimal detection threshold developed in Section 3.3 is still valid for this detector. So that, in the above development we can say that $\bullet' = \bullet'$. The statistics of the detection variable $T_{pn}(\mathbf{y})$ are equated in 9, and are summarized in (24).

$$T_{pn}(\mathbf{y}) = \begin{cases} \mathcal{N}(0, \mathbf{s}^{\mathsf{T}}\mathbf{R}^{-1^{\mathsf{T}}}\mathbf{s}) & : \text{para } \mathcal{H}_0 \\ \mathcal{N}(\mathbf{s}^{\mathsf{T}}\mathbf{R}^{-1}\mathbf{s}, \mathbf{s}^{\mathsf{T}}\mathbf{R}^{-1^{\mathsf{T}}}\mathbf{s}) & : \text{para } \mathcal{H}_1 \end{cases} \tag{24}$$

As the matrix $\mathbf{R}$ is toeplitz Manolakis et al. (2000), it is known that $\mathbf{R}^{\mathsf{T}} = \mathbf{R}$ Strang (1988). Besides, as $(\mathbf{R}^{-1})^{\mathsf{T}} = (\mathbf{R}^{\mathsf{T}})^{-1}$, we conclude that $(\mathbf{R}^{-1})^{\mathsf{T}} = \mathbf{R}^{-1}$. So,

$$\mathsf{T}_{\mathsf{pn}}(\mathbf{y}) = \begin{cases} \mathcal{N}(0, \mathbf{s}^{\mathsf{T}}\mathbf{R}^{-1}\mathbf{s}) & : \text{para } \mathcal{H}_0 \\ \mathcal{N}(\mathbf{s}^{\mathsf{T}}\mathbf{R}^{-1}\mathbf{s}, \mathbf{s}^{\mathsf{T}}\mathbf{R}^{-1}\mathbf{s}) & : \text{para } \mathcal{H}_1 \end{cases} \tag{25}$$

Now, from equations (23) and (25) we see that both depends on the autocorrelation matrix ($\mathbf{R}$) of the correlated Gaussian noise that models the recycled paper background processed by the PS channel. In the next section we determine the values of that matrix and point out some considerations on the matrix.

5. Estimation of the R matrix

As shown in Section 4.1, the developed detector is dependent on the autocorrelation matrix of the correlated Gaussian noise that models the recycled paper background processed by the PS channel. For that reason we need to estimate the $\mathbf{R}$ matrix. As discussed in (Therrien, 1992, Chap. 6), the simplest but effective way of estimating a correlation matrix is by means of the autocorrelation method. Thus, we define this method to perform the estimation of the $\mathbf{R}$ matrix.

The estimation procedure using the autocorrelation method can be summarized as following. First, we generate a Gaussian noise with mean 150 and variance 16.5 (in accordance with Section 4) and processed it by the PS channel. After, we obtained $\mathsf{N_s}$ pixel values, $\mathsf{x}[0], \mathsf{x}[1], \ldots, \mathsf{x}[\mathsf{N_s}-1]$. In order to estimate the autocorrelation matrix $\mathbf{R}$ of dimension $\mathsf{P} \times \mathsf{P}$, we formed the data matrix $\mathbf{X}$ of dimension $(\mathsf{N_s} + \mathsf{P} - 1) \times \mathsf{P}$.

$$\mathbf{X} = \begin{bmatrix} x[0] & 0 & \cdots & 0 \\ x[1] & x[0] & \cdots & 0 \\ \vdots & \vdots & \ddots & \vdots \\ x[P-1] & x[P-2] & \cdots & x[0] \\ x[P] & x[P-1] & \cdots & x[1] \\ \vdots & \vdots & & \vdots \\ x[N_s-1] & x[N_s-2] & \cdots & x[N_s-P] \\ 0 & x[N_s-1] & \cdots & \vdots \\ \vdots & \vdots & \ddots & \vdots \\ 0 & 0 & \cdots & x[N_s-1] \end{bmatrix} \tag{26}$$

The estimation of the autocorrelation matrix $\mathbf{R}$ is given by

$$\mathbf{R} = \frac{1}{\mathsf{N_s}} \mathbf{X}^{\mathsf{H}} \mathbf{X} \tag{27}$$

where $\mathbf{X}^{\mathsf{H}}$ means the conjugate transpose of the matrix $\mathbf{X}$.

The $\mathbf{R}$ matrix defined in equation (27) is Toeplitz Therrien (1992) but it is not sparse. Considering the size of an A4 page document ($\approx 7000 \times 5000$ pixels), the size of the logo could not be so small in order to be visually recognizable. This means the $\mathbf{R}$ matrix, which is proportional to the logo size, will be large. For instance, for a 128×128 pixels logo (which is relatively small), the $\mathbf{R}$ matrix will have 16384×16384 elements. In the detection process of equation (23) this matrix needs to be inverted, which means a very high computational cost for a large matrix. Therefore, we analyzed the values of the **R** matrix running simple experiments and we could realize that this matrix can be approximated by an sparse matrix keeping the first 50 values and zeroing the others. In Fig. 10 we illustrate the distribution of the values of matrix **R** with dimension 400 $\times$ 400 elements. Fig. 11 depicts the plot of a line of the **R** matrix.

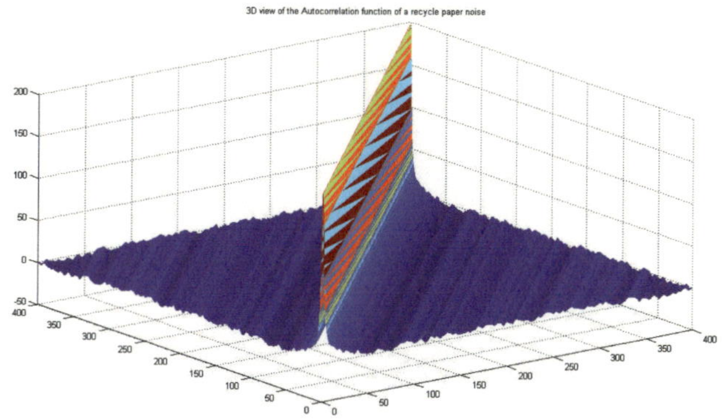

Fig. 10. Plot of the values of the **R** matrix with 400 $\times$ 400 elements.

As this matrix is Toeplitz, only a line is enough to characterize it at all Strang (1988).

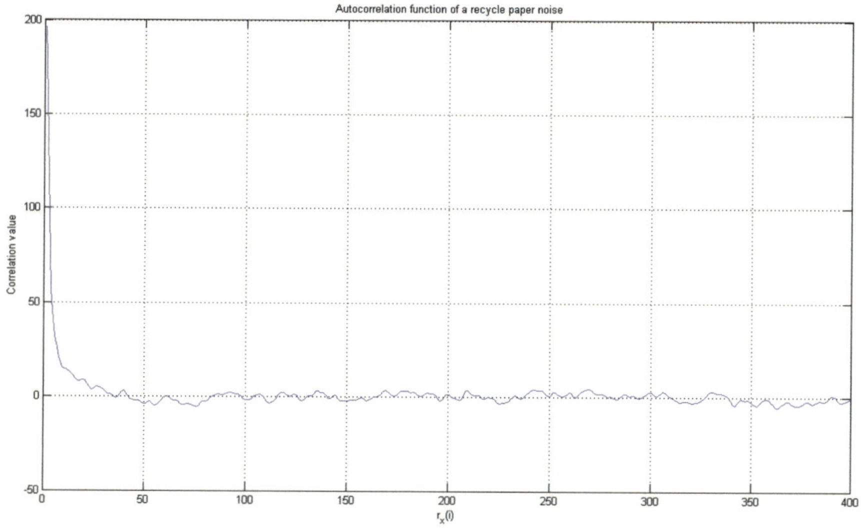

Fig. 11. Plot of a line of the **R** matrix.

6. Experiments

In this section we provide experiments to show the performance of the proposed method. It is important to comment that for the experiments presented in this paper we have used the multifunctional HP M1120, HP PSC1510, and the printers HP P1005, HP LJ-1100. For those devices, the typical values for parameter of equations (1) and (21) are

- $\bullet^2_{\eta_e} = 0.01$

- $\bullet_r^2 = 0.15$

6.1 On characters segmentation

We have pointed out at Section 3.2 that characters segmentation brings a significant improvement on the detection error probability. To notice the improvement obtained by the detector after characters segmentation, we present in Fig. 12 a comparison of the correlation plots. In Fig. 12(a) we have a plot of the correlation values without characters segmentation, and in Fig. 12(b) the segmentation was performed before the detection process. In both plots the dashed line represents the optimal detection threshold obtained from equation (5) with appropriate values for the means and variances for each case. The error probability associated to each detection is $Pe = 3.5 \times 10^{-39}$ in the case of characters segmentation before correlation, and $Pe = 3.71 \times 10^{-30}$ when segmentation is not employed.

6.2 Experiments with real logos

In this part of the experiments we present results obtained from using a real logo. This logo is shown in Fig. 13.

In Fig. 14 we show part of a marked document after printing and scanning with an HP multifunctional LaserJet device model M1120. The logo has only 10% of his total energy which is very transparent and permits reading the text without any difficulty. This document has originally 300ppi. The printer resolution was set to 600dpi and the scanning resolution to 300ppi. The result of the detection process is presented in Fig. 15.

These experiments illustrate that the robustness of the method is not significantly compromised even for a logo with reduced energy.

6.3 Position error experiment

The proposed method suffers from some specific geometric distortions that occurs in the PS channel. These distortions are not properly modeled on the PS channel model described in section 2.2. Therefore, during the logo detection process in a document processed by the PS channel, some little distortions due to the printing and scanning processes will occur. Besides, as the logo image is, in general, correlated, our position estimation strategy may generate an error. This error was model in section 3.6. Here we demonstrate how to evaluate this error and determine the size of the insertion region to be considered both in the insertion and in the detection process. In Fig. 13 it is shown the digital logo used for this experiment. First we compute the logo autocorrelation $C_x[n]$. This is presented in Fig. 16. As already explained in section 3.6, the peak of the correlation of the original logo with the document logo will suffer a disturbance from the total noise present in the document. Considering the CLT, we assume that the total noise present in the document has a Gaussian pdf. Thus $r \approx \mathcal{N}(0, \bullet_r^2)$, where r represents the total noise of the document. This noise includes the electronic noise, small imperfections in the paper, dirt particles present on the paper, small geometric distortions like small rotations inherent to the PS process, among others. This noise was evaluated during some experiments and we assume that, typically, it has $\bullet_r^2 = 0.15$.

The next step is to evaluate the variation of the value of the n correlations taking into account the action of the total noise over the correlations. After, determine until which point there is a possibility of a correlation value be greater than the value em $n = 0$. In the case of the logo of

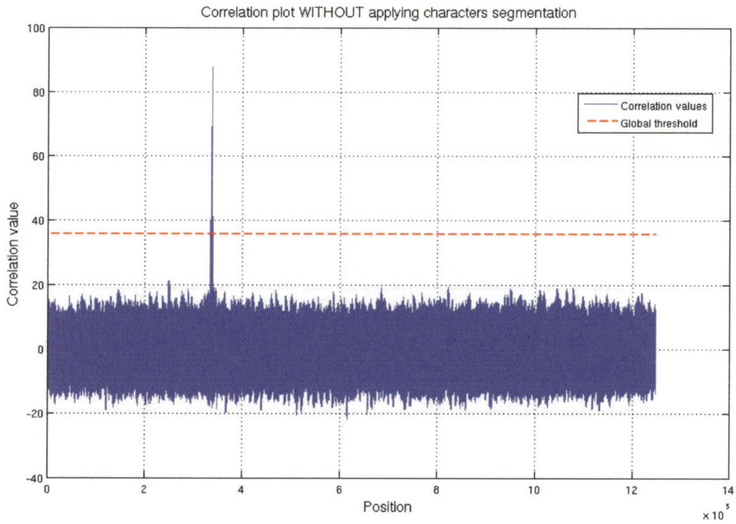

(a) Correlation before characters segmentation.

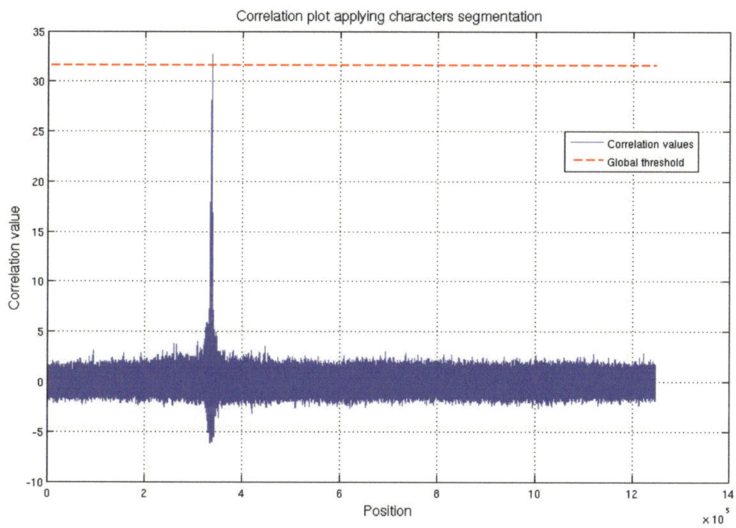

(b) Correlation after characters segmentation.

Fig. 12. Detection level before and after characters segmentation.

Fig. 13, the first six correlation values can, depending on the influence of the noise, assume a value greater than the correlation in $n = 0$. In Table 1 the correlation values and the variation of them for the logo are presented.

Analyzing the values of Table 1, we note that for the first tree correlations ($n = 3$) there is a possibility of the values be greater than the central value ($n = 0$). Therefore, for this logo it is necessary to consider an insertion region of 7×7 pixels in order to correctly decode the message. This means that we have to create a mapping table known by the transmitter and the

Fig. 13. Real logo used in the experiments.

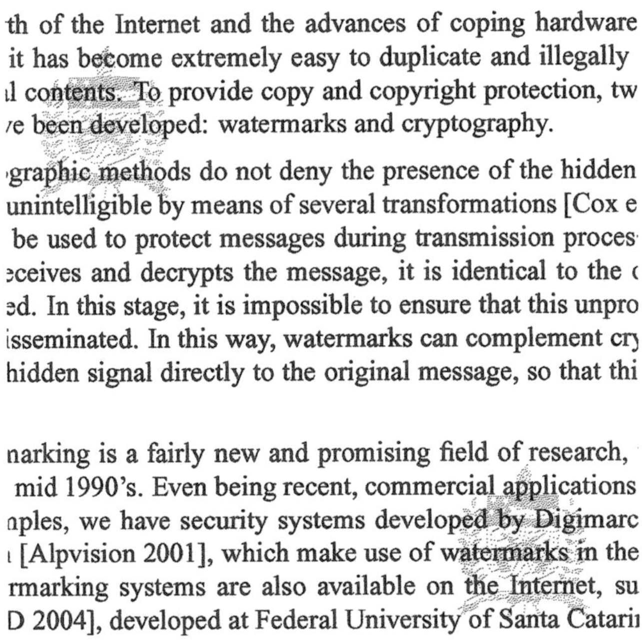

th of the Internet and the advances of coping hardware
it has become extremely easy to duplicate and illegally
l contents. To provide copy and copyright protection, tw
ve been developed: watermarks and cryptography.

graphic methods do not deny the presence of the hidden
unintelligible by means of several transformations [Cox e
be used to protect messages during transmission proces
eceives and decrypts the message, it is identical to the
ed. In this stage, it is impossible to ensure that this unpro
isseminated. In this way, watermarks can complement cry
hidden signal directly to the original message, so that thi

narking is a fairly new and promising field of research,
mid 1990's. Even being recent, commercial applications
nples, we have security systems developed by Digimarc
[Alpvision 2001], which make use of watermarks in the
rmarking systems are also available on the Internet, su
D 2004], developed at Federal University of Santa Catari

Fig. 14. A watermarked document after PS channel process.

receiver, for instance, in order to map all the 7×7 pixels of the insertion region to the specific insertion point.

6.4 Experiment using recycled paper

Here we present an experiment to illustrate the applicability of the method for documents printed on recycled paper as described in section 4. In Fig. 17(a) it is shown part of a document printed on a recycled paper. This document was authenticated with one logo in position $(51, 51)$. The authenticated version is presented in Fig. 17(b). For this case, the logo has 50% of his total energy. This amount of energy is necessary in order to keep the logo visible and still detectable. The detection plot shown in Fig. 18 was obtained after detection using equation (23). The optimal threshold was calculated from equation (6) and is represented in

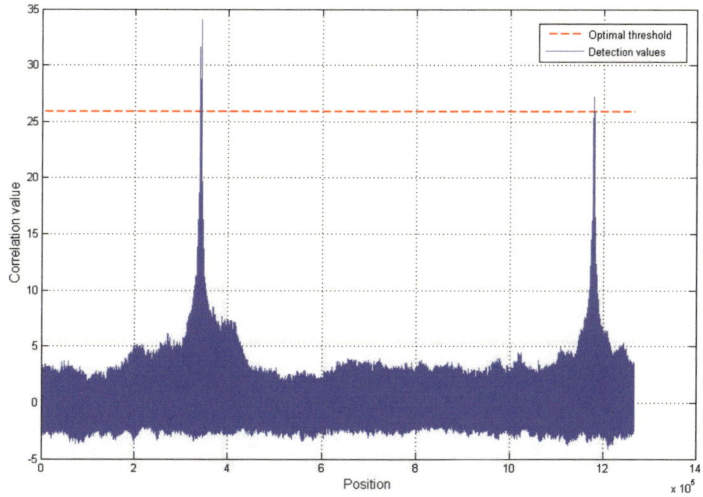

Fig. 15. Detection plot of Fig. 14.

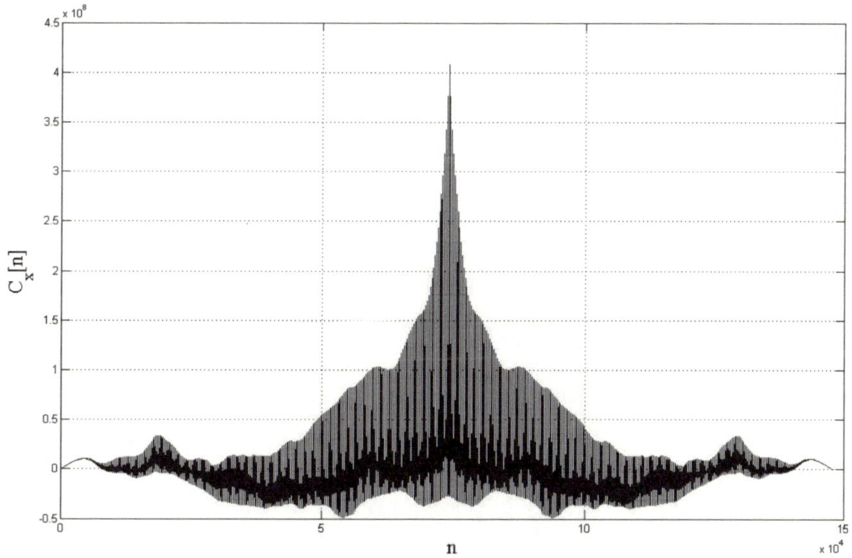

Fig. 16. Autocorrelation of the logo presented in Fig. 13.

n	$C_x[n]$	min $C_x[n]$	max $C_x[n]$
0	4.082E+08	3.470E+08	4.695E+08
1	3.762E+08	3.198E+08	4.327E+08
2	3.424E+08	2.910E+08	3.937E+08
3	3.181E+08	2.704E+08	3.659E+08
4	2.962E+08	2.518E+08	3.406E+08
5	2.774E+08	2.358E+08	3.190E+08
6	2.594E+08	2.205E+08	2.983E+08
7	2.432E+08	2.068E+08	2.797E+08

Table 1. Correlation values, their minimum and maximum in accordance with the total noise variance $\bullet_r^2$ for the logo of Fig. 13.

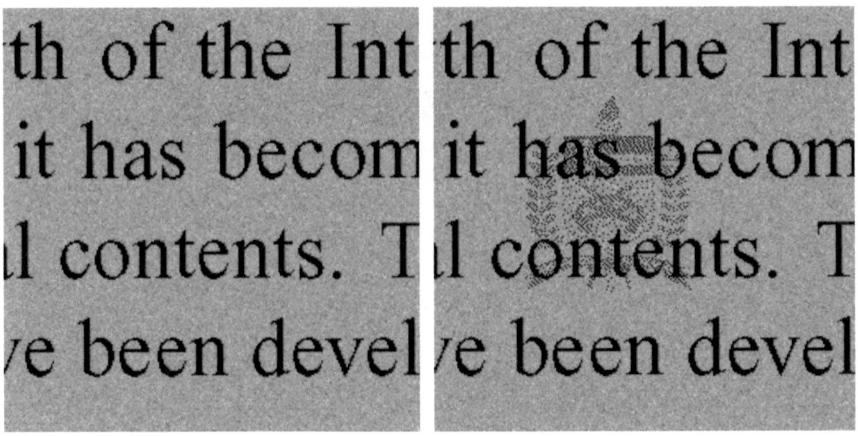

(a) Original document. (b) Authenticated document.

Fig. 17. Example of a document printed on recycle paper.

the graphics as a horizontal dashed line. Analyzing the detection data, we determined the correlation peak on (51,51). This corresponds to the exact insertion position of the logo. So that, we can correctly decode the message conveyed.

6.5 Performance of the detector for documents printed on recycled paper

In the detection theory the way to compare detectors performance is by the receiver operating characteristics (ROC) curves Kay (1998). The ROC curves are basically the plot of the detection probability (P_d) versus the false alarm probability (P_{fa}) of the detector.

To support the development of the optimal detector presented in section 4.1, and to show the better performance of the GMF against the MF for the case where the authenticated document has been printed on recycle paper we present here a comparison of both detectors by means of the ROC curves. For this experiment we simulate the detection of a logo inserted in a document printed on a recycled paper. This document was processed by the PS channel in accordance of the model presented in Fig. 1. We have performed tens of thousands of realizations of the detection process. At the end, we were able to determine the detection probability and the false alarm probability of the whole process for a specific range

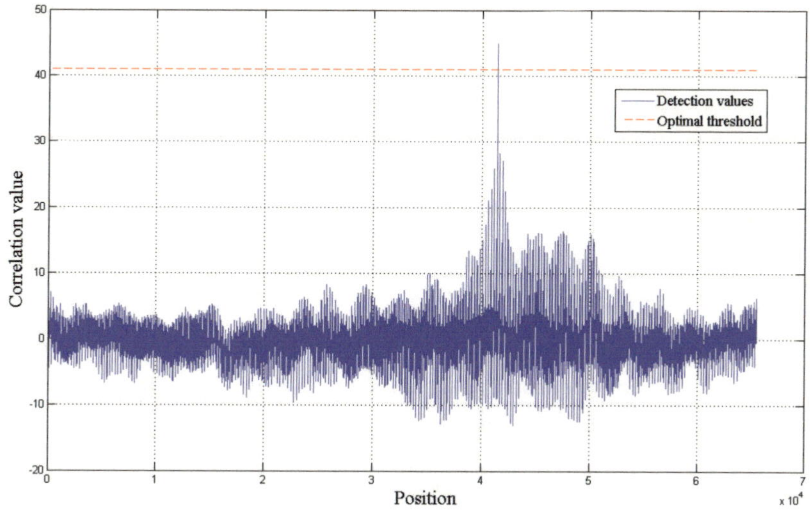

Fig. 18. Detection plot for experiment using recycled paper.

of detection threshold values. In Fig. 19 it is presented the ROC curves of the experiment. It is important to note that this is not a theoretical curve. It was obtained by a real detection process.

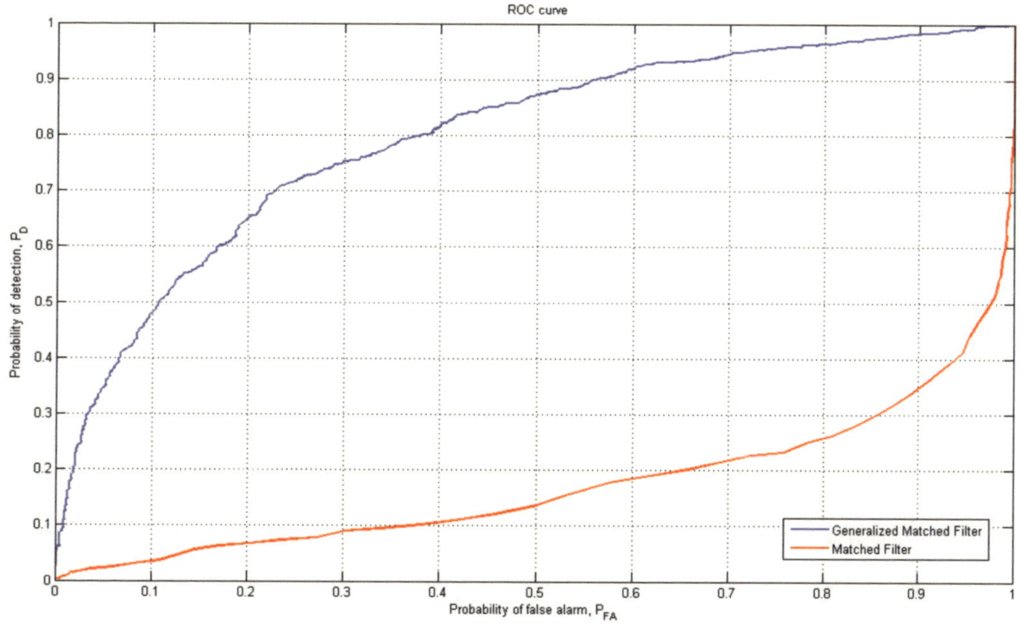

Fig. 19. ROC curves comparing the GMF against the MF for detection of logos inserted in recycled paper.

As expected, analyzing Fig. 19, we note that the MF has a very poor performance compared to the GMF in the case of document printed on recycled paper. This proves us the applicability of the developed detector.

6.6 A complete example

Now let us present a complete example to characterize the usage of the proposed method. Given we need to authenticate an identification card (ID) as that shown in Fig. 20 (this example ID has 1243×717 pixels) with a binary string computed from a hashing function Stinson (1995) using important parts of the card text plus a private key. Let us consider that after this hashing process we got a string of 39 bits, $b = 100000010101000101101111110110100101000$. Following the coding scheme presented in Borges & Mayer (2006a) we first convert the bit string into his decimal representation, which is $Z = 277708533032$. Now, suppose we are interesting in inserting two logos on that card. So, we have $K = 2$. For our example, the mapping function will be $Z = c_1 a_1 + c_2 a_2$. As suggested in Borges & Mayer (2006a) we define the coefficients $c_i = N^{i-1}, i = 1, \ldots, N$, where N is the total amount of pixels of the document. So that, $c_1 = 1$ and $c_2 = 1243 \times 717 = 891231$. The positions a_1 and a_2 that represent the message b can be calculated by

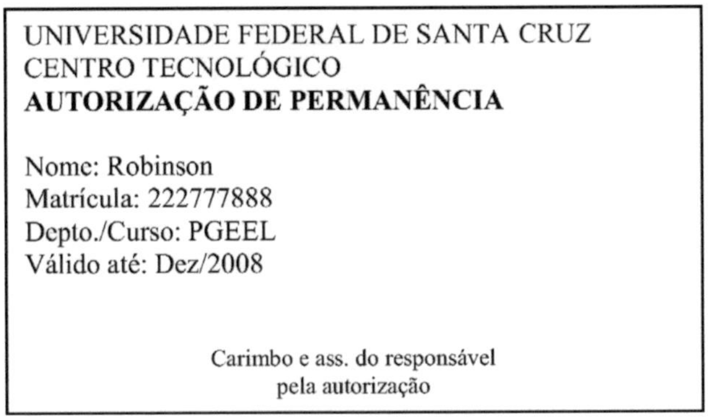
UNIVERSIDADE FEDERAL DE SANTA CRUZ
CENTRO TECNOLÓGICO
AUTORIZAÇÃO DE PERMANÊNCIA

Nome: Robinson
Matrícula: 222777888
Depto./Curso: PGEEL
Válido até: Dez/2008

Carimbo e ass. do responsável
pela autorização

Fig. 20. Example of a card to be authenticated by our method.

$$a_2 = \left\lfloor \frac{Z}{C_2} \right\rfloor = 311601 \tag{28}$$

$$a_1 = \left\lfloor \frac{Z - a_2 c_2}{c_1} \right\rfloor = 62201 \tag{29}$$

It is important to notice that a_1 and a_2 are positions of the 1D vector representation of the document image. In the 2D image, a conversion is needed and it gives us the pixels $(51, 51)$ for a_1, and (251,851) for a_2. To assure good transparency of the logos, their energy will be reduced to only 20%. In Fig. 21 we can see the ID card authenticated with two logos conveying 39 bits of information. This figure represents the ID card already processed by the PS channel.

For this case, the optimal threshold calculated is $\bullet = 90.8$. The detection values are depicted in Fig. 22. In Fig. 23 we show with black points the estimated positions found by the detector. More specifically, the insertion points estimated from the correlation peaks correspond to the points $(52, 52)$ and $(253, 852)$. In accordance with the experiment in section 6.3, for the logo used we need to consider an insertion region of 7×7 pixels. In this experiment both points were identified inside of the 7×7 region. This guarantee we can correctly decode the message.

Fig. 21. Example of a card authenticated with 39 bits using the method presented in this paper.

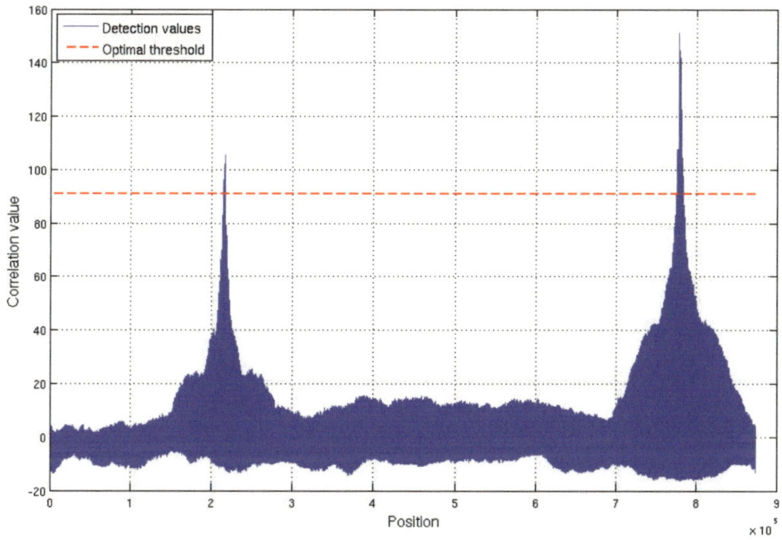

Fig. 22. Detection plot of the Fig. 21.

Fig. 23. Estimation of the logos position. The black points indicate the estimated positions.

7. Conclusion

We have presented a novel hardcopy watermarking technique to authenticate text documents. The proposed method provides two forms of application: (i) authentication of documents encoding relevant information of the document itself, or (ii) use of a document just to convey a hidden message that do not have any relation to the document. We proposed a simple and effective PS channel model for our problem. Experiments illustrated the robustness of the method to the PS channel interferences. The proposed character segmentation allows the detection of very low energy logos inserted into text documents and also allows it to cooperatively work with other techniques, such as barcodes, without significantly interfering on the performance of each other. Also we have investigated the applicability of the method for documents printed on recycled paper. A new detector was derived for this application and the better performance of this one was presented.

Future work will involve the improvement of the character segmentation, and the development of a more realistic capacity equation for the method. Also, we believe the detection process could be improved by the knowledge of the whole authentication process and noise involved in the process.

8. Acknowledgments

The author would like to thanks to Prof. Joceli Mayer and the Electrical Engineering Graduate Program from Federal University of Santa Catarina, Brazil, for the support.

9. Appendix: Detector statistics

This appendix derives the results presented in equation (24).

The mean of $\mathsf{T}_{\mathsf{pn}}(\mathbf{y})$ to the hypothesis $\mathcal{H}_0$ ($\bullet_{\mathsf{pn}|\mathcal{H}_0}$) is given by the expectation $\mathsf{E}\{\mathsf{T}_{\mathsf{pn}}(\mathbf{y}); \mathcal{H}_0\}$, therefore

$$\begin{aligned} \bullet_{\mathsf{pn}|\mathcal{H}_0} &= \mathsf{E}\{\bullet^{\mathsf{T}}\mathbf{R}^{-1}\mathbf{s}\} \\ &= \mathsf{E}\{\bullet^{\mathsf{T}}\}\mathbf{R}^{-1}\mathbf{s} \\ &= 0. \end{aligned} \tag{30}$$

The mean of $\mathsf{T}_{\mathsf{pn}}(\mathbf{y})$ to the hypothesis $\mathcal{H}_1$ ($\bullet_{\mathsf{pn}|\mathcal{H}_1}$) is given by the expectation $\mathsf{E}\{\mathsf{T}_{\mathsf{pn}}(\mathbf{y}); \mathcal{H}_1\}$, therefore

$$\begin{aligned} \bullet_{\mathsf{pn}|\mathcal{H}_1} &= \mathsf{E}\{(\mathbf{s} + \bullet)^{\mathsf{T}}\mathbf{R}^{-1}\mathbf{s}\} \\ &= \mathsf{E}\{\mathbf{s}^{\mathsf{T}}\mathbf{R}^{-1}\mathbf{s} + \bullet^{\mathsf{T}}\mathbf{R}^{-1}\mathbf{s}\} \\ &= \mathbf{s}^{\mathsf{T}}\mathbf{R}^{-1}\mathbf{s} + \mathsf{E}\{\bullet^{\mathsf{T}}\mathbf{R}^{-1}\mathbf{s}\} \\ &= \mathbf{s}^{\mathsf{T}}\mathbf{R}^{-1}\mathbf{s} + \mathsf{E}\{\bullet^{\mathsf{T}}\}\mathbf{R}^{-1}\mathbf{s} \\ &= \mathbf{s}^{\mathsf{T}}\mathbf{R}^{-1}\mathbf{s} \end{aligned} \tag{31}$$

The variance of $\mathsf{T}_{\mathsf{pn}}(\mathbf{y})$ to the hypothesis $\mathcal{H}_0$ ($\bullet^2_{\mathsf{pn}|\mathcal{H}_0}$) is given by the expectation $\mathsf{E}\{\mathsf{T}_{\mathsf{pn}}(\mathbf{y})^2;\mathcal{H}_0\} - \mathsf{E}\{\mathsf{T}_{\mathsf{pn}}(\mathbf{y});\mathcal{H}_0\}^2$, therefore

$$\begin{aligned}
\bullet^2_{\mathsf{pn}|\mathcal{H}_0} &= \mathsf{E}\{\mathsf{T}_{\mathsf{pn}}(\mathbf{y})^2;\mathcal{H}_0\} - \mathsf{E}\{\mathsf{T}_{\mathsf{pn}}(\mathbf{y});\mathcal{H}_0\}^2 \\
&= \mathsf{E}\{\mathsf{T}_{\mathsf{pn}}(\mathbf{y})^2;\mathcal{H}_0\} \\
&= \mathsf{E}\{(\mathbf{y}^{\mathsf{T}}\mathbf{R}^{-1}\mathbf{s})^2\} \\
&= \mathsf{E}\{(\bullet^{\mathsf{T}}\mathbf{R}^{-1}\mathbf{s})^2\} \\
&= \mathsf{E}\{\bullet^{\mathsf{T}}\mathbf{R}^{-1}\mathbf{s}\bullet^{\mathsf{T}}\mathbf{R}^{-1}\mathbf{s}\}.
\end{aligned}$$

Now, letting $\mathbf{a} = \mathbf{R}^{-1}\mathbf{s}$ we have

$$\begin{aligned}
\bullet^2_{\mathsf{pn}|\mathcal{H}_0} &= \mathsf{E}\{\bullet^{\mathsf{T}}\mathbf{a}\bullet^{\mathsf{T}}\mathbf{a}\} \\
&= \mathsf{E}\{(\bullet^{\mathsf{T}}\mathbf{a})^{\mathsf{T}}\bullet^{\mathsf{T}}\mathbf{a}\} \\
&= \mathsf{E}\{\mathbf{a}^{\mathsf{T}}\bullet\bullet^{\mathsf{T}}\mathbf{a}\} \\
&= \mathbf{a}^{\mathsf{T}}\mathbf{R}\mathbf{a} \\
&= \left(\mathbf{R}^{-1}\mathbf{s}\right)^{\mathsf{T}}\mathbf{R}\left(\mathbf{R}^{-1}\mathbf{s}\right) \\
&= \mathbf{s}^{\mathsf{T}}\mathbf{R}^{-1^{\mathsf{T}}}\mathbf{s}
\end{aligned} \tag{32}$$

The variance of $\mathsf{T}_{\mathsf{pn}}(\mathbf{y})$ to the hypothesis $\mathcal{H}_1$ ($\bullet^2_{\mathsf{pn}|\mathcal{H}_1}$) is given by the expectation $\mathsf{E}\{\mathsf{T}_{\mathsf{pn}}(\mathbf{y})^2;\mathcal{H}_1\} - \mathsf{E}\{\mathsf{T}_{\mathsf{pn}}(\mathbf{y});\mathcal{H}_1\}^2$, therefore

$$\begin{aligned}
\bullet^2_{\mathsf{pn}|\mathcal{H}_1} &= \mathsf{E}\{\mathsf{T}_{\mathsf{pn}}(\mathbf{y})^2;\mathcal{H}_1\} - \mathsf{E}\{\mathsf{T}_{\mathsf{pn}}(\mathbf{y});\mathcal{H}_1\}^2 \\
&= \mathsf{E}\{(\mathbf{y}^{\mathsf{T}}\mathbf{R}^{-1}\mathbf{s})^2\} - (\mathbf{s}^{\mathsf{T}}\mathbf{R}^{-1}\mathbf{s})^2 \\
&= \mathsf{E}\{\mathbf{y}^{\mathsf{T}}\mathbf{R}^{-1}\mathbf{s}\mathbf{y}^{\mathsf{T}}\mathbf{R}^{-1}\mathbf{s}\} - (\mathbf{s}^{\mathsf{T}}\mathbf{R}^{-1}\mathbf{s})^2 \\
&= \mathsf{E}\{(\mathbf{s}^{\mathsf{T}}\mathbf{R}^{-1}\mathbf{s} + \bullet^{\mathsf{T}}\mathbf{R}^{-1}\mathbf{s})(\mathbf{s}^{\mathsf{T}}\mathbf{R}^{-1}\mathbf{s} + \bullet^{\mathsf{T}}\mathbf{R}^{-1}\mathbf{s})\} - (\mathbf{s}^{\mathsf{T}}\mathbf{R}^{-1}\mathbf{s})^2 \\
&= \mathsf{E}\{(\mathbf{s}^{\mathsf{T}}\mathbf{R}^{-1}\mathbf{s})^2 + \mathbf{s}^{\mathsf{T}}\mathbf{R}^{-1}\mathbf{s}\bullet^{\mathsf{T}}\mathbf{R}^{-1}\mathbf{s} + \bullet^{\mathsf{T}}\mathbf{R}^{-1}\mathbf{s}\mathbf{s}^{\mathsf{T}}\mathbf{R}^{-1}\mathbf{s} + \\
&\quad + (\bullet^{\mathsf{T}}\mathbf{R}^{-1}\mathbf{s})^2\} - (\mathbf{s}^{\mathsf{T}}\mathbf{R}^{-1}\mathbf{s})^2 \\
&= \mathsf{E}\{\mathbf{s}^{\mathsf{T}}\mathbf{R}^{-1}\mathbf{s}\bullet^{\mathsf{T}}\mathbf{R}^{-1}\mathbf{s} + \bullet^{\mathsf{T}}\mathbf{R}^{-1}\mathbf{s}\mathbf{s}^{\mathsf{T}}\mathbf{R}^{-1}\mathbf{s} + (\bullet^{\mathsf{T}}\mathbf{R}^{-1}\mathbf{s})^2\} \\
&= \mathsf{E}\{\mathbf{s}^{\mathsf{T}}\mathbf{R}^{-1}\mathbf{s}\bullet^{\mathsf{T}}\mathbf{R}^{-1}\mathbf{s}\} + \mathsf{E}\{\bullet^{\mathsf{T}}\mathbf{R}^{-1}\mathbf{s}\mathbf{s}^{\mathsf{T}}\mathbf{R}^{-1}\mathbf{s}\} + \\
&\quad + \mathsf{E}\{\bullet^{\mathsf{T}}\mathbf{R}^{-1}\mathbf{s}\bullet^{\mathsf{T}}\mathbf{R}^{-1}\mathbf{s}\} \\
&= \mathbf{s}^{\mathsf{T}}\mathbf{R}^{-1}\mathbf{s}\mathsf{E}\{\bullet^{\mathsf{T}}\}\mathbf{R}^{-1}\mathbf{s} + \mathsf{E}\{\bullet^{\mathsf{T}}\}\mathbf{R}^{-1}\mathbf{s}\mathbf{s}^{\mathsf{T}}\mathbf{R}^{-1}\mathbf{s} + \\
&\quad + \mathsf{E}\{\bullet^{\mathsf{T}}\mathbf{R}^{-1}\mathbf{s}\bullet^{\mathsf{T}}\mathbf{R}^{-1}\mathbf{s}\} \\
&= \mathsf{E}\{\bullet^{\mathsf{T}}\mathbf{R}^{-1}\mathbf{s}\bullet^{\mathsf{T}}\mathbf{R}^{-1}\mathbf{s}\} \\
&= \mathbf{a}^{\mathsf{T}}\mathbf{R}\mathbf{a} \\
&= \left(\mathbf{R}^{-1}\mathbf{s}\right)^{\mathsf{T}}\mathbf{R}\left(\mathbf{R}^{-1}\mathbf{s}\right) \\
&= \mathbf{s}^{\mathsf{T}}\mathbf{R}^{-1^{\mathsf{T}}}\mathbf{s}
\end{aligned} \tag{33}$$

10. References

Borges, P. & Mayer, J. (2006a). Analysis of position based watermarking, *Pattern Analysis and Applications* 9(1): 70–82.

Borges, P. V. K. & Mayer, J. (2003). Position based watermarking, *Proc. of the 3rd Int. Symp. on Image and Signal Processing and Analysis. ISPA 2003*, Vol. 2, pp. 997–1002.

Borges, P. V. & Mayer, J. (2006b). Document watermarking via character luminance modulation, *IEEE International Conference on Acoustic, Speech and Signal Processing*.

Brassil, J. T., Low, S. & Maxemchuk, N. F. (1999). Copyright protection for the electronic distribution of text documents, *Proc. of the IEEE* 87(7): 1181–1196.

Braudaway, G. W., Magerlein, K. A. & Mintzer, F. (1996). Protecting publicly-available images with a visible image watermark, *Technical Report RC 20336 (89918) 1/15/96*, IBM Research Division.

Gonzalez, R. C. (1992). *Digital Image Processing*, Addison Wesley.

Kay, S. M. (1998). *Fundamentals of Statistical Signal Processing: Detection Theory*, Prentice Hall.

Manolakis, D. G., Ingle, V. K. & Kogon, S. M. (2000). *Statistical and Adaptive Signal Processing: Spectral Estimation, Signal Modeling, Adaptive Filtering and Array Processing*, McGraw-Hill.

M.S. Kankanhalli, R. Lil, R. R. (1999). Adaptive visible watermarking of images, *in* I. C. Press (ed.), *Proc. IEEE Int. Conf. on Multimedia Computing and Systems*, pp. 68–73.

Norris, M. & Smith, E. H. B. (2004). Printer modeling for document imaging, *Proc. of the Int. Conf. on Imaging Science, System and Technology, CISST'04*.

Otsu, N. (1979). A threshold selection method from gray-level histograms, *IEEE Transactions on Systems, Man, and Cybernetics* 9(1): 62–66.

Quintela, N. D. & Pérez-González, F. (2003). Visible encryption: using paper as a secure channel, *Proc. of SPIE, USA*.

Stinson, D. R. (1995). *Cryptography: Theory and Practice*, CRC Press.

Strang, G. (1988). *Linear Algebra and Its Applications*, 3 edn, Brooks Cole.

Therrien, C. W. (1992). *Discrete Random Signals and Statistical Signal Processing*, Signal Processing Series, Prentice Hall.

Víllan, R., Voloshynovskiy, S., Koval, O. & Pun, T. (2005). Multilevel 2d bar codes: towards high capacity storage modules for multimedia security and management, *Proc. of SPIE, Electronic Imaging, USA*.

Víllan, R., Voloshynovskiy, S., koval, O., Vila, J., Topak, E., Deguillaume, F., Rytsar, Y. & Pun, T. (2006). Text data-hiding for digital and printed documents: theoretical and practical considerations, *Proc. of SPIE, Elect. Imaging*.

Wu, M. & Liu, B. (2004). Data hiding in binary image for authentication and annotation, *IEEE Trans. on Multimedia* 6(4): 528–538.

Y. Hu, S. K. (2003). An image fusion-based visible watermarking algorithm, *in* I. Press (ed.), *Proc. Int. Symp. Circuits and Systems*, pp. 25–28.

Zitová, B. & Flusser, J. (2003). Image registration methods: a survey, *Image and Vision Computing* 21(11): 977–1000.

9

Comparison of "Spread-Quantization" Video Watermarking Techniques for Copyright Protection in the Spatial and Transform Domain

Radu Ovidiu Preda and Nicolae Vizireanu
Politehnica University of Bucharest
Romania

1. Introduction

In spite of the existence of watermarking technique for all kinds of digital data, most of the literature addresses the watermarking of still images for copyright protection and only some work is extended to video watermarking. Video watermarking is distinct from image watermarking, because there is more data available to both the attacker as well as to the watermarker. This additional data volume allows the payload to be more redundantly and reliably embedded.

Video watermarking schemes are characterized by the domain that the watermark is being embedded or detected, their capacity, the perceptual quality of the watermarked videos and their robustness to particular types of attacks. They can be divided into three main groups according to the domain in which the watermark is embedded: spatial domain, frequency domain and compressed domain watermarking. An overview of video watermarking techniques can be found in (Gwenael & Dugelay, 2003).

The spatial domain algorithms embed the watermark directly into the pixel values and no transforms are applied to the host signal during the embedding process. The most common techniques to insert the watermark into the host data in the spatial domain is via Least Significant Bit modification, Spread Spectrum Modulation and Quantization Index Modulation.

The easiest way to embed a watermark in the spatial domain is the LSB method. If each pixel in an image is represented by an 8-bit value, the image/frame can be sliced up in 8 bit planes. The least significant bit plane does not contain visually significant information and can easily be replaced by the watermark bits. There are also some more sophisticated algorithm that makes use of LSB modification (Kinoshita, 1996). These techniques are not very robust to attacks because the LSB plane can be easily replaced by random bits, removing the watermark.

Spread spectrum watermarking views watermarking as a problem of communication through a noisy channel. As a means to combatting this noise or interference, spread-spectrum techniques are employed to allow reliable communication in such noisy environments. In this case, the watermark data is coded with a pseudorandom code sequence to spread its power spectrum in the image or video, thus increasing its robustness to attacks. One of the first methods was the one-dimensional spread spectrum approach (Hartung & Girod, 1998). Here, the watermark is a pseudo-random sequence spread over the video frames by direct spatial domain addition. The watermark is repeatedly embedded throughout the video in a sequential manner. Other more complicated spread-spectrum methods were proposed in (Celik et al., 2008), (Altun et al., 2009), (Maity, S.P. & Maity, S., 2009).

Quantization IndexModulation (QIM) refers to a class of data hiding schemes that exploit Costa's (Costa, 1983) now famous findings by embedding information in the choice of quantizers. Over the past few years, QIM-based data hiding has received increasing attention from the data hiding community because it is more robust than techniques such as spread spectrum and LSB modification. State of the art proposed QIM schemes include Chen and Wornell's QIM and dither modulation (Chen & Wornell, 2001), Eggers et al's scalar Costa scheme (SCS) (Eggers et al., 2003), Jie and Zhiqiang's color image QIM scheme (Jie & Zhiqiang, 2009) and Kalantari and Ahadi's logarithmic QIM scheme (Kalantari & Ahadi, 2010).

For frequency domain watermarking, the most common transforms being used are the Discrete Cosine Transform (DCT), Discrete Fourier Transform (DFT) and Discrete Wavelet Transform. The main advantage offered by transform domain techniques is that they can take advantage of special properties of the alternate domains to address the limitations of pixel-based methods or to support additional features. For instance, a watermarking scheme in the DCT domain achieves better implementation compatibility with popular video coding algorithms such as MPEG. Also, they have better resistance to compression based attacks. Generally, the main drawback of transform domain methods is their higher computational requirements.

Image and video watermarking in the Discrete Cosine Transform domain is very popular, because the DCT is still the most popular domain for digital image processing. The DCT allows an image to be broken up into different frequency sub-bands, making it much easier to embed watermarking information into the middle frequency sub-bands of an image or video frame. One of the first DCT based algorithms, upon which many variations have been based, is presented in (Cox et al., 1997). The watermark is a normally distributed sequence of real numbers added to the full-frame DCT of each video frame. More advanced techniques were also proposed in (Suhail & Obaidat, 2003), (Liu, L. et al., 2005), (Yang et al., 2008). The choice of the DCT coefficients for watermark embedding is a compromise between the quality degradation of the image/frame (frequency of the coefficients should be high) and the resilience of the watermarking scheme to attacks (frequency of the coefficients should be low).

Lately, algorithms in the Wavelet domain have gained more popularity due to their excellent spatial localization, frequency spread, and multi-resolution characteristics (Barni et al., 2001), (Reddy & Chatterji, 2005), (Ellinas & Kenterlis, 2006), (Zou et al., 2006), (El-Taweel, 2007), (Coria et al., 2008), (Preda & Vizireanu, 2011). The Discrete Wavelet Transform (DWT) separates an image into a lower resolution approximation image (LL) as well as horizontal (HL), vertical (LH) and diagonal (HH) detail components. The process can then be repeated to compute multiple scale wavelet decompositions. Many embedding techniques in the wavelet domain use similar approaches to those in the DCT domain.

Watermarking schemes performed in the compressed domain include those for MPEG 1-4 (Liu Z. et al., 2004), (Biswas et al., 2005), (Preda & Vizireanu, 2007) and H.26x (Zhang et al., 2007) compressed videos. Video watermarking techniques that use MPEG/H.26x coding structures as primitive components are primarily motivated with the goal of integrating watermarking and compression to reduce overall real-time video processing complexity. Such methods usually embed the watermark directly into the VLC code by modifying the transform domain coefficients (Biswas et al., 2005), (Preda & Vizireanu, 2007), (Zhang et al., 2007) or the motion vector information (Liu Z. et al., 2004). The main drawback of such methods is that they are bound to a specific compression standard and any transcoding to a different format would destroy the watermark.

The goal of this chapter is to compare the performances of three different proposed video watermarking schemes in the spatial, DCT and Wavelet domain. A lot of research has been done lately in developing new and improved watermarking techniques, but there is a difficulty in comparing the research results, because independent researchers use very different watermarks, watermark capacity, test videos, parameters for watermark embedding and extraction and attacks with different parameters to test the robustness of their schemes. There is a need to compare the watermarking methods in different domains. Our chapter addresses this issue by proposing three approaches in the spatial, DCT and Wavelet domain that have similar specifications, like watermark, watermark capacity, test videos, attacks with the same parameters. All approaches embed the same watermark (binary image) with spatial and temporal redundancy and use a blind method for watermark extraction.

The rest of this chapter is organized as follows: Section 2 describes the three proposed video watermarking techniques, providing detailed diagrams and description of the watermark embedding and extraction strategies. Section 3 contains the experimental results and a detailed comparison of the proposed methods in terms of perceptual quality and robustness to different attacks. Finally, Section 4 presents the conclusions of our work and possible future research.

2. Proposed "Spread-Quantization" video watermarking techniques

This section presents our watermarking schemes in the spatial, Discrete Cosine Transform (DCT) and Wavelet domain. First we will summarize some common properties of the proposed algorithms and then, in Subsections 2.1 to 2.3 the detailed embedding and extraction schemes will be presented for every method.

The proposed watermarking techniques are a combination of spread-spectrum and quantization based watermarking. That is why we call them "spread-quatization" techniques.

Our methods embed the watermark into the luminance values of the pixels or into some selected coefficients in a transform domain, thus all algorithms will first do a conversion of the RGB (Red, Green, Blue) color space into the YC_bC_r (ITU-R BT.601) color space, as shown in Equation (1):

$$\begin{aligned} Y &= 0.257R + 0.504G + 0.098B + 16 \\ C_b &= -0.148R - 0.291G + 0.439B + 128 \\ C_r &= 0.439R + 0.368G - 0.071B + 128 \end{aligned} \tag{1}$$

After the watermark embedding, the video is converted back to the RGB format using Equation (2):

$$\begin{aligned} R &= 1.164(Y-16)+1.596(C_r-128) \\ G &= 1.164(Y-16)-0.813(C_r-128)-0.391(C_b-128) \\ B &= 1.164(Y-16)+2.018(C_b-128) \end{aligned} \tag{2}$$

To improve the resilience of the proposed algorithms to attacks, two protection mechanisms are used:

- The watermark is coded using a low complexity error correction code (m,n), where n is the dataword length and m is the codeword length. Using the error correction code, the useful size of the watermark will be m/n times smaller in comparison to the case when no error correction code is used.
- The same watermark is redundantly embedded in a number of k frames. Thus, the useful size of the watermark will be k times smaller, but the resilience to attacks is improved. At the watermark decoder, after extracting the watermark sequence w_i' of size P' bits from every frame of a number of k frames, a bit of the useful watermark $w'(j)$ is computed using Equation (3).

$$w'(j) = \begin{cases} 0, & \text{if } \sum_{i=1}^{k} w_i'(j) \le \frac{k}{2} \\ 1, & \text{if } \sum_{i=1}^{k} w_i'(j) > \frac{k}{2} \end{cases}, \quad j \in \{1,2,\ldots,P'\} \tag{3}$$

2.1 Video watermarking scheme in the spatial domain

The watermark embedding process, illustrated in Fig. 1, is described in the following steps:

1. The original video is partitioned into groups of k frames.
2. Every frame of the group is converted to the YC_bC_r format as in Equation (1).
3. The binary image matrix is transformed into a binary row vector w of size $P = h \times v$.
4. To protect the watermark against bit errors, a Hamming error correction code (m,n) with codeword length of m bits and data-word length of n bits is applied to the vector w. The size of the resulting watermark vector w_c is:

$$P' = P\frac{m}{n} \tag{4}$$

The binary sequence w_c is partitioned into a number of $\frac{F}{k}$ sequences $w_c(j)$ of size $P'\frac{k}{F}$, where $j = \overline{1,\frac{F}{k}}$, F is the number of frames of the video and k is the number of redundant frames. The dimensions h and v of the watermark are chosen so that $P'\frac{k}{F}$ is an integer. The same sequence $w_c(j)$ will be inserted into every frame of a group j of k frames.

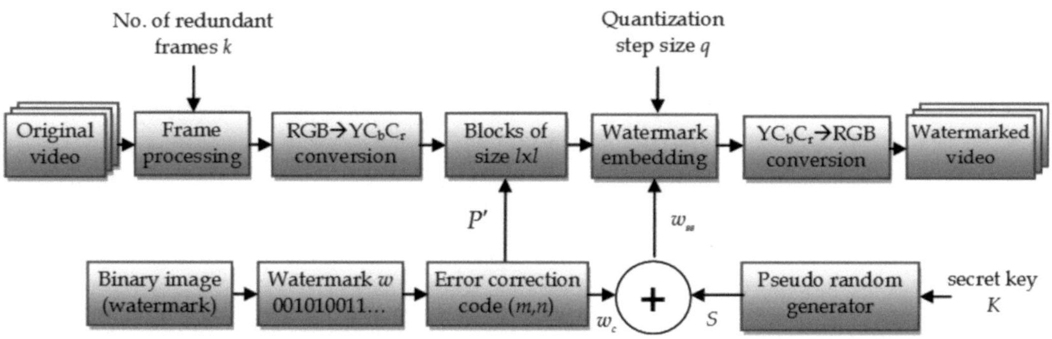

Fig. 1. Block diagram of the spatial watermark encoder

5. The size l of a square bloc of $l \times l$ luminance values is calculated to embed a bit of the watermark:

$$l = \left[\sqrt{\frac{MNC}{P'k}} \right] \tag{5}$$

where [.] is the integer part operator.

6. A spread-spectrum technique is used to spread the power spectrum of the watermark data, thus, increasing its robustness against attacks. First a binary pseudo-random sequence $S = \{ s_r | s_r \in \{0,1\}, r = 1,...,l^2 \}$ of size l^2 with equal number of zeros and ones is generated using the Mersenne-Twister algorithm proposed in (Matsumoto & Nishimura, 1998) with the use of the last 64 bits of the secret key K as seed for the generator. This method generates numbers with a period of $(2^{19937} - 1)/2$.
7. For every bit of the watermark $w_c(j)$, the corresponding spread spectrum sequence is:

$$w_{ss} = \begin{cases} [s_1, s_2, ..., s_{l^2}], \text{ if } w_c = 0 \\ [\overline{s}_1, \overline{s}_2, ..., \overline{s}_{l^2}], \text{ if } w_c = 1 \end{cases} \tag{6}$$

8. A sequence S (representing one bit of the original watermark) is embedded in every bloc of $l \times l$ luminance values.
9. A bit of S is embedded into the luminance value of the pixel of the same index by rounding its value to an even or odd quantization level. Rounding to an even quantization level embeds a "0", while rounding to an odd quantization level embeds a "1", as shown in Equation 6:

$$L_w(i,j) = \left[\frac{L}{2q} \right] \cdot 2q + q \cdot w \cdot sign\left(L(i,j) - \left[\frac{L(i,j)}{2q} \right] \cdot 2q \right), \tag{7}$$

where $L(i,j)$ is the original luminance value, $L_w(i,j)$ is the watermarked luminance value, q is the quantization step size and $sign()$ is defined as:

$$sign(x)=\begin{cases}-1, & if\ x\le 0\\ 1, & if\ x>0\end{cases} \tag{8}$$

Wat. bit	Pseudo-random sequence S	Spread spectrum watermark $w_{ss}=S\oplus w$	Quant. step size	Original luminance block	Watermarked luminance block
w=0	$\begin{bmatrix}0&1&1&0\\1&0&1&0\\0&1&0&1\\1&1&0&0\end{bmatrix}$	$\begin{bmatrix}0&1&1&0\\1&0&1&0\\0&1&0&1\\1&1&0&0\end{bmatrix}$	q=4	$\begin{bmatrix}224&75&86&20\\62&45&12&123\\45&5&68&74\\145&59&247&23\end{bmatrix}$	$\begin{bmatrix}224&76&84&24\\60&48&12&120\\48&4&72&76\\148&60&248&24\end{bmatrix}$
w=1		$\begin{bmatrix}1&0&0&1\\0&1&0&1\\1&0&1&0\\0&0&1&1\end{bmatrix}$			$\begin{bmatrix}228&72&88&20\\64&44&16&124\\44&8&68&72\\144&56&244&20\end{bmatrix}$

Table 1. Example of embedding a watermark bit into a block of 4x4 luminance pixels

10. The video is converted back to the RGB format using Equation 2, obtaining the watermark video.

The choice of the quantization step q is a tradeoff between the perceptual quality of the watermarked video (q must have a small value) and the resilience of the watermarking scheme to attacks (q must have a big value). An example of embedding a watermark bit into a block of 4x4 pixels is given in Table 1.

The watermark extraction process, shown in Fig. 2, implies the following steps:

1. The watermarked video is partitioned into groups of k frames.
2. Every frame of the group is converted to the YC_bC_r format using Equation 1.
3. Every luminance frame is partitioned into square blocks of $l\times l$ luminance values.
4. A bit of the spread spectrum sequence w_{ss}' of size l^2 is extracted from every luminance value of a block of size $l\times l$ using Equation (9):

$$w'=\mathrm{mod}2\left(round\left(\frac{L_w(i,j)}{q}\right)\right), \tag{9}$$

   where w' is the extracted watermark bit, $L_w(i,j)$ is the luminance value of the pixel at position (i,j), q is the quantization step size and *mod2* is the modulo2 function.
5. Using the 64 bit seed from the secret key K the binary sequence S is generated locally.
6. The extracted watermark bit for the corresponding block is:

$$w_b'=\begin{cases}0, & \text{if } \sum_{r=1}^{l^2}\left|w_{ss,r}'-s_r\right|\le\frac{l^2}{2}\\ 1, & \text{if } \sum_{r=1}^{l^2}\left|w_{ss,r}'-s_r\right|>\frac{l^2}{2}\end{cases} \tag{10}$$

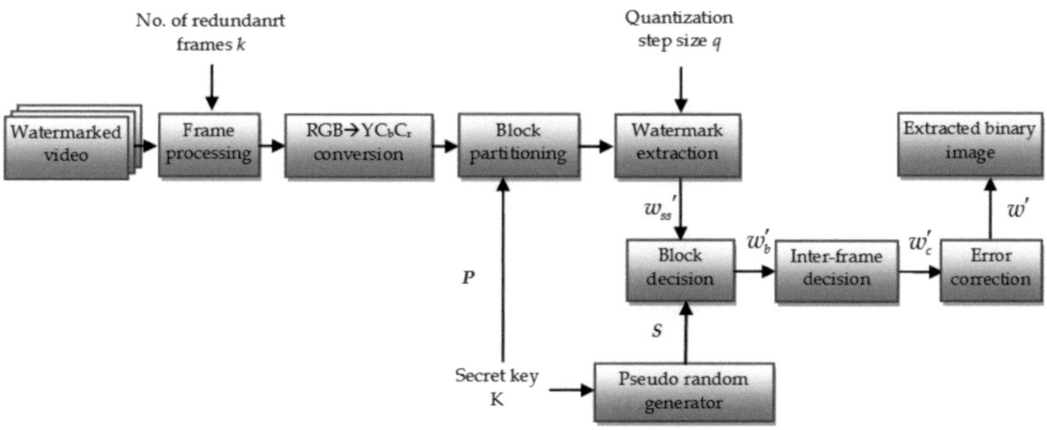

Fig. 2. Block diagram of the spatial watermark decoder

7. A binary sequence $w'_{c,i}(j)$ is extracted from every frame of a group of k frames, where $i = \overline{1,k}$. The sequence $w'_c(j)$ is computed from $w'_{c,i}(j)$ using Equation (11):

$$w'_c(j) = \begin{cases} 0, & \text{if } \sum_{i=1}^{k} w'_{c,i}(j) \le \frac{k}{2} \\ 1, & \text{if } \sum_{i=1}^{k} w'_{c,i}(j) > \frac{k}{2} \end{cases}, \quad j \in \{1,2,\ldots,P'\} \tag{11}$$

8. The resulting watermark bitstream w'_c of size P' is error corrected and the watermark w' of size P is obtained.
9. The extracted binary image is obtained by reshaping the vector w' to a matrix of size $h \times v$.

The choice of the quantization step size q is a tradeoff between the perceptual quality of the watermarked video (q should have a small value) and the resilience of the watermarking scheme to attacks (q should have a big value).

2.2 Video watermarking scheme in the Discrete Cosine Transform domain (DCT)

For this method, the watermark is redundantly inserted in the DCT domain. Compared to the previous method in the spatial domain this technique works with blocks of 8x8 luminance pixels. Every Y block is transformed into a 8x8 DCT coefficient block. To insert the watermark, only 22 DCT coefficients from every block are used, as shown in Fig. 3, where the white coefficients are ignored and only the gray coefficients are used for redundant watermark embedding. Instead of step 6 of the spatial domain embedding strategy, this algorithm calculates the number b of 8x8 DCT coefficient blocks, where the same watermark bit can be redundantly embedded, as shown in Equation (12).

$$b = \left\lfloor \frac{1}{64} \frac{MNF}{P'k} \right\rfloor \tag{12}$$

where MxN is the resolution of the video, F is the number of frames of the video, k is the number of redundant frames, P' is the watermark size after applying the error correction code and [.] is the the integer part operator.

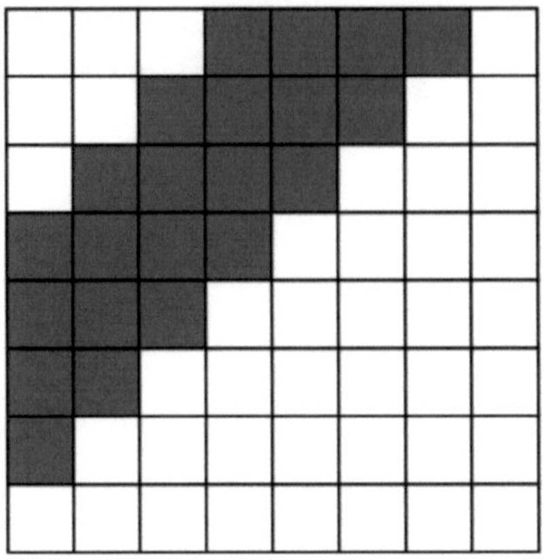

Fig. 3. DCT coefficient selection for watermark embedding

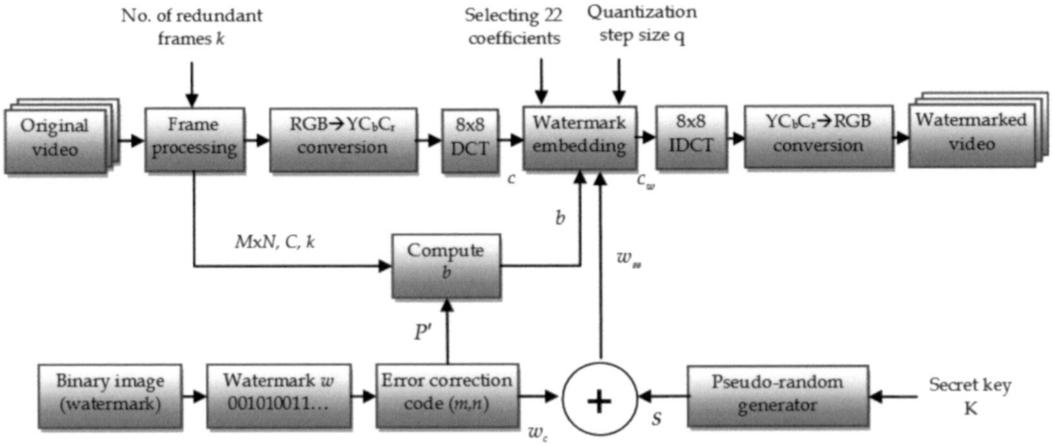

Fig. 4. Block diagram of the DCT watermark encoder

The binary pseudo-random sequence S generated using the secret key K has a fixed size, equal to the number of DCT coefficients selected from every 8x8 coefficient block.

$$S = \{s_r | s_r \in \{0,1\}, r = 1,...,22\} \quad (13)$$

The same watermark bit will be inserted in a number of 22 DCT coefficients using the spread-spectrum sequence $w_{ss}(i)$ obtained using Equation (14).

$$w_{ss} = \begin{cases} [s_1, s_2, ..., s_{22}], \text{ if } w_c = 0 \\ [\bar{s}_1, \bar{s}_2, ..., \bar{s}_{22}], \text{ if } w_c = 1 \end{cases} \quad (14)$$

Every coefficient of index i is quantized to an even or odd number of quantization step sizes according to the value of the bit $w_{ss}(i)$, using Equation (15). The watermark embedding process is illustrated in Fig. 4.

$$c_w(i) = \left[\frac{c(i)}{2q}\right] \cdot 2q + q \cdot w_{ss}(i) \cdot sign\left(c(i) - \left[\frac{c(i)}{2q}\right] \cdot 2q\right), \; i = 1,2,...,22 \tag{15}$$

where $c(i)$ is the original DCT coefficient and $c_w(i)$ is the watermarked DCT coefficient.

At the decoder side (Fig. 5) first the number b of DCT coefficient blocks is calculated. From every coefficient selected according to Fig. 3 a bit is extracted using Equation (16), resulting in a sequence $w'_{ss}(j)$ of 22 bits from every block.

$$w' = \mathrm{mod}2\left(round\left(\frac{c_w}{q}\right)\right) \tag{16}$$

The spread-spectrum sequence w''_{ss} corresponding to an inserted watermark bit is obtained from b blocks of coefficients as in Equation (17).

$$w''_{ss,r} = \begin{cases} 0, & \text{if } \sum_{j=1}^{b} w'_{ss,r}(j) \le \frac{b}{2} \\ 1, & \text{if } \sum_{j=1}^{b} w'_{ss,r}(j) > \frac{b}{2} \end{cases}, \quad r \in \{1,2,\ldots,22\} \tag{17}$$

Then the pseudo-random bit sequence S is locally generated using the secret key K. The extracted watermark bit w_b' corresponding to a group of b coefficient blocks is computed in Equation (18).

$$w_b' = \begin{cases} 0, & \text{if } \sum_{r=1}^{22} \left|w''_{ss,r} - s_r\right| \le 11 \\ 1, & \text{if } \sum_{r=1}^{22} \left|w''_{ss,r} - s_r\right| > 11 \end{cases} \tag{18}$$

A binary sequence $w'_b(j)$ is extracted from every frame of a group of k frames, with $j = 1,2,...,k$. Every bit of the sequence w'_c corresponding to a group of k frames is determined using Equation (19):

$$w'_c(i) = \begin{cases} 0, & \text{if } \sum_{j=1}^{k} w'_b(j) \le \frac{k}{2} \\ 1, & \text{if } \sum_{j=1}^{k} w'_b(j) > \frac{k}{2} \end{cases}, \quad i = 1,2,\ldots,P' \tag{19}$$

The bit sequence $w'_c(i)$ is then error corrected obtaining the extracted watermark sequence w'.

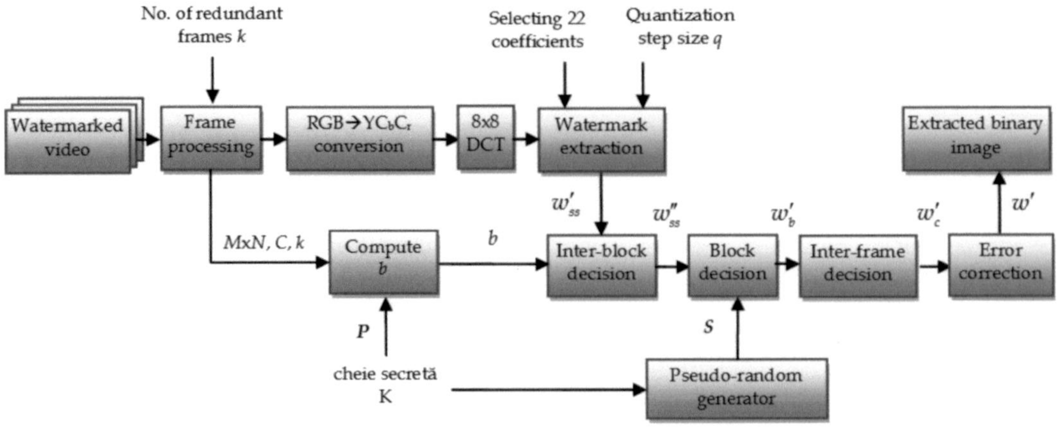

Fig. 5. Block diagram of the DCT watermark decoder

2.3 Video watermarking scheme in the wavelet domain

For this method the watermark is embedded in the selected wavelet coefficients of the luminance Y of every frame of the video. The wavelet decomposition of the luminance is done using the 2D Discrete Wavelet Transform. We have chosen a Wavelet decomposition on L=3 resolution levels. The watermark is embedded in the wavelet coefficients of the LH, HL and HH sub-bands of the second Wavelet decomposition level. The choice of the second decomposition level is a tradeoff between the invisibility of the watermark and the resilience to attacks. A watermark embedded in the wavelet coefficients of the LH_1, HL_1 and HH_1 sub-bands is very sensitive to attacks, because these sub-bands contain the finest details of the frame. On the other hand, if we embed the watermark in the LH_3, HL_3 and HH_3 sub-bands, the perceptual quality of the video will be significantly altered. For these reasons, the best choice for watermark embedding is the second wavelet decomposition level. Fig. 6 shows the sub-bands (gray color) selected for watermark embedding.

For videos of resolution $M \times N$, the number of selected wavelet coefficients for a frame is:

$$C = 3\frac{MN}{2^{2(L-1)}} \tag{20}$$

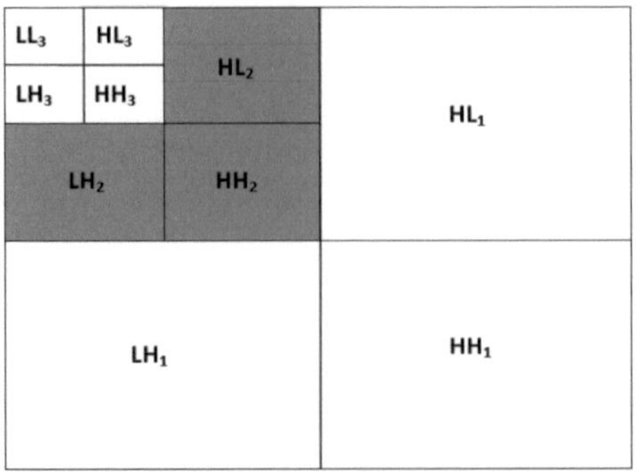

Fig. 6. Wavelet sub-bands selected for watermark embedding

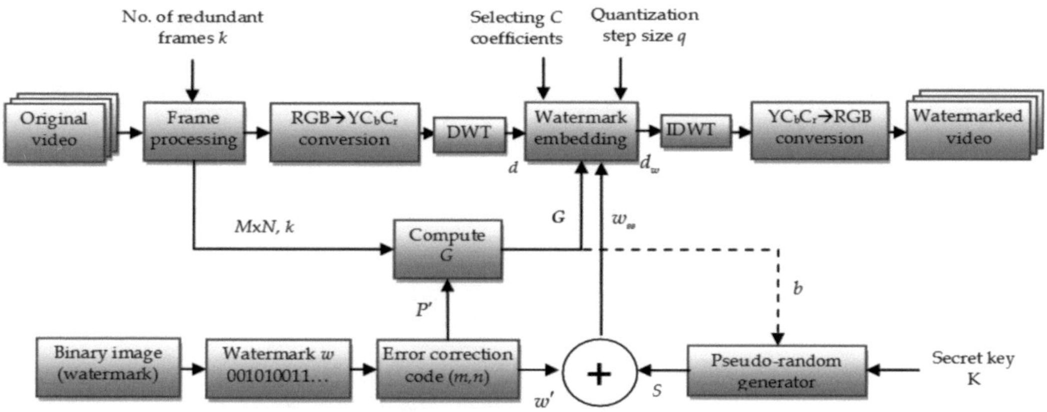

Fig. 7. Block diagram of the wavelet watermark encoder

The maximum capacity of the watermarking scheme is $C' = FC$ where F is the number of video frames and can be achieved by embedding a watermark bit in every selected wavelet coefficient. For example, for CIF videos of resolution 352x288 and 30 frames/s, the maximum capacity is 556kb/s. This maximum capacity is not needed in most applications, thus we will reduce it to improve the robustness of the scheme. Fig. 7 shows the block diagram of our Wavelet based watermark embedding scheme and is described in the following steps:

1. The binary image matrix is transformed into a binary row vector w of size $P = h \times v$.
2. To protect the watermark against bit errors, a Hamming error correction code with codeword length of m bits and dataword length of n bits is applied to vector w. The size of the resulting watermark vector w' is:

$$P' = P\frac{m}{n} \tag{21}$$

3. A same spread-spectrum technique is used to spread the power spectrum of the watermark data, thus, increasing its robustness against attacks. First the binary pseudorandom code sequence $S = \{s_j | s_j \in \{0,1\}, j = 0,1,...,G\}$ with equal number of zeros and ones is generated using the Mersenne-Twister algorithm with the use of 64 bits of the secret key K as seed for the generator. For every bit of the watermark w', the corresponding spread spectrum sequence is:

$$w_{ss}(i) = \begin{cases} [s_1, s_2, ..., s_G], & if\ w'(i) = 0 \\ [\bar{s}_1, \bar{s}_2, ..., \bar{s}_G], & if\ w'(i) = 1 \end{cases}, \quad i = 1, ..., P' \tag{22}$$

4. Every sequence $w_{ss}(i)$ (representing one bit of the original watermark) is embedded into a number G of wavelet coefficients, every bit of $w_{ss}(i)$ in a wavelet coefficient. The number G depends on the number C of the selected wavelet coefficients, the number of frames F of the original video and the size P' of the watermark:

$$G = \left[\frac{C \cdot F}{P'}\right] \tag{23}$$

where [.] is the integer part operator.

5. A bit of the binary sequence S is embedded in the selected wavelet coefficient by rounding its value to an even or odd quantization level. Rounding to an even quantization level embeds a "0", while rounding to an odd quantization level embeds a "1", as shown in Equation (5):

$$d_w = \left[\frac{d}{2q}\right] \cdot 2q + q \cdot w \cdot sign\left(d - \left[\frac{d}{2q}\right] \cdot 2q \right), \tag{24}$$

where d is the original wavelet coefficient, d_w is the watermarked wavelet coefficient and q is the quantization step size.

6. After the entire watermark has been embedded, the 2D Inverse Discrete Wavelet Transform is computed for every frame to obtain the watermarked video.

The watermark extraction process, shown in Fig. 8, implies the following steps:

1. Wavelet decomposition of the watermarked, possibly attacked video;
2. Selection of the wavelet coefficients used for embedding;
3. Computation of the parameter G using the information about the size of the watermark provided by the secret key K;
4. From every coefficient selected according to Fig. 6 a bit is extracted according to Equation (25), resulting in a sequence $w'_{ss}(j)$ of G bits from every group.

$$w' = \mathrm{mod}_2\left(round\left(\frac{d_w}{q} \right) \right), \tag{25}$$

where d_w is the watermarked wavelet coefficient.

5. Using the 64 bit seed from the secret key K the binary sequence S of size G is generated.
6. The extracted watermark bit $w''(i)$ corresponding to a group of G wavelet coefficients is computed in Equation (26).

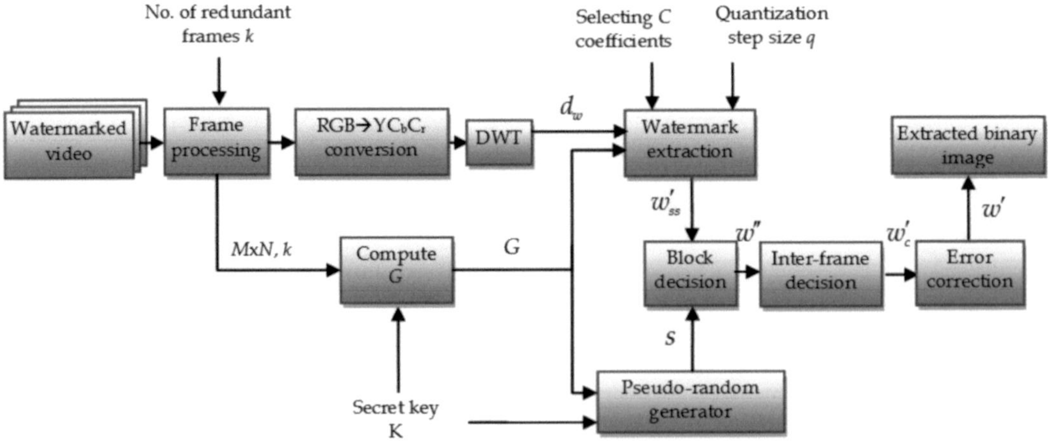

Fig. 8. Block diagram of the wavelet watermark decoder

$$w''(i) = \begin{cases} 0, if \sum_{j=1}^{G} [w'_j(i) - s_j] \leq \frac{G}{2} \\ 1, if \sum_{j=1}^{G} [w'_j(i) - s_j] > \frac{G}{2} \end{cases}, i = 1, ..., P' \tag{26}$$

7. The resulting watermark bitstream of size P' is error corrected and the watermark w' of size P is obtained.
8. The extracted binary image is obtained by reshaping the vector w' to a matrix of size $h \times v$.

To improve the resilience of the algorithm against temporal attacks we embedded the same watermark redundantly in every *k* frames. Thus, the number of wavelet coefficients used for embedding a watermark bit is decreased from G to *G/k*.

3. Comparison of the proposed "Spread-Quantization" video watermarking techniques

The simulation results were conducted on the first 27 frames of the videos "stefan", "forman" and "bus" in RGB uncompressed avi format, of resolution 352x288 (Common Intermediate Format), 24 bits/pixel and frame rate of 30 frames/s. The binary image used as watermark is shown in Fig. 9. The resolution of the image depends on the error correction code used, the number of redundant frames and the resolution of the initial video.

Fig. 9. Binary image used as watermark

We have conducted the experiments for every proposed method using the quantization step sizes $q = 2$, $q = 4$ and $q = 8$, no redundant frame embedding, embedding of the same watermark in $k = 3$ and $k = 9$ frames, without using an error correction code and using a Hamming (7,4) error correction code.

First we wanted to test the perceptual quality of the watermarked videos. To compare the watermarked video with the original one, we computed the mean Peak Signal to Noise Ration (PSNR) of all frames of the video.

$$PSNR = \frac{\sum_{i=1}^{F} PSNR(i)}{F} \tag{27}$$

where F is the number of frames of the video.

The PSNR results are shown in Fig. 10. We can see that the best quality for every quantization step size chosen is obtained using the Wavelet approach, followed by the DCT and the spatial method. The PSNR results for the spatial watermarking scheme are quite low for quantization with bigger quantization step sizes (for $q = 4$ and $q = 8$ below the accepted

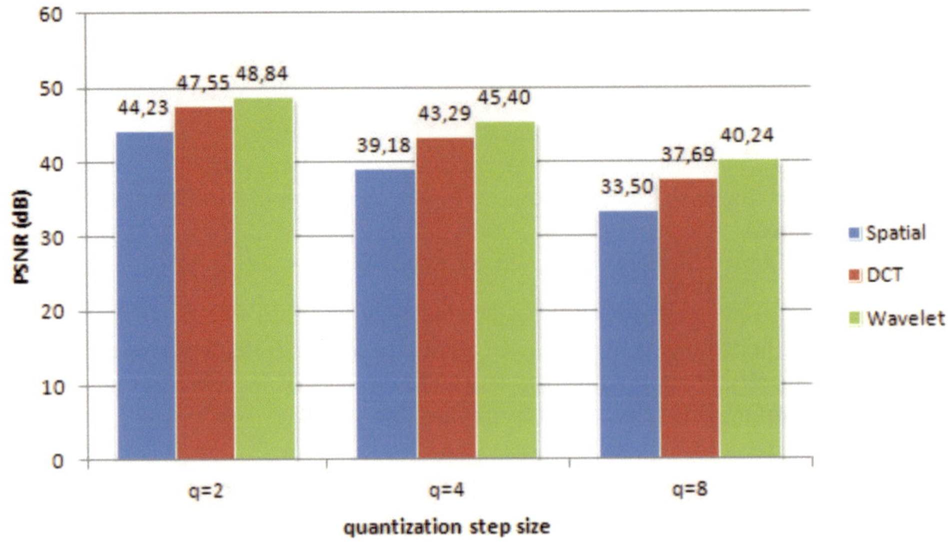

Fig. 10. PSNR values for the three proposed methods for different quantization step sizes

value of 40 dB). For $q = 8$ only the wavelet based technique achieves a PSNR value higher than 40 dB.

For a visual comparison, Figure 11 shows the fifth frame of the original stefan video and the corresponding watermarked frames for the three proposed methods using the quantization step sizes $q = 2$, $q = 4$ and $q = 8$.

Next, we wanted to test the robustness of the proposed watermarking schemes. For this purpose we have carried out a range of eight attacks on the watermarked videos (see Table 2). The parameters of the attacks were chosen in such a manner, that the visual degradation of the attacked videos is acceptable, because, by attacking a watermarked video, an attacker wants to destroy the watermark, but not the video quality.

To evaluate the robustness objectively, we have calculated the mean values of the decoding BER for the watermarks extracted from all test videos after they were attacked:

$$BER = \frac{1}{P}\sum_{j=1}^{P}\left|w_{out}(j) - w_{in}(j)\right|, \tag{28}$$

where w_{out} is the extracted watermark, w_{in} is the original watermark and P is the size of the watermark. We have plotted 9 different graphs (Fig. 12 - 20), where we represented the mean decoding BER for every method and every attack. The variables are the quantization step size q (chosen 2, 4 and 8) and the number of frames k used for embedding the same watermark (chosen 1, 3 and 9). For $q = 2$ no error correction code was used, because the corresponding BER values are quite high and the Hamming (7,4) error correction would not work for such high bit error rates. For $q = 4$ and $q = 8$, where the BER values are lower, we used the Hamming (7,4) error coreection code, which can correct single bit errors.

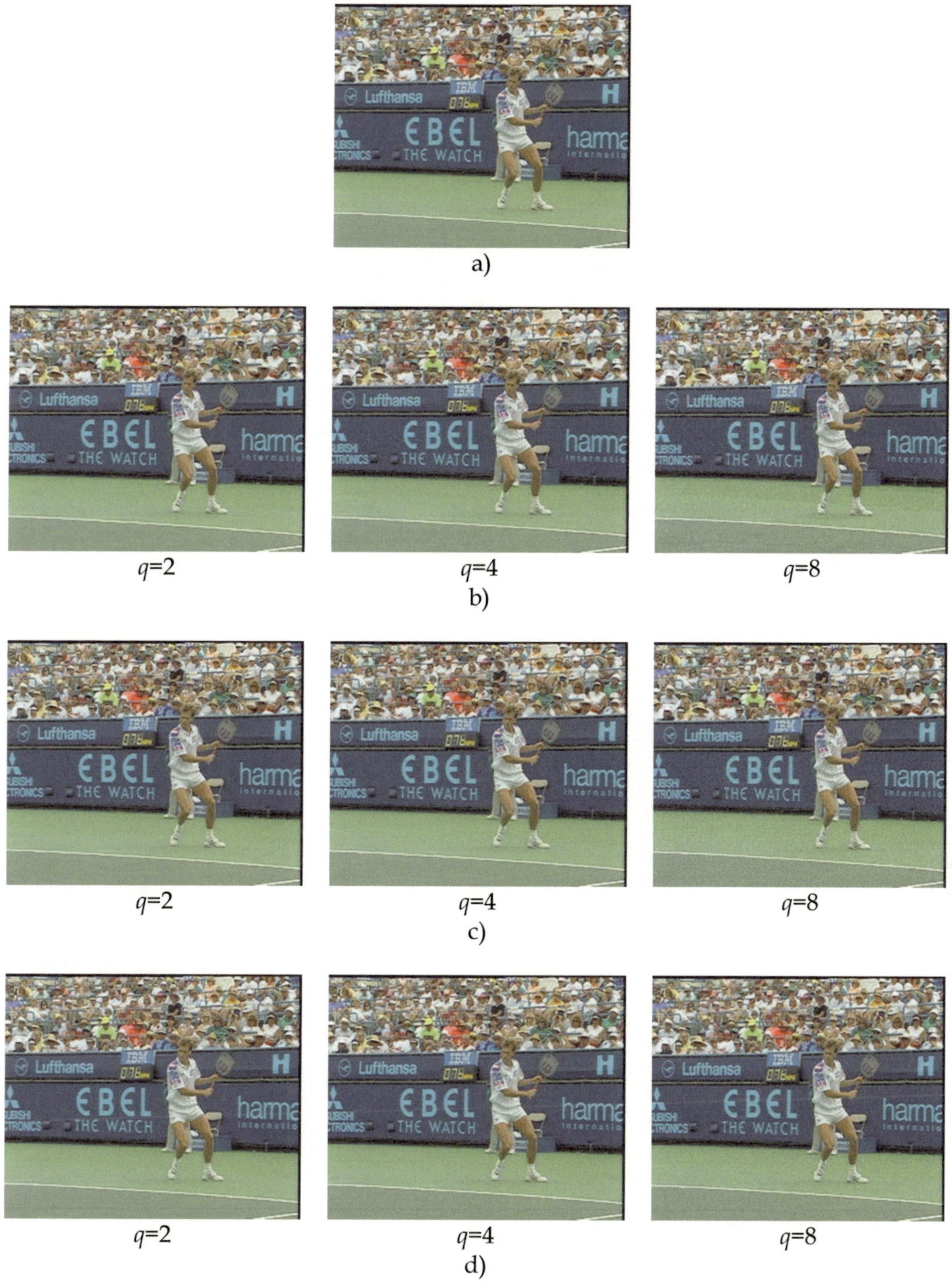

Fig. 11. Visual comparion of the proposed methods. The fifth frame of a) the original "stefan" video, b) the watermarked video using the spatial approach, c) the watermarked video using the DCT approach and d) the watermarked video using the Wavelet approach

Attack	Parameters
Blurring	blocks of 2x2 pixels
Brightening	adding Y_0=6 to the luminance of every pixel
Addition of Gaussian noise	mean 0 and variance 0,0003
Median filtering	using a 3x3 pixel neighborhood
Addition of "salt and pepper" noise	density 0,3%
Frame averaging	20% of the frames were averaged, where the current frame is the mean of the previous, current and next frame of the video
JPEG compression of every frame	quality factor Q=60
MPEG-2 compression	4 Mbps
MPEG-2 compression	2 Mbps

Table 2. Attacks against the watermarking schemes

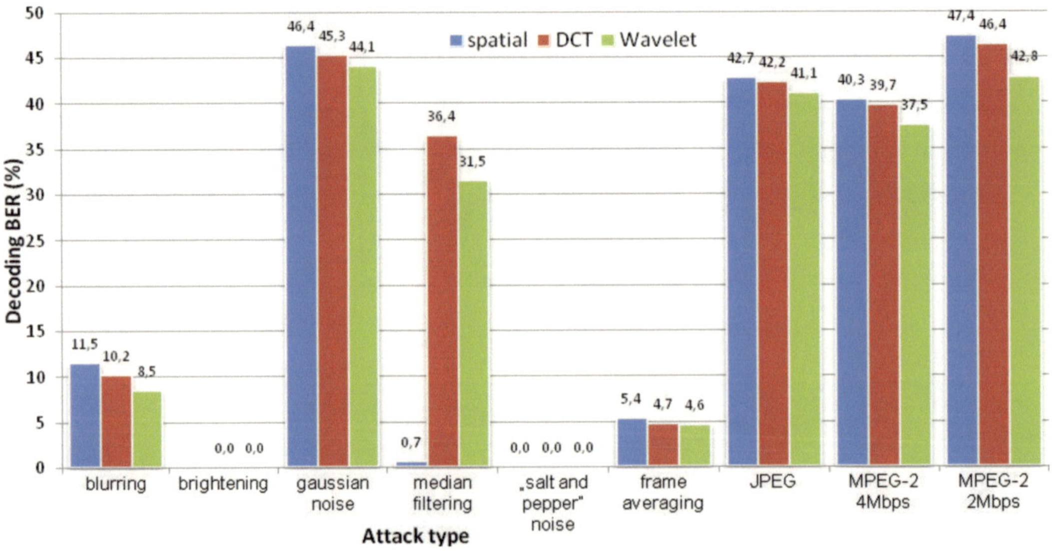

Fig. 12. Comparison of the decoding BER (%) for the proposed methods using $q = 2$, no redundant frame embedding and no error correction code

The method working in the spatial domain is very vulnerable to the brightening attack. For example by adding Y=6 to every luminance value, the decoding BER is 100% for every combination of parameters. We didn't represent this value on the graphs, because we didn't want to scale all BER values to 100%. On the other hand, the spatial embedding method has the best resilience to median filtering attacks. The DCT based technique is more vulnerable to the median filtering attack than the other two methods.

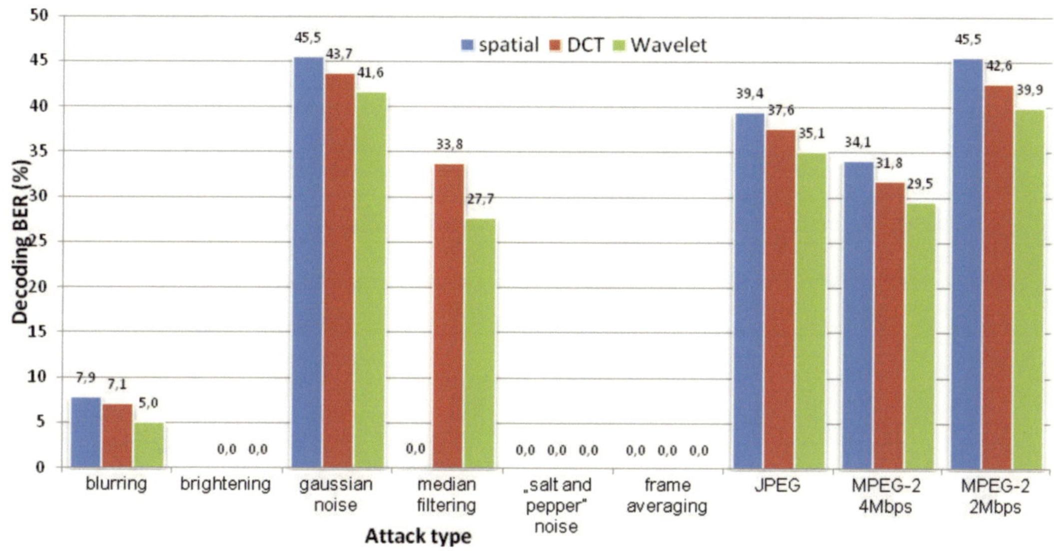

Fig. 13. Comparison of the decoding BER (%) for the proposed methods using $q = 2$, $k = 3$ and no error correction code

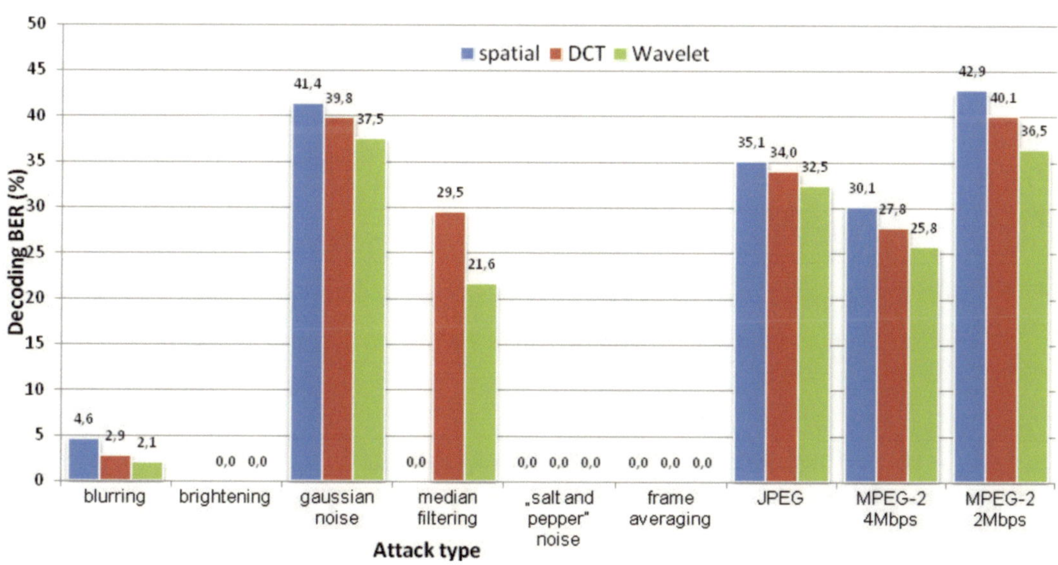

Fig. 14. Comparison of the decoding BER (%) for the proposed methods using $q = 2$, $k = 9$ and no error correction code

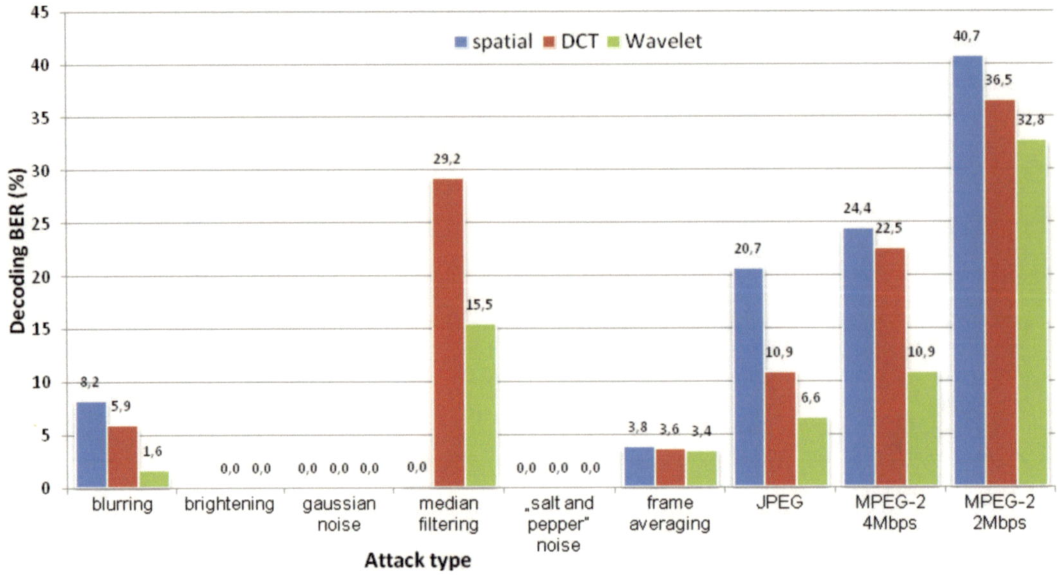

Fig. 15. Comparison of the decoding BER (%) for the proposed methods using $q = 4$, no redundant frame embedding and the Hamming (7,4) error correction code

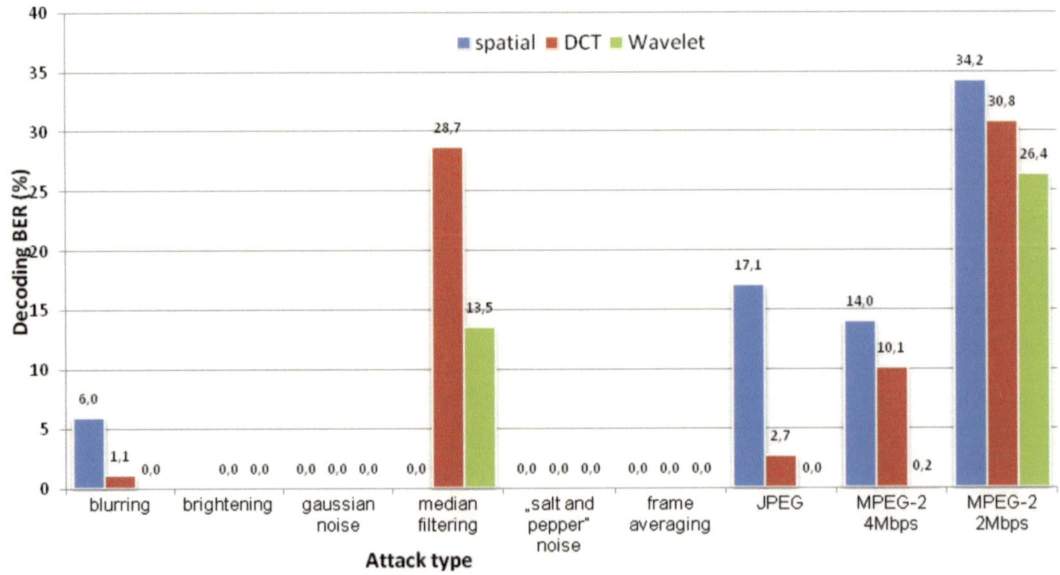

Fig. 16. Comparison of the decoding BER (%) for the proposed methods using $q = 4$, $k = 3$ and the Hamming (7,4) error correction code

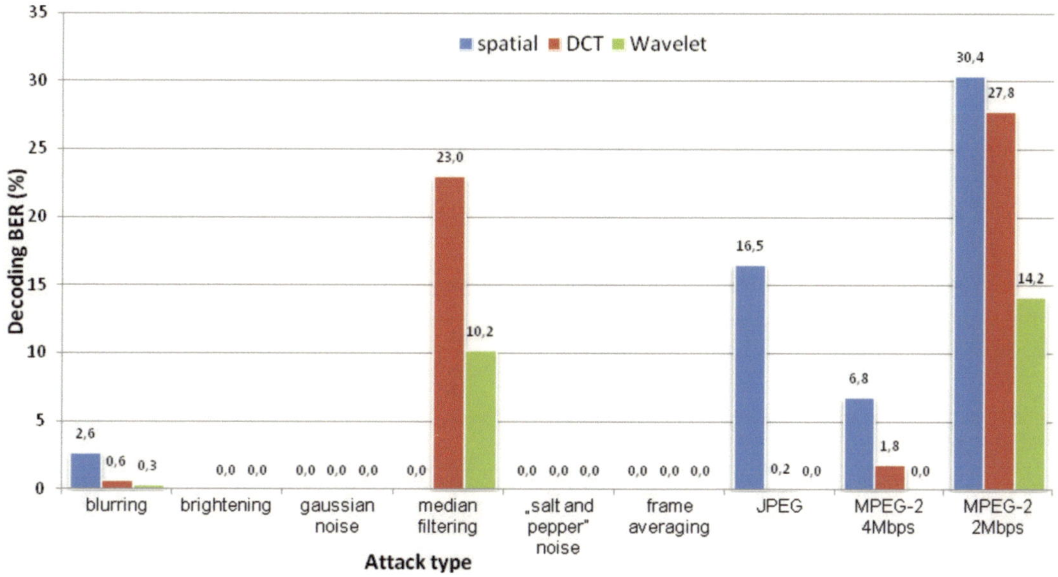

Fig. 17. Comparison of the decoding BER (%) for the proposed methods using $q = 4$, $k = 9$ and the Hamming (7,4) error correction code

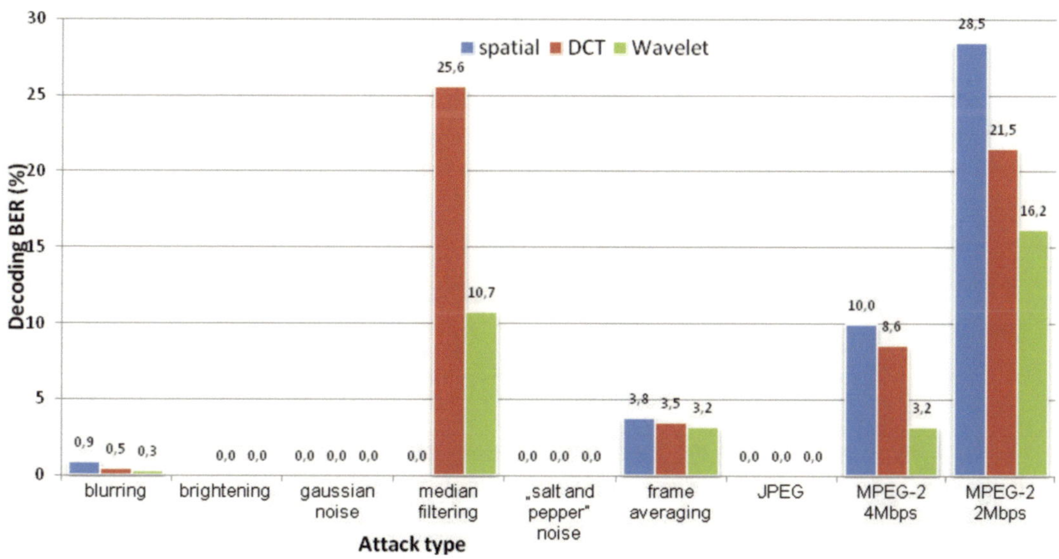

Fig. 18. Comparison of the decoding BER (%) for the proposed methods using $q = 8$, no redundant frame embedding and the Hamming (7,4) error correction code

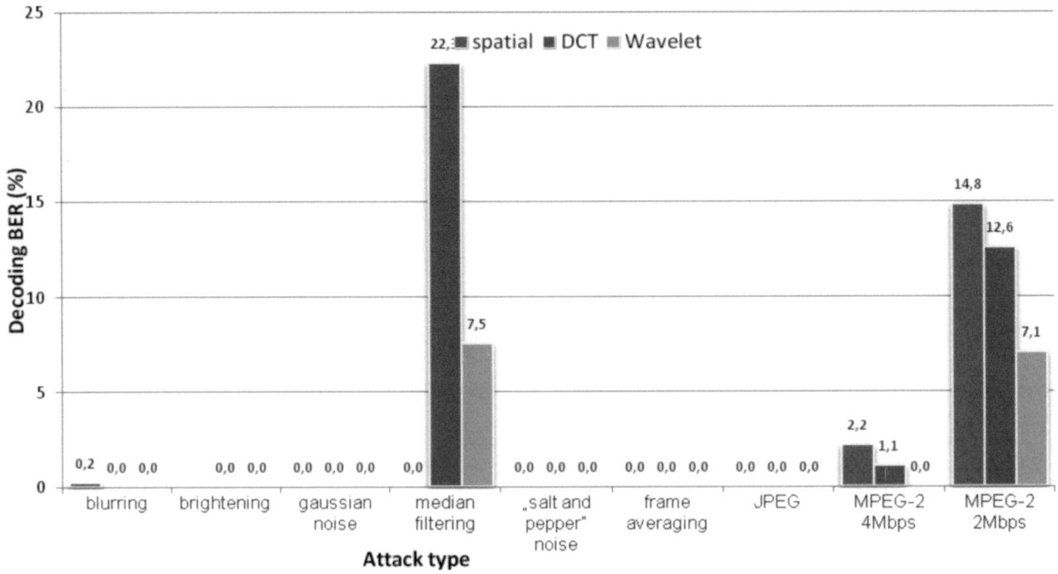

Fig. 19. Comparison of the decoding BER (%) for the proposed methods using $q = 8$, $k = 3$ and the Hamming (7,4) error correction code

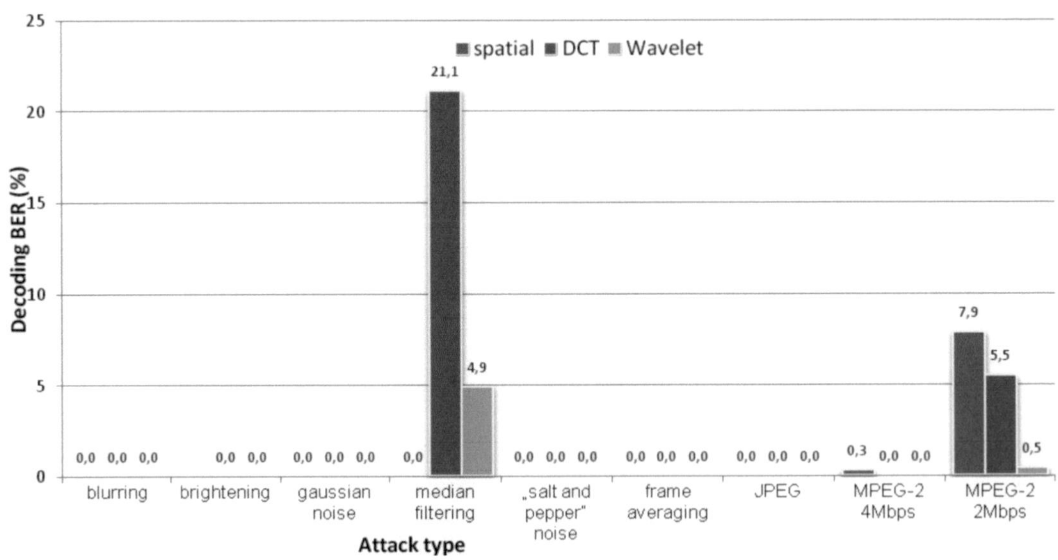

Fig. 20. Comparison of the decoding BER (%) for the proposed methods using $q = 8$, $k = 9$ and the Hamming (7,4) error correction code

Method	Original watermark	Blurr	Brighten	Gaussian noise	Median filtering
spatial	©PREDA	©PREDA	©PREDA	©PREDA	©PREDA
DCT	©PREDA	©PREDA	©PREDA	©PREDA	©PREDA
Wavelet	©PREDA	©PREDA	©PREDA	©PREDA	©PREDA

Method	Salt and pepper noise	Frame averaging	JPEG Q=60	MPEG-2 4 Mbps	MPEG-2 2 Mbps
spatial	©PREDA	©PREDA	©PREDA	©PREDA	[illegible]
DCT	©PREDA	©PREDA	©PREDA	©PREDA	©PREDA
Wavelet	©PREDA	©PREDA	©PREDA	©PREDA	©PREDA

Table 3. Watermarks extracted from the watermarked "stefan" video after various attacks for $q = 4$, $k = 3$ and Hamming (7,4) error correction

Method	Original watermark	Blurr	Brighten	Gaussian noise	Median filtering
spatial	©PREDA	©PREDA	©PREDA	©PREDA	©PREDA
DCT	©PREDA	©PREDA	©PREDA	©PREDA	©PREDA
Wavelet	©PREDA	©PREDA	©PREDA	©PREDA	©PREDA

Method	Salt and pepper noise	Frame averaging	JPEG Q=60	MPEG-2 4 Mbps	MPEG-2 2 Mbps
spatial	©PREDA	©PREDA	©PREDA	©PREDA	©PREDA
DCT	©PREDA	©PREDA	©PREDA	©PREDA	©PREDA
Wavelet	©PREDA	©PREDA	©PREDA	©PREDA	©PREDA

Table 4. Watermarks extracted from the watermarked "stefan" video after various attacks for $q = 8$, $k = 3$ and Hamming (7,4) error correction

The best overall resilience is achieved by the method working in the wavelet domain, being the only technique with perfect decoding of the watermark for $q = 8$, $k = 9$ and Hamming (7,4) error correction. The second most resilient method is the DCT techniques, followed by the spatial technique.

Tables 3 and 4 contain the watermarks extracted after each attack from the video sequence "stefan", using the three different approaches, k=3 redundant frames, Hamming (7,4) error correction code, $q = 4$ and $q = 8$, respectively. These tables show the advantage of using a binary image as watermark. We can see that the extracted watermarks can be identified easily for bit error rates below approximately 15%.

4. Conclusion

In this chapter we have compared three blind "spread quantization" video watermarking techniques in the spatial, DCT and wavelet domain. The original watermark and the original, unwatermarked videos are not required for the watermark extraction process. The methods are combinations of spread-spectrum and quantization based techniques. All three schemes embed the watermark in the luminance channel or in the transform coefficients of the luminance. The watermarks used are binary images, containing the copyright information. The watermark is protected against singular bit errors using a Hamming error correction code.

The spatial domain technique embeds a watermark bit by spreading it in a luminance block. The actual embedding into a luminance value is done using a quantization based approach.

The DCT domain technique spreads the same watermark bit into a number of 8x8 DCT blocks. In every DCT block only 22 middle frequency DCT coefficients are used for embedding. The wavelet based technique embeds the same watermark bit into a number of detail wavelet coefficients of the middle wavelet sub-bands.

The resilience of the schemes is improved by redundantly embedding the same watermark in a number of k video frames.

We have tested the perceptual quality of the watermarked videos and the resilience of the schemes to eight different attacks in the spatial, temporal and compressed domain, for different quantization step sizes and different number of redundant frames.

The experimental results show, that the wavelet domain technique achieves the highest video quality and the best robustness to most attacks, followed by the DCT and spatial domain techniques. The spatial domain method is most vulnerable to the brightening attack and the DCT method to the median filtering attack. The wavelet based technique achieves very good overall scores, being the best candidate for robust video watermarking.

Future research directions include the improvement of our wavelet based watermarking techniques in terms of robustness to the proposed attacks, but also to other temporal and geometric attacks. The quality of the watermarked videos could also be improved by using a Human Visual System (HVS) approach. These techniques are usually time consuming and a tradeoff has to be made between the perceptual quality of the watermarked videos and the arithmetical complexity of the scheme.

5. References

Altun, H. O.; Orsdemir, A.; Sharma, G.; Bocko, M. F. (February 2009). Optimal Spread Spectrum Watermark Embedding via a Multistep Feasibility Formulation, *IEEE Transactions on Image Processing*, vol. 18, no. 2, pp. 371-387

Barni, M.; Bartolini, F. & Piva, A. (2001). Improved wavelet-based watermarking through pixel-wise masking, *IEEE Transactions on Image Processing*, vol. 10, no. 5, pp. 783-791

Biswas, S.; Das, S.R. & Petriu, E.M. (2005). An adaptive compressed MPEG-2 video watermarking scheme, *IEEE Transactions on Instrumentation and Measurement*, vol. 54, no. 5, pp. 1853-1861

Celik, M.U.; Lemma, A.N., Katzenbeisser, S., van der Veen, M. (September 2008). Lookup-Table-Based Secure Client-Side Embedding for Spread-Spectrum Watermarks, *IEEE Transactions on Information Forensics and Security*, vol. 3, no. 3, pp. 475-487

Chen, B. & Wornell, G. W. (May 2001). Quantization index modulation: A class of provably good methods for digital watermarking and information embedding, *IEEE Transactions on Information Theory*, vol. 47, no. 4, pp. 1423–1443

Coria, L.E.; Pickering, M.R., Nasiopoulos, P. & Ward, R.K. (September 2008). A Video Watermarking Scheme Based on the Dual-Tree Complex Wavelet Transform, *IEEE Transactions on Information Forensics and Security*, vol. 3, no. 3, pp. 466-474

Costa, M. H. M. (May 1983). Writing on dirty paper, *IEEE Transactions on Information Theory*, vol. IT-29, no. 3, pp. 439–441

Cox, I. J.; Kilian, J., Leighton, F. T. & Shamoon, T. (December 1997). Secure spread spectrum watermarking for multimedia, *IEEE Transactions on Image Processing*, vol. 6, no. 12, pp. 1673–1687

Eggers, J. J.; Bauml, R., Tzschoppe, R. & Girod, B. (2003). Scalar Costa scheme for information embedding, *IEEE Transactions On Signal Processing*, vol. 51, no. 4, pp. 1003–1019

Ellinas, J. N. & Kenterlis, P. (2006). A Wavelet-Based Watermarking Method Exploiting the Contrast Sensitivity Function, *International Journal of Signal Processing*, vol. 3, no. 4, pp. 266-272

El-Taweel, G. S.; Onsi, H. M., Samy, M. & Darwish, M.G. (2007). Secure and Non-Blind Watermarking Scheme for Color Images Based on DWT, *GVIP Special Issue on Watermarking*, 2007

Gwenael, A. D. & Dugelay, J. L. (April 2003). A guide tour of video watermarking, *Signal Processing: Image Communications*, vol. 18, no. 4, pp. 263–282

Hartung, F. & Girod, B. (May 1998). Watermarking of uncompressed and compressed video, *Signal Processing*, vol. 66, no. 3, pp. 283–301.

Jie, N. & Zhiqiang, W. (June 2009). A new public watermarking algorithm for RGB color image based on Quantization Index Modulation, *International Conference on Information and Automation, ICIA '09*, pp.837-841

Kalantari, N.K.; Ahadi, S.M. (June 2010). A Logarithmic Quantization Index Modulation for Perceptually Better Data Hiding, *IEEE Transactions on Image Processing*, vol. 19, no. 6, pp. 1504-1517

Kinoshita, H. (September 1996). An image digital signature system with ZKIP for the graph isomorphism, *Proceedings of IEEE International Conference on Image Processing*, vol. 3, Lussane, Switzerland

Liu, L.; Li, R. & Gao, Q. (August 2005). A robust video watermarking scheme based on DCT, *Proceeding of the IEEE International Conference on Machine Learning and Cybernetics*, vol. 8, pp. 5176-5180

Liu, Z.; Liang, H., Niu, X. et al. (2004). A Robust Video Watermarking in Motion Vectors, *7th International Conference on Signal Processing*, vol. 3, pp. 2358-2361

Maity, S. P. & Maity, S. (April 2009). Multistage Spread Spectrum Watermark Detection Technique Using Fuzzy Logic, *IEEE Signal Processing Letters*, vol. 16, no. 4, pp. 245-248

Matsumoto, M. & Nishimura, T., (1998). Mersenne Twister: A 623-Dimensionally Equidistributed Uniform Pseudorandom Number Generator, *ACM Transactions on Modeling and Computer Simulation*, vol. 8, no. 1, pp. 3-30

Preda, R. O. & Vizireanu, N. (2007). Blind Watermarking Capacity Analysis of MPEG2 Coded Video, *8th International Conference on Telecommunications in Modern Satellite,*

Cable and Broadcasting Services, IEEE TELSIKS 2007, Nis, Serbia and Montenegro, pp. 465-468

Preda, R. O. & Vizireanu, D. N. (2011). Robust wavelet-based video watermarking scheme for copyright protection using the human visual system, *Journal of Electronic Imaging*, vol. 20, no. 1, 013022, DOI: 10.1117/1.3558734

Reddy, A. A. & Chatterji, B. N. (2005). A new wavelet based logo-watermarking scheme, *Pattern Recognition Letters*, vol. 26, no. 7, pp. 1019-1027

Suhail, M.A. & Obaidat, M.S. (October 2003). Digital Watermarking-Based DCT and JPEG Model, *IEEE Transactions on Instrumentation & Measurement*, vol. 52, no. 5, pp. 1640-1647

Yang, C.; Huang, H. & Hsu, W. (July 2008). An adaptive video watermarking technique based on DCT domain, *8th IEEE International Conference on Computer and Information Technology, CIT 2008*, pp. 589-594

Zhang, J.; Ho, A., Qiu, G. & Marziliano, P. (February 2007). Robust video watermarking of H.264/AVC, *IEEE Transactions on Circuits and System-II: Express Briefs*, vol. 54, pp. 205–209

Zou, D.; Shi, Y.Q., Ni, Z. & Su, W. (October 2006). A Semi-Fragile Lossless Digital Watermarking Scheme Based on Integer Wavelet Transform, *IEEE Transactions on Circuits and Systems for Video Technology*, vol. 16, no. 10, pp. 1294-1300

10

AWGN Watermark in Images and E-Books – Optimal Embedding Strength

Vesna Vučković[1] and Bojan Vučković[2]
[1]*Faculty of Mathematics, University of Belgrade*
[2]*Serbian Academy of Sciences and Arts, Belgrade*
Serbia

1. Introduction

During the last twenty years, a lot of methods for grayscale images robust watermarking were proposed.

One important watermarking algorithms class is based on spread spectrum technique (Cox et al., 1997, 2008; Feng et al., 2005, 2006; Mora-Jimenez & Navia-Vazquez, 2000; Perez-Freire & Perez-Gonzalez, 2009; Ruanaidh & Pun, 1998; Ruanaidh & Csurka, 1999) - embedding by spreading the information about each message bit across several image pixels, or across the whole image. Watermark embedding in such manner is usually performed by adding of some pseudorandom data vector to the image.

Among such algorithms an interesting class form those based on additive white Gaussian noise (AWGN) embedding, with blind detection, based on correlation between image and embedded message. In (Cox et al., 2008) authors devoted a lot of space to these techniques. In our text for them we use the term *AWGN watermarks*.

Important property of digital watermark, dedicated to copyright protection, is its *robustness*. The watermark needs to remain detectable after common image operations (lossy compression, contrast/brightness changing, cropping, rotation...). In this text we call these operations (*image*) *modifications* (or *distortions*).

AWGN watermarking algorithm exhibits good robustness characteristics against many image modifications.

Clearly, **not every individual watermark embedded by robust technique - robust:** for this, it needs to be embedded **strongly enough**. However, strongly embedded watermark will damage image quality. It is important to find a real measure for embedding strength.

This is our text theme: for AWGN watermarking algorithm, **we determine** *optimal* **embedding strength** - minimal one that ensures message detectability after expected modification.

Important example is determining optimal strength if modification is lossy compression.

Namely, saving watermarked image in lossy compressed format inevitably destroys part of watermark data. That's why the big part of this text is dedicated to lossy compression.

Practically all results and derived formulas here are originally ours, and they are published already in (Vučković, 2008, 2010a, 2010b, 2011).

Sections 2-4 are dedicated to the simplest AWGN algorithm – *spatial domain* embedding. In section 2 we briefly outline AWGN watermark algorithm in spatial domain, described in (Cox et al., 2008). In section 3 we discover optimal strength for effective embedding in spatial domain. Section 4 deals with determining necessary embedding strength for message to survive the expected lossy compression.

In section 5 we consider the same algorithm within the transform domain. We show that optimal strength is equal in spatial and transform domain if watermark is embedded over the whole image. Then, we briefly speak about embedding in some image coefficients, in block DCT transform domain.

In section 6 we give a short analysis of embedding strength determining for other image modifications.

Section 7 deals with color images and e-books watermarking.

Section 8 concludes this text.

It is assumed that our text reader has some prior knowledge – especially from linear algebra, image processing – including lossy compression, and probability theory – normal distribution.

2. AWGN watermark algorithm

Here, we briefly outline AWGN watermark algorithm, as it is described in (Cox et al., 2008) (spatial domain embedding).

Later, we will analyze other variants of this algorithm too (embedding in different domains and image coefficients). However, this stays in essence the same algorithm: we add white Gaussian noise to image (or subimage) in some domain; we test the correlation in the same domain in which the watermark is embedded.

2.1 Embedding

Inputs into embedding program are the original image, the message bit and the watermark key. The *watermark key* is a secret number, same for the embedder and the detector. Embedder output is the watermarked image.

We present the grayscale image c_0, of $m \times n$ pixels, with one $m \times n$ matrix or (same in fact) with one mn vector. In this text we will use terms *image vector, image matrix* and *image* as synonyms (if this doesn't make confusion).

We embed one message bit (binary one or zero) into the image according to formulas:

$$\begin{aligned} c_{w1} &= c_0 + \alpha \cdot r_w \\ c_{w0} &= c_0 - \alpha \cdot r_w \end{aligned} \tag{1}$$

Image vectors c_{w1} and c_{w0} arise from embedding of binary one or binary zero into the image, c_0 is the original image vector before embedding, α is the embedding strength coefficient ($\alpha>0$) and r_w is the reference pattern.[1]

The *reference pattern* is pseudorandom vector chosen in accordance with N(0,1) (*standard normal distribu1tion*), of the same dimension as c_0. In its generation, watermark key is used as the pseudorandom generator seed.

2.2 Detection

Inputs to the detector are the image and the watermark key (the same as in the embedder). Its output is the detected watermark message. As a detection measure, we use a linear correlation between the image and the reference pattern:

$$\mathrm{lc}(c, r_w) = \frac{c \bullet r_w}{\|r_w\| \cdot \|r_w\|} \tag{2}$$

($\bullet$ denotes the dot product, and $\| \;\|$ - the vector norm).

The detector compares the computed linear correlation value with the threshold value τ, set in advance, and replies that it is embedded:

$$\begin{array}{llll} - & \text{binary one} & \text{if} & \mathrm{lc}(c, r_w) \geq \tau \\ - & \text{binary zero} & \text{if} & \mathrm{lc}(c, r_w) \leq -\tau \\ - & \text{nothing} & \text{if} & \left|\mathrm{lc}(c, r_w)\right| < \tau \end{array} \tag{3}$$

2.3 Embedding of longer message

We embed a k bits message into the image by repeatedly (k times) embedding one bit. We name this *embedding of message bits one over another*.

An alternative solution is *embedding into subimages*: we divide the image into disjoint subimages, and then we embed one bit message into each subimage. Under *subimage* term we mean any subset of image pixels set. Subimages may, but need not, be composed of adjacent pixels.

Different variants of the stated methods are also possible. For example, we may embed several message bits into every subimage.

2.4 Optimal embedding strength

It is not easy to produce good imperceptible digital watermark, because it needs to satisfy two opposite requests:

---

[1] More precisely, resultant values in matrices must be from permissible set of image pixels values. Therefore, it is more precise to say $c_{w1}=[c_0+\alpha \cdot r_w]_8$ and $c_{w0}=[c_0-\alpha \cdot r_w]_8$. Sign $[\;]_8$ designates "squeezing" of the result vector coordinates into 8-bits values, i.e. into values from the set {0,1,2...255}. However here, for the purpose of simplicity, we will ignore this (small!) diference.

- *Detectability* – in any case it needs to be detectable
- *Fidelity* – it needs to be imperceptible for casual observer.

These two demands are mutually confronted. If watermark is embedded stronger, then it's more likely it will be detectable. In the other hand, if watermark is strongly embedded, it will be more noticeable. Detectability is surely more important condition – "essential requirement". Thus, we need to determine *optimal* embedding strength – minimal one that guaranties detectability.

In some situations it may be expected that watermarked image will be subjected (from embedding to detection moment) to some modification. Under these circumstances it is also useful to know optimal strength – minimal one that ensures watermark detectability after this (expected) modification.

Two concepts are closely related to watermark detectability: effective and robust embedding.

Watermark is embedded *effectively* if it is detectable immediately after embedding.

If message is detectable in digital image that is after embedding subjected to some modification, we say the watermark is *robust* against undergone modification.

3. Embedding effectiveness

Embedding strength coefficient α and detection threshold τ directly influence the embedding effectiveness.

Coefficient α needs to be big enough (effective embedding), but not too big (quality request).

If we reduce the detection threshold τ (set it to be close to, or maybe equal to zero), embedding will be more effective (the detector will report in higher percent of embedding cases the image as watermarked). But, if the threshold τ is too small, the detector may reply that the image is watermarked, even when this is not true.

It is very important to find the real measure – to set the threshold τ and the coefficient α, in a way that *false negative* probabilities (non-effective embedding) and *false positive* ones (case when the detector reports that image is watermarked when this is not true) are acceptably low. Also, watermark must not be embedded too strongly to have the fidelity affected.

In subsection 3.1, we determine optimal value of coefficient α for effective embedding of one bit message. In subsection 3.2, we determine it for a longer message.

3.1 Effective embedding of one bit message

3.1.1 Deviation of $lc(c_0,r)$ from zero – parameter σ_{lc}

In searching for optimal embedding strength, we begin with well known facts for normal distribution:

- If X_1 and X_2 are normally distributed random variables: $X_1 \sim N(\mu_1,\sigma_1^2)$, $X_2 \sim N(\mu_2,\sigma_2^2)$, then their linear combination is also normally distributed:

$$aX_1+bX_2\sim N(a\mu_1+b\mu_2,a^2\sigma_1^2+b^2\sigma_2^2) \quad (4)$$

- For distribution $N(\mu, \sigma^2)$, the *68–95–99,7 rule* (*empirical rule, 3-sigma rule*) states that nearly all values drawn from it lie within 3 standard deviations of the mean:

$$\begin{aligned} &- \text{ within interval } (\mu-\sigma,\mu+\sigma) && \text{are about 68\% of values,} \\ &- \text{ within interval } (\mu-2\cdot\sigma,\mu+2\cdot\sigma) && \text{are about 95\% of values,} \\ &- \text{ within interval } (\mu-3\cdot\sigma,\mu+3\cdot\sigma) && \text{are about 99,7\% of values} \end{aligned} \quad (5)$$

- If X_1, X_2, ..., X_k are independent *standard normal* random variables (i.e. $X_i\sim N(0,1)$, $i=1,...,k$), then the sum of their squares is χ^2 (chi-square) variable with k degrees of freedom. Its mathematical expectation is k.

In following text, we'll use symbols for reference patterns and images:

- r - an arbitrary reference pattern
- r_w - reference pattern that is to be embedded
- c_0 – original image (or image where r_w is not embedded)
- c - image - input into the detector (r_w may, but need not be embedded in it)

All coordinates of $r=(r(1),r(2),...,r(mn))$ are drawn from distribution $N(0,1)$. Mathematical expectation for $\|r\|$ is $\sqrt{mn}$. For image $c_0=(c_0(1),c_0(2),...,c_0(mn))$ and reference pattern r, linear correlation is

$$lc(c_0,r)=\frac{c_0\bullet r}{\|r\|^2}=\frac{\sum_{i=1}^{mn} c_0(i)\cdot r(i)}{mn} \quad (6)$$

Therefore $lc(c_0,r)$, as linear combination of random variables $r=(r(1),r(2),...,r(mn))$ has values from distribution $N(0,\sigma_{lc}^2)$, where:

$$\sigma_{lc}=\frac{\sqrt{(c_0(1))^2+(c_0(2))^2+...+(c_0(mn))^2}}{mn}=\frac{\sqrt{E(c_0)}}{mn} \quad (7)$$

Value $E(c_0)= (c_0(1))^2+(c_0(2))^2+...+(c_0(mn))^2$ is called *energy of image* c_0.

Then,

- in interval $(-\sigma_{lc}, \sigma_{lc})$ are 68% of linear correlation values,
- in interval $(-2\cdot\sigma_{lc},2\cdot\sigma_{lc})$ are 95% of linear correlation values,
- in interval $(-3\cdot\sigma_{lc},3\cdot\sigma_{lc})$ are almost all of linear correlation values.

3.1.2 Parameter α setting

According to empirical rule, it is $|lc(c_0,r_w)|\leq 3\cdot\sigma_{lc}$ with probability 0.997 ("almost 1").

Parameter σ_{lc} - the standard deviation of a sample (linear correlations between the original image and reference patterns) **is the basis for correct setting of parameters α and τ**, for effective embedding.

The biggest embedding strength is needed

- when $lc(c_0,r_w)=-3\cdot\sigma_{lc}$ and we embed binary one, and
- when $lc(c_0,r_w)=3\cdot\sigma_{lc}$ and we embed binary zero

Thus, if we choose

$$\alpha=3\cdot\sigma_{lc}+\tau \tag{8}$$

then almost every reference pattern will be effectively embedded with strength α.

Such embedding, in which α is set in advance, and the reference pattern is embedded with this strength (without consideration for linear correlation value between the image and the reference pattern that **is to be embedded**), we call a *fixed strength embedding.*

The fixed strength embedding is quite bigger than necessary. Better result we get if we consider the linear correlation between the image and the pattern that is to be embedded. In this case, we talk about an algorithm with the *embedding strength adjustment.*

Let $l_0=lc(c_0,r_w)$ and we embed the binary one. If $l_0<\tau$, we set $\alpha=\tau-l_0$. If $l_0\geq\tau$, we set $\alpha=0$ (not necessary to embed anything). Thus,

$$\begin{aligned}&- \quad \text{if we embed binary one, then } \alpha=\max(\tau-l_0,0)\\&- \quad \text{if we embed binary zero, then } \alpha=\max(\tau+l_0,0)\end{aligned} \tag{9}$$

Embedding with strength α makes in image *mean square error*

$$\mathrm{MSE}(c_0,c_w)=\frac{1}{mn}\sum_{i=1}^{mn}[c_w(i)\text{-}c_0(i)]^2=\frac{1}{mn}\sum_{i=1}^{mn}\alpha^2[r_w(i)]^2=\alpha^2 \tag{10}$$

3.1.3 Detection threshold τ setting

To avoid false positive error, τ needs to be bigger than the biggest correlation between the image and not embedded reference patterns.

If we set $\tau=3\cdot\sigma_{lc}$, the linear correlation between the original image (c_0) and reference pattern would be in interval $(-\tau,\tau)$, almost with probability p=1. In other words, we could be almost 100% sure that the detector would not respond with a false positive error.

The threshold should not be larger than $3\cdot\sigma_{lc}$: this is not only needless, but also affects the fidelity (a stronger embedding would be needed for the detector to recognize the message).

We have to consider the possibility of a false positive error when the message is quite short (as here, the message being one bit long). If it is longer, the false positive error is not a big problem (we will explain more about this topic in subsubsection 3.2.1), and τ could be set quite smaller.

3.1.4 Parameter σ_{lc} dependence on the image dimension

The image c_k derived from k equal images, c, with energies E(c), has energy $E(c_k)=k\cdot E(c)$ and dimension $\dim(c_k)=k\cdot\dim(c)$. Its σ_{lc} parameter is

$$\sigma_{lc}(c_k) = \frac{\sqrt{E(c_k)}}{\dim(c_k)} = \frac{\sqrt{k \cdot E(c)}}{k \cdot \dim(c)} = \frac{\sqrt{E(c)}}{\sqrt{k} \cdot \dim(c)} = \frac{1}{\sqrt{k}} \cdot \sigma_{lc}(c) \quad (11)$$

So, parameter σ_{lc} is lower for larger images. Therefore, in an image with larger dimension, we have to embed our message with a lower strength. In the previous case, it is

$$\alpha_k = \alpha/\sqrt{k} \text{ and } \tau_k = \tau/\sqrt{k} \quad (12)$$

Taking the fidelity of image into account, it is obvious that in larger image we can embed a longer message.

3.2 Effective embedding of longer message

3.2.1 Threshold τ setting for longer message

The threshold τ for a longer message may be smaller than $3 \cdot \sigma_{lc}$ (value recommended in case of one bit message). For example, for $\tau = \sigma_{lc}$, for roughly 68% of possible reference patterns, the linear correlation between the image and the reference pattern is inside the interval $(-\tau, \tau)$. So, the false positive may appear in 'every third' case. If we insist that every message bit must be detected for confirmation of message presence, it will be almost impossible to detect the message if it is not embedded (for detection of non-existing message, it is necessary for all reference patterns to arise a false positive, and in a longer message this is almost impossible).

So, in the case of longer message it is permitted a quite smaller τ value.

3.2.2 Message bits embedding one over another

Due to the fact that reference patterns are mutually uncorrelated, embedding of new pattern will not substantially change linear correlation between the image and previously embedded patterns (linear correlation is resistant against white Gaussian noise):

$$lc(c_0 + r_1 + r_2, r_1) = \frac{(c_0 + r_1) \bullet r_1 + r_2 \bullet r_1}{\|r_1\| \cdot \|r_1\|} \approx \frac{(c_0 + r_1) \bullet r_1 + 0}{\|r_1\| \cdot \|r_1\|} = lc(c_0 + r_1, r_1) \quad (13)$$

Hence, if we embed message bits one over another, we can take same value for α as in the case of only one information bit.[2]

We embed k bits into image $c_0 = (c_0(1), c_0(2), \ldots, c_0(mn))$, in a way that for each bit we add (or subtract) the corresponding reference pattern $r_j = (r_j(1), r_j(2), \ldots, r_j(mn))$ $(j=1,2,\ldots,k)$, multiplied by embedding strength α_j. The resultant image is $c_w = (c_w(1), c_w(2), \ldots, c_w(mn))$. We obtain each image pixel with (sign '+' is for binary one, '-' for binary zero embedding):

$$c_w(i) = c_0(i) + \sum_{j=1}^{k} (\pm\alpha_j \cdot r_j(i)) \ (i=1,2,\ldots,mn) \quad (14)$$

[2] (Of course, if we neglect the fact that for one bit embeddind we get $\tau = 3 \cdot \sigma_{lc}$, and presume that we can take here smaller value of τ, as well).

Such embedding is localized in space. Only corresponding coordinates of the original image and reference pattern influence on resultant pixel value.

Reference patterns coordinates take values from distribution N(0,1). Therefore, their linear combination

$$R(i) = \sum_{j=1}^{k} (\pm\alpha_j \cdot r_j(i)) \quad (i=1,2,...,mn) \tag{15}$$

takes values from $N(0,\sigma^2)$, where

$$\sigma = \sqrt{\alpha_1^2 + \alpha_2^2 + ... + \alpha_k^2} \tag{16}$$

Also, coordinates of vector $r_s=(r_s(1), r_s(2),..., r_s(mn))$, where

$$r_s(i) = \frac{R(i)}{\sqrt{\alpha_1^2 + \alpha_2^2 + ... + \alpha_k^2}} \quad (i=1,2,...,mn) \tag{17}$$

are liable to N(0,1) distribution, and therefore, **r_s is reference pattern.**

Thus, **embedding of k reference patterns r_j one over another, with strengths** α_j (j=1,2,...,k), **is equal with embedding one reference pattern, r_s, with strength** $\beta = \sqrt{\alpha_1^2 + \alpha_2^2 + ... + \alpha_k^2}$, or

$$c_w = c_0 + \beta \cdot r_s \tag{18}$$

Mean square error of this embedding is

$$MSE(c_0,c_w)=\beta^2=\alpha_1^2+\alpha_2^2+...+\alpha_k^2 \tag{19}$$

If all patterns are embedded with the same strength, $\alpha_1=\alpha_2=...=\alpha_k=\alpha$, then the total embedding strength is $\beta = \sqrt{k} \cdot \alpha$.

Example 1: If k=2, $\alpha_1=3$, $\alpha_2=4$, then $r_s = \frac{3 \cdot r_1 + 4 \cdot r_2}{5}$. (Embedding of two patterns with strengths 3 and 4 makes the same MSE as embedding of one pattern, with strength $\beta = \sqrt{3^2 + 4^2} = 5$).

Example 2: If $\alpha=2$ and we embed the message of k=25 bits (one over another, with fixed strength embedding), then $\beta = \sqrt{k} \cdot \alpha = 10$, i.e. embedding of 25 patterns with strength 2 is equivalent to embedding of one pattern with strength 10.

3.2.3 Embedding into subimages

We divide image c_0 of mn pixels into k disjoint subimages $c_0^1, c_0^2, ..., c_0^k$, of $mn^1, mn^2,..., mn^k$ pixels, respectively ($mn = \sum_{j=1}^{k} mn^j$). For each subimage, the coefficient σ_{lc}^j (j=1,2,...,k) is

$$\sigma_{lc}^{j} = \frac{\sqrt{E(c_0^j)}}{mn^j} \tag{20}$$

If it is possible to divide this image into k parts of equal dimensions and energies, then all subimages will have the same $\sigma_{lc}{}^{j}$ parameter value:

$$\sigma_{lc}^{j} = \frac{\sqrt{E(c_0^j)}}{mn^j} = \frac{\sqrt{E(c_0)/k}}{mn/k} = \sqrt{k}\cdot\frac{\sqrt{E(c_0)}}{mn} = \sqrt{k}\cdot\sigma_{lc} \tag{21}$$

In this case, the overall strength for k bits message, when embedding into k subimages, is equal to the strength for one bit message, multiplied by $\sqrt{k}$. Embedding strength in this case is equal as if the message is embedded one bit over another.

4. Robustness against lossy compression

Next we give an estimate of the strength coefficient α for watermark, to survive the lossy compression.

In subsection 4.1 we consider the case of one bit, and in subsection 4.2 - of a longer message. For the purpose of simplicity, we only discuss the case of binary one embedding. The contents of this section may be used with small changes for the case of binary zeros.[3]

4.1 Robustness against compression – one bit message

4.1.1 Embedding strength parameter after compression (α')

With next experiment we try to find which part of watermark will be destroyed by lossy compression.

1. We embed k reference patterns r(1), r(2),..., r(k) (one by one) into the image c_0 with strength α (value α is the same for all of them). In a way, we get k watermarked images (with binary one embedded) $c_w(1), c_w(2),..., c_w(k)$.
2. Then, we subject each of these k images to expected lossy compression (same for all k images), and we get k compressed watermarked images $c_{wn}(1), c_{wn}(2),..., c_{wn}(k)$.
3. For each of them we calculate linear correlation with corresponding reference pattern (the one that is previously embedded in it).

In Fig. 1, linear correlation values of these images with reference patterns are shown (c_0 is the first page scan of the Ruđer Bošković's book '*Elementa geometriae*', α=3, k=20, compression is DjVu Photo, made by program DjVu Solo 3.1 - LizardTech, Inc). Graphic abscissa presents arrays indexes, and ordinate - their values.

The dotted line presents linear correlation values between the **original image** and reference patterns. The dashed line presents linear correlation values between **watermarked images** and corresponding reference patterns. The solid line presents the linear correlation values between **compressed watermarked images** and corresponding reference patterns.

---

[3] We can observe case with binary zero as the opposite pattern embedding. Opposite pattern of r_w is $-r_w$, and it also possesses all of reference pattern properties (takes values from distribution N(0,1)).

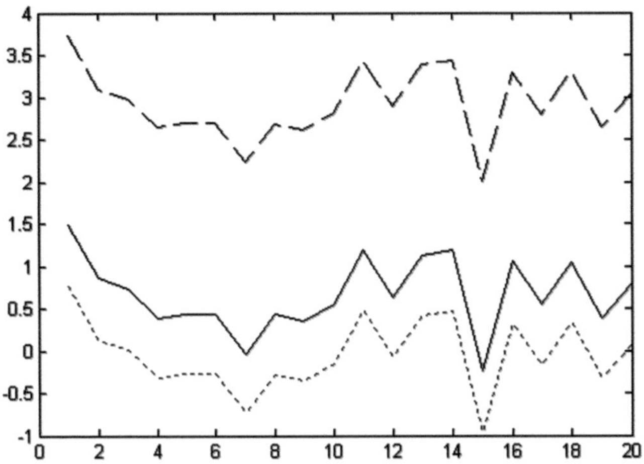

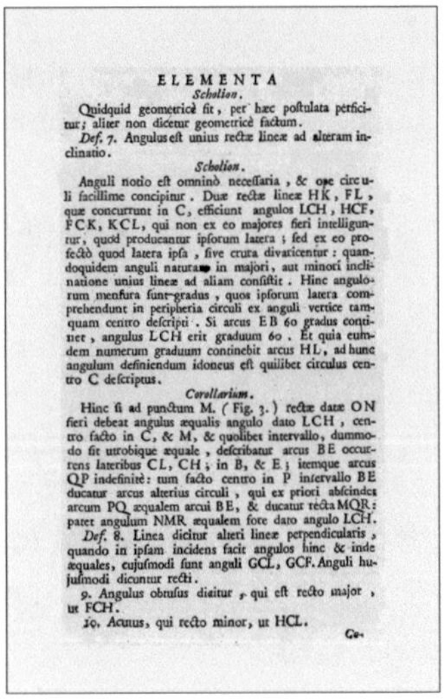

ELEMENTA

Scholion.

Quidquid geometricè fit, per hæc poſtulata perficitur; aliter non dicetur geometricè factum.

Def. 7. Angulus eſt unius rectæ lineæ ad alteram inclinatio.

Scholion.

Anguli notio eſt omninò neceſſaria, & ope circuli facillime concipitur. Duæ rectæ lineæ HK, FL, quæ concurrunt in C, efficiunt angulos LCH, HCF, FCK, KCL, qui non ex eo majores fieri intelliguntur, quod producantur ipſorum latera; ſed ex eo profectò quod latera ipſa, ſive crura divaricentur: quandoquidem anguli naturam in majori, aut minori inclinatione unius lineæ ad aliam conſiſtit. Hinc angulorum menſura ſunt gradus, quos ipſorum latera comprehendunt in peripheria circuli ex anguli vertice tamquam centro deſcripti. Si arcus EB 60 gradus continet, angulus LCH erit graduum 60. Et quia eumdem numerum graduum continebit arcus HL, ad hunc angulum definiendum idoneus eſt quilibet circulus centro C deſcriptus.

Corollarium.

Hinc ſi ad punctum M. (Fig. 3.) rectæ datæ ON fieri debeat angulus æqualis angulo dato LCH, centro facto in C, & M, & quolibet intervallo, dummodo ſit utrobique æquale, deſcribatur arcus BE occurrens lateribus CL, CH; in B, & E; itemque arcus QP indefinitè: tum facto centro in P intervallo BE ducatur arcus alterius circuli, qui ex priori abſcindet arcum PQ æqualem arcui BE, & ducatur recta MQR: patet angulum NMR æqualem fore dato angulo LCH.

Def. 8. Linea dicitur alteri lineæ perpendicularis, quando in ipſam incidens facit angulos hinc & inde æquales, cujuſmodi ſunt anguli GCL, GCF. Anguli hujuſmodi dicuntur recti.

9. Angulus obtuſus dicitur, qui eſt recto major, ut FCH.

10. Acutus, qui recto minor, ut HCL.

Ge-

Fig. 1. Linear correlation between the image (original, watermarked and compressed watermarked) and corresponding reference patterns (left), for the first page of the book "*Elementa geometriae*" (right)

We can see from this graphic, that for each reference pattern r(i), (i=1,2,...,k) stands:

- Embedding of binary one with strength α raises linear correlation value between the image and the reference pattern by α
- Lossy compression reduces linear correlation by constant, i.e. it erases constant part of watermark. Thus, after lossy compression, it remains the constant part of watermark.

(Clearly, binary zero embedding reduces linear correlation value for α, and lossy compression raises it by constant – it erases constant part of watermark).

We introduce new concept: *embedding strength coefficient after compression,* α'. α' **is part of** α **that survives after lossy compression.**

For all of twenty reference patterns, the effect is the same: for our image and α=3, after DjVu Photo compression, it survived α'=0.75.

After repeating our experiment for other compression techniques (for various intensities, for JPEG compression and compression used in PDF and DjVu files making), we get the same conclusion:

For given image and compression intensity, α' is constant for fixed α coefficient (it doesn't depend on reference pattern embedded, nor on linear correlation value of original image with it).

Surely, for given α coefficient, value α' is smaller in more intensive compression. For example, α' is bigger for JPEG 70% compression than for JPEG 40%.

4.1.2 Coefficient α setting for a robust watermark

If we wish the watermark to be robust against lossy compression, we need to modify statements (8) and (9) (subsubsection 3.1.2: *Parameter α setting*) and replace each α with α':

- in the case of fixed embedding strength: $\alpha'=3\cdot\sigma_{lc+\tau}$
- in the case of embedding strength adjustment: $\alpha'=\max(\tau-l_0,0)$ (for binary one), $\alpha'=\max(\tau+l_0,0)$ (for binary zero embedding)

The procedure of deriving α' from α is "natural", because it matches to the events chronology: α and α' are "cause and effect":

1. We embed watermark with strength α;
2. We compress the image;
3. We read α'.

In order to derive α from α', we have to try with different α values, by using watermarks made from **arbitrary (but only one) reference pattern**.

Steps for α setting:

1. For our image, we set τ and (desired value of) α'
2. In our image we embed watermark for several α values; to get several watermarked images.
3. We expose these images to expected lossy compression.
4. The detector calculates α' for each compressed watermarked image. Then, we compare obtained α' values with desired value. α that corresponds α' value, closest to desired one, is appropriate.

4.2 Robustness of a longer message

If we embed k patterns into the image, each with own embedding strength coefficient α_i (i=1, 2... k), we have:

$$c_w = c_0 + \sqrt{\alpha_1{}^2 + \alpha_2{}^2 + ... + \alpha_k{}^2} \cdot r_s = c_0 + \beta \cdot r_s \tag{22}$$

$$r_s = \frac{\pm\alpha_1 r_1 \pm \alpha_2 r_2 \pm ... \pm \alpha_k r_k}{\beta} \tag{23}$$

After compression, we have:

$$c_{wn} \approx c_0 + \beta' \cdot r_s, \quad \beta' = \sqrt{(\alpha_1')^2 + (\alpha_2')^2 + ... + (\alpha_k')^2} \tag{24}$$

The overall strength coefficient remaining after compression is β' (the coefficient that corresponds to β for our image and compression technique).

$$p = \beta' / \beta, \quad \beta' = p \cdot \beta = \sqrt{(p\cdot\alpha_1)^2 + (p\cdot\alpha_2)^2 + ... + (p\cdot\alpha_k)^2} \tag{25}$$

Thus, $\frac{\alpha_1'}{\alpha_1} = \frac{\alpha_2'}{\alpha_2} = \ldots = \frac{\alpha_k'}{\alpha_k} = \mathrm{p}$

The procedure for coefficients α_i (i=1,2,...,k) setting is:

1. For our image, we set parameters τ and α_i' (i=1,2,...,k);
2. We calculate $\beta' = \sqrt{(\alpha_1')^2 + (\alpha_2')^2 + \ldots + (\alpha_k')^2}$
3. We obtain β from β' and calculate $\mathrm{p} = \frac{\beta'}{\beta}$
4. $\alpha_i = \frac{\alpha_i'}{\mathrm{p}}$ (i=1,2,...,k)

Example 3: Let $\alpha_1'=3$, $\alpha_2'=4$. Then $\beta' = \sqrt{3^2 + 4^2} = 5$

If for given image and compression technique, to coefficient $\beta'=5$ corresponds $\beta=10$, then

$$\mathrm{p} = \frac{\beta'}{\beta} = \frac{1}{2}, \qquad \alpha_1 = \frac{\alpha_1'}{\mathrm{p}} = 6, \qquad \alpha_2 = \frac{\alpha_2'}{\mathrm{p}} = 8$$

Example 4: We embed k=16 message bits (binary ones) into the image c_0='*Fishingboat*' (512×512 pixels).

$$\sigma_{lc} = \frac{\sqrt{E(c_0)}}{(512 \cdot 512)} = 0.25 \qquad \text{We take } \tau=0.25$$

$\alpha' =$ [0, 0.18, 0, 0.17, 0.41, 0.54, 0.19, 0.58, 0.42, 0.58, 0.64, 0.66, 0.14, 0.57, 0.31, 0.05]

(using embedding strength adjustment)

$\beta'=1.65$ $\beta=5.4$ p=0.3 $\alpha_i=\alpha'_i/\mathrm{p}$ (i=1,2,...,k)

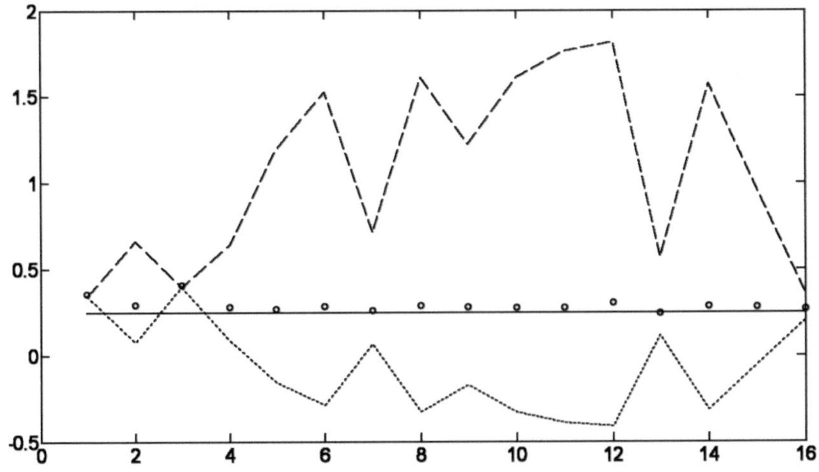

Fig. 2. Linear correlation between the image (original, watermarked and compressed watermarked) and k=16 embedded reference patterns

Fig. 2 shows linear correlation values between the image and each of embedded patterns. The dotted line presents linear correlation values for the original image; the dashed line is for the watermarked image. Roundels present linear correlation values between the compressed watermarked image and embedded reference patterns. We can see that their ordinates are near the threshold τ value (solid line). So, they are the smallest values needed for the detector to recognize after compression the image as watermarked.

Example 5: The same test is done for 64 bits message. The watermark also survives DjVu Photo compression. Overall embedding strength is β=6.94. In Fig. 3, the compressed original (without watermark) and compressed watermarked image could be seen.

Fig. 3. Compressed original and compressed watermarked image (*"Fishingboat"*, 512×512 pixels, k=64 message bits, DjVu Photo compression)

5. AWGN watermark in transform domain

Many authors suggest watermark embedding in transform, instead of spatial domain. In addition, they propose using transform domain that will be used during lossy compression. Goal is to achieve greater watermark robustness against expected compression.

5.1 Optimal embedding strength in transform domain

In this subsection we apply the described watermarking algorithm in transform domain (embedding and detection occur in transform, instead of spatial domain). We show that there is no difference from the viewpoint of effective embedding of AWGN watermark, between watermarking in spatial and in transform (DCT, block DCT, Fourier or arbitrary wavelet) domain.

First of all, most of nowadays used transforms in image processing and in compression are orthogonal (or at least unitary) linear transforms.

Linear transform f respects addition and scaling. Therefore,

$$f(c_0+\alpha\cdot r)=f(c_0)+\alpha\cdot f(r) \tag{26}$$

Orthogonal transform f preserves the inner product and consequently, it preserves vectors lengths and angles between vectors. Therefore,

$$\|c_0\| = \|f(c_0)\| \quad \text{and} \quad \|r\| = \|f(r)\| \tag{27}$$

$$\cos(c_0,r)=\cos(f(c_0),f(r)) \tag{28}$$

So, we have

$$lc(c_0,r)=lc(f(c_0),f(r)) \tag{29}$$

Also, for orthogonal (and unitary as well) linear transforms applies *Parseval's (energy) identity*:

$$\text{If} \quad b_0=f(c_0), \quad \text{then} \quad E(b_0)=\sum_{i=1}^{mn}(b_0(i))^2=\sum_{i=1}^{mn}(c_0(i))^2=E(c_0) \tag{30}$$

Orthogonal transform maps reference pattern r=(r(1),r(2),...,r(mn)) (i.e. vector with coordinates taken from distribution N(0,1)), into vector f(r) from distribution N(0,1), i.e. **orthogonal transform maps reference pattern to reference pattern**.

Standard deviations from zero of linear correlations between vector c_0 and reference patterns in spatial and transform domain are equal:

$$\sigma_{lc}(c_0)=\sigma_{lc}(f(c_0)) \tag{31}$$

It is all the same if we embed AWGN watermark into an image with strength α in spatial or in transform domain. **Correlation values and MSE too, will be the same in both domains.**

Also, there is no difference between spatial and transform domains in AWGN watermark robustness against lossy compression.

5.2 AWGN watermark embedding into subimage in transform domain

As in spatial domain, it is possible to embed watermark in some **part of coefficients** in transform domain (here also, we call it *embedding into subimage*).

Technically, there is not any difference in optimal strength setting, speaking of subimage and of the whole image. Effective embedding strength we determine by dimension and energy of image (or image part) in that AWGN watermark is to be embedded. Robustness against lossy compression we determine by these coefficients properties in the regard to expected compression.

However, for images in spatial and in transform domain, there is a great difference in **energy distribution**. While in spatial domain, image energy is mainly distributed evenly over entire matrix, in transform domain it is concentrated in some of its elements. Illustration of this fact may be seen in Fig. 4, on example of block DCT (transform used in JPEG compression). Here, for presentation of matrices in DCT domain, we use solution proposed in (Vučković, 2008):

- matrix elements with value 0 are presented in black color
- positive elements are presented in nuances from black to white

- negative elements are colored in nuances from black to yellow
- because of big difference between image elements in block DCT domain (second and fourth objects in Fig. 4), they are presented with logarithmed magnitudes

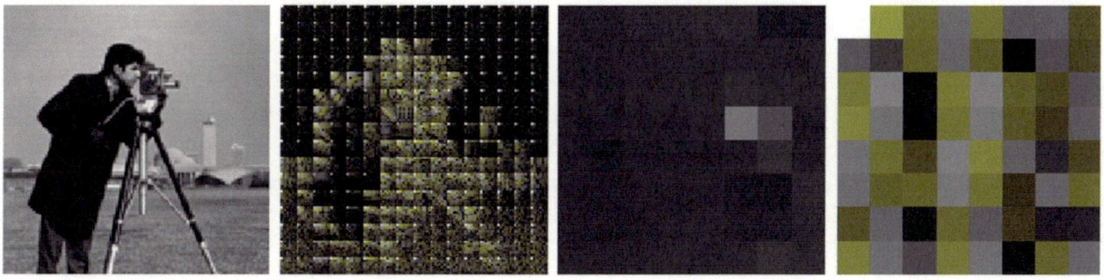

Fig. 4. Image '*Cameraman*' in spatial and in block DCT domain; one 8×8 block in spatial and in block DCT domain

As we can see, in block DCT domain, energy of each block is concentrated in its upper left corner. On the other hand, JPEG compression damages elements in lower right corner much more intensively.

Block DCT domain, which is the basis of JPEG compression, is used frequently in watermark embedding. At description of such embedding, we use term *image subchannel* (Eggers and Girod introduced it in (Eggers & Girod, 2001)). *Subchannel* is vector that in block DCT domain has for coordinates - elements, with same index in blocks. Subchannels are ordered according to zigzag order (Fig. 5). Thus, subchannel 1 consists of all DC blocks elements; subchannel 10 consists of all elements that are in the position 10 in the block (zigzag order).

So, the image of dimension m×n in (8×8) block DCT domain may be presented with 64 subchannels: [4]

$$s_j=(s_j(1),s_j(2),\ldots,s_j(nbl)),\ (j=1,2,\ldots,64)),\ \text{where } nbl=mn/64 \qquad (32)$$

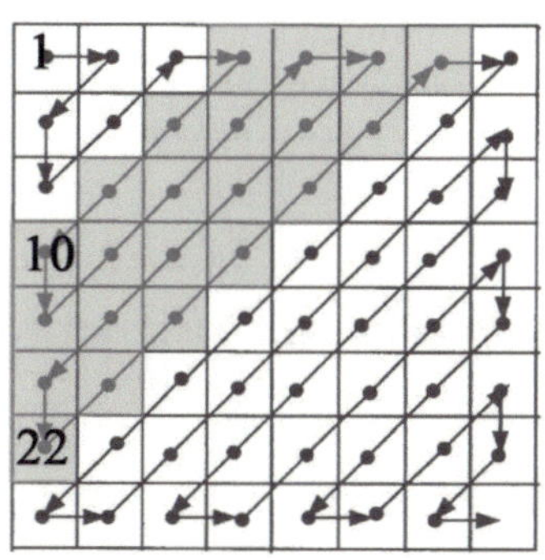

Fig. 5. Zigzag order; coefficients 1, 10, 22 in zigzag order; region of subchannels 10-22 (colored in gray)

[4] Here, for the purpose of simplicity, we assume that image dimensions are multiples of 8, in order to make the partition in 8×8 blocks possible.

In (Vučković, 2010a, 2010b) we described in detail our investigations results in connection with embedding into subchannels in block DCT domain. We analyzed case of embedding into group of (first 32) subchannels and embedding into some of individual subchannels (specifically, subchannels 1, 10 and 22). Here, we briefly outline conclusions obtained.

In block DCT domain, image energy is concentrated in upper left corner of the block. For example, in image '*Cameraman*', even 99.76% of whole image energy is concentrated in its first 32 subchannels. Therefore, with described algorithm, it is needed twice higher strength for effective embedding in first 32 subchannels than into the whole image. In this way we embed in 50% image coefficients, so the mean square error in this case is two times higher comparing with embedding into all of coefficients.

Embedding in lower right block corner is effective even with very small strength. However, even at very low compression, these coefficients will be destroyed. Therefore, embedding into those coefficients is not recommended.

Embedding in vicinity of subchannel 1 is not good solution, because of extremely high energy which requires big embedding strength (and this badly influences image quality).

Our explorations (Vučković, 2010a, 2010b) confirmed earlier (Eggers-Girod, 2001), that for effective and robust (against JPEG compression) and imperceptible watermark, it is the best to embed it in several coefficients in upper left block part (somewhere in the region of subchannels 10-22 - see Fig. 5). Such embedding showed also good robustness against compression techniques different from JPEG (for example, against DjVu compression).

6. AWGN watermark and other image modifications

Image modifications are organized (Cox et al., 2008) in two classes - valumetric and geometric distortions.

6.1 Valumetric distortions

Valumetric distortions are simpler than geometric ones. They change individual pixels values. These modifications include additive noise, amplitude changes, linear filtering and lossy compression.

6.1.1 Additive noise

This modification has effect of a random signal adding. For watermarked image, additive noise adding is defined by:

$$c_{w1} = c_w + s = c_0 + \alpha \cdot r + s, \tag{33}$$

where s is a random vector chosen from some distribution, independently of c_0 and r.

Clearly,

$$lc(c_{w1}, r) = lc(c_w, r) + lc(s, r) \approx lc(c_w, r) \tag{34}$$

(because s is uncorrelated with r).

Thus, an additive noise does not affect AWGN watermark (AWGN algorithm is robust against this image modification).

AWGN watermark is also robust against **brightness changing** ($c_{w1}=c_w+n\cdot J$, where J is matrix of ones and n is integer).

6.1.2 Amplitude changing

It may be presented by the formula

$$c_{w1}=\nu\cdot c_w, \tag{35}$$

where $\nu>0$ is scaling factor. Such operation causes **brightness and contrast changing**.

After this modification, linear correlation value is equal to starting one, multiplied by factor ν. Depending on factor ν, watermark detectability will increase (if $\nu>1$), or diminish (if $\nu<1$).

6.1.3 Linear filtering

It is given by

$$c_{w1}=c_w*f, \tag{36}$$

where f is a filter, and $*$ designates convolution. Many common image operations are performed using linear filters. Examples of them are **blurring** and **sharpening** effects.

Linear filtering and lossy compression are more complex operations than the previous two, because changes that they cause are not strictly localized (pixel change depends on certain number of surrounding pixels too).

6.2 Geometric distortions

This class of image modifications includes many image distortions (rotation, spatial scaling, translation, skew or shear, cropping, perspective transformation, and changes in aspect ratio).

These modifications are more complicated than valumetric, because they displace information about pixels in image matrix. They usually change matrix dimensions as well. Therefore, here is not possible readily to detect the watermark. Yet, with these modifications, information about embedded message is not lost, but only "**masked**". For each geometric distortion, before detection, we need to perform one **correction procedure**.

For illustration, we depict one geometric modification - image rotation by an angle φ. Many inferences of this analyze could be applied to other modifications.

With modifications that erase a part of image data (for example crop operation, or other operation with erasing several columns or rows), after correction procedure, we'll have original image matrix with locally erased data (some elements are erased, but other are untouched). Then, it is possible to calculate accurately parameter σ_{lc} for untouched image part. For example, if prior to watermark embedding we know that image will be subjected to crop operation with reducing complete image area to its quarter, the watermark needs to be embedded twice stronger, to be detectable after cropping.

6.2.1 Robustness against rotation

In the case of image rotation, one of several different correction procedures may be used prior to detection. If watermarked image is rotated by angle φ, to make watermark detection possible, we may do one of the following:

- Compare (using linear correlation) rotated image with the reference pattern that is also rotated by φ
- Before detection, rotate the rotated image by angle $-\varphi$ and crop it to its original dimension; and then, compare it with reference pattern, that is also rotated by angles φ and $-\varphi$ and cropped to original dimension
- Image rotated by φ and then by $-\varphi$ (and then cropped to original image dimensions), (we may) compare with the original reference pattern.

Linear correlation values for image and reference pattern (unrotated and rotated) are presented in Fig. 6, for image "*Cameraman*". Reference pattern r_w is embedded with strength α=5. Then, image is subjected to rotation by angle φ=10°.

In each row we present image and pattern for which the correlation is calculated. So, for each example it is specified which image and pattern (and their dimensions) we deal with, and also the linear correlation value for them. In the first figure row, watermarked image and embedded reference pattern are presented. Second, third and fourth row contain information about three previously stated solutions of correction and detection.

The rotation practically does not reduce linear correlation value, if it is calculated for image and reference pattern that are rotated in the same manner. However, if we compare the rotated image (after restoration to original position by rotation in opposite direction and cropping to original dimension) with the original reference pattern, certain watermark amount will be lost (α' value will be considerably less than embedding strength value α).

It should be noted that in cases where not all details of distortion occurrence are known, the latest solution is usually only possible.

Experiments have confirmed (Vučković, 2010a) that stated inference for lossy compression (subsubsection 4.1.1: *Embedding strength parameter after compression (α'))* stays also for rotation (and other distortions too). For our image and embedding strength α, after given modification, remaining strength α' **doesn't depend on the reference pattern nor on its correlation with the original image**. Hence, to set embedding strength α needed that after expected modification remains α', **it is sufficient to experiment with only one reference pattern**.

The procedure of determining the necessary embedding strength α may be performed in the next steps:

1. We determine α' using procedure given in subsubsection 4.1.2 (*Coefficient α setting for a robust watermark*)
2. By experimenting with only one reference pattern, we determine the necessary embedding strength α, that after expected modification, remaining strength is at least α'.

$c_w(256,256)$ watermarked image ('*Cameraman*')

$r_w(256,256)$ - embedded reference pattern

$lc(c_w,r_w)= 5.787$

$c_{wr}(297,297)$ - watermarked image, rotated by φ (=10°)

$r_{wr}(297,297)$ - reference pattern, rotated by φ

$lc(c_{wr},r_{wr})= 5.815$

c_{wr1} (256,256) - watermarked image, rotated by φ and -φ, after cropping to original dimensions

r_{wr1} (256,256) - reference pattern, rotated by φ and -φ, after cropping to original dimensions

$lc(c_{wr1},r_{wr1})= 5.592$

c_{wr1} (256,256) - watermarked image, rotated by φ and -φ, after cropping to original dimensions

$r_w(256,256)$ - (embedded) reference pattern

$lc(c_{wr1},r_w)= 1.953$

Fig. 6. Linear correlation values for image and reference pattern (unrotated and rotated)

7. Color images and e-books

7.1 Digital watermark and color image

Each color image can be regarded as three grayscale images combination (one for each of red/ green/ blue components). Therefore, it is not too complicated to generate results for grayscale images to use for color images. Of course, for better results we need to consider human visual system (HVS) characteristics:

- Human eye notices changes in green color nuances best, a bit worse it discerns changes in red, and changes in blue it discerns worst. That's why some authors recommend watermark embedding mostly in blue color channel (because human eye is the least sensitive there).
- Human eye better notices changes in brightness than in color nuances. Hence, JPEG standard uses different compression intensities for those components. For good watermark algorithm, this fact should be considered.

7.2 Watermark for e-books

Electronic book (e-book) is the digital equivalent of a printed book. In our *Virtual library* (Mijajlović & Vasiljević, 2008), e-books are in PDF format. On Internet, DjVu format is used often as well.

PDF books in Virtual library, from the viewpoint of digital watermark embedding, may be classified as:

- E-books produced by **scanning**; their pages are images (book pages scans). Watermark may be embedded into them in the same manner as in other images.
- E-books originated from **DOC or TeX files**; their image pages are not bitmapped images. Hence before embedding, they need to be converted to bitmaps.

7.2.1 PDF e-books produced by scanning

Embedding procedure for PDF e-books:

1. We scan book pages – results are bitmapped (e.g., TIFF) images.
2. In each book page (TIFF file) we embed watermark – result is watermarked (TIFF) page.
3. We combine watermarked (TIFF) pages into one PDF file – watermarked e-book.

Detection:

1. Book page in which we search for watermark we extract from PDF file and save as (e.g.) TIFF image.
2. We detect the watermark message in this image.

7.2.2 PDF e-books originated from DOC and TeX files

These PDF pages need at first to be converted to bitmaps; this can be done by conversion of PDF pages into (e.g.) TIFF images. Then we may proceed with just described procedure (7.2.1).

However, by converting pages into images, we lose possibility of text retrieving in the file. This problem can be overcome by using some OCR procedure.

7.2.3 Problem with black-white books

Proposed algorithm is not suitable for simple black-white images (as book pages usually are). In big white image regions (for example, page margins) a large part of embedded data will be destroyed by "squeezing" operation: values that, after adding of white noise to image matrix become greater than 255, after "squeezing" return to 255. Also, it is very easy to remove watermark data from these image regions (for example, with eraser in Photoshop).

Pages in e-books produced by scanning usually aren't black-white, but grayscale (or color) images; even their margins are not completely white, and watermarking is possible for them. Problem is emphasized with second mentioned e-books class. Watermarking makes sense only if these books aren't purely textual files but they contain some amount of pictures, in which watermark could be embedded.

With black-white text pages there exists another problem, which makes them especially inconvenient for watermarking: watermark can be removed simply by text retyping from them.

8. Conclusion

This text contains integrated results of several earlier papers.

For given grayscale image and AWGN watermark, we described procedure for optimal embedding strength setting. We analyzed optimal strength for effective embedding, and also watermark robust against expected image modification.

We analyzed AWGN watermark embedding cases, into the whole image and into images, in spatial and transform domains and robustness of such embedding against expected compression.

For other image modifications, procedures for optimal strength setting are similar as in the case of compression. For each geometric modification, however, we need prior detection to perform one correction procedure.

Obtained results we applied to color images and e-books. AWGN algorithm is not applicable on black-white e-books that originate from DOC or TeX files, because watermark may be removed from them by simply retyping of text.

9. Acknowledgment

The work presented here was supported by the Serbian Ministry of Education and Science (project III44006).

10. References

Cox, I.J., Kilian, J., Leighton, F.T. & Shamoon, T. (1997): Secure spread spectrum watermarking for multimedia, *IEEE Transactions on Image Processing,* 6(12), pp. 1673-1687

Cox, I . & Miller, M., Bloom, J., Fridrich, J. & Kalker, T. (2008): *Digital Watermarking and Steganography*, Morgan Kaufmann Publishers, ISBN 978-0-12-372585-1

Eggers, J. & Girod, B. (2001): Quantization effects on digital watermarks, *Signal Processing* 81 (2001) pp. 239–263

Feng, G., Jiang, L., Wang, D. & He, C. (2005): Quickly tracing detection for spread spectrum watermark based on effect estimation of the affine transform, *Pattern Recognition,* Volume 38 Issue 12, December, 2005, pp. 2530 - 2536

Feng, G., Jiang, L., He, C. & Xue, Y. (2006): Chaotic spread spectrum watermark of optimal space-filling curves, *Chaos, Solitons and Fractals* 27, pp. 580–587

Mijajlović, Ž. & Vasiljević, D. (2008): Web page *Virtual library eLibrary,* Available from http://elibrary.matf.bg.ac.rs/

Mora-Jimenez, I. & Navia-Vazquez, A. (2000); A new spread spectrum watermarking method with self-synchronization capabilities,, *Proceedings 2000 International Conference on Image Processing*, pp. 415 - 418 vol. 1 , Print ISBN: 0-7803-6297-7

Perez-Freire, L. & Perez-Gonzalez, F. (2009): Spread-Spectrum Watermarking Security, *IEEE Transactions on Information Forensics and Security,* March 2009, Vol. 4, Issue: 1, pp. 2 - 24, ISSN: 1556-6013

Ruanaidh, J.J.K.O. & Pun, T. (1998): Rotation, scale and translation invariant spread spectrum digital image watermarking, *Signal Processing* 66 No. 3, May 1998, pp. 303-317, ISBN: 0818681837

Ruanaidh, J.J.K.O. & Csurka, G. (1999): A Bayesian approach to spread spectrum watermark detection and secure copyright protection for digital image libraries, *IEEE Computer Society Conference on Computer Vision and Pattern Recognition (CVPR'99)* - Volume 1, 1999, pp. 1207-1212, Print ISBN: 0-7695-0149-4

Vučković, V. (2008): Image and its matrix, matrix and its image, *Review of the National Center for Digitization*, Issue: 12, pp. 17-31, ISSN: 1820-0109, http://www.ncd.matf.bg.ac.yu/casopis/12/NCD12017.pdf

Vučković, V. (2010a): Embedding strength criteria for AWGN watermark, robust against expected distortion, *Computing and Informatics*, Vol. 29, no. 3 (2010), pp. 357–387, ISSN 1335-9150

Vučković, V. (2010b): *AWGN watermark optimal strength (Optimalna snaga žiga belog Gausovog šuma)* - doctoral dissertation, Faculty of Mathematics, Belgrade, 2010, http://elibrary.matf.bg.ac.rs/bitstream/handle/123456789/1073/PhDVVuckovic.pdf

Vučković, V. (2011): Digital watermark in digital images and e-books, *Review of the National Center for Digitization* 19, pp. 1–6, ISSN: 1820-0109, http://elib.mi.sanu.ac.rs/files/journals/ncd/19/ncd19001.pdf